ANTHROPOLOGICAL PAPERS OF
THE UNIVERSITY OF ARIZONA
NUMBER 9

WILLIAM W. WASLEY
and
ALFRED E. JOHNSON

SALVAGE ARCHAEOLOGY IN PAINTED ROCKS RESERVOIR WESTERN ARIZONA

with
appendices
by
Hugh C. Cutler
Mary Elizabeth King

THE UNIVERSITY OF ARIZONA PRESS
TUCSON 1965

A Project
of the

Inter-Agency Archeological Salvage Program

Completed under Contract Nos.
14–10–333–352, 14–10–333–554, and 14–10–0333–667

between
Arizona State Museum and National Park Service

LC Card Catalog Number 64–63815

PREFACE

On the subject of bias in archaeological reporting Jennings (1957: 9) once commented:

> It seems desirable to have the bias set forth early in the study, not because bias is an improper attribute in a study–indeed, study of any material seems improbable or impossible if bias is lacking–but in order that the reader be fully aware, at the outset, of the nature and extent of the reporter's views.

It would appear that perhaps three major biases, and probably a number of minor ones, affected our archaeological thinking at the very outset of work in the Painted Rocks Reservoir.

One of the major biases stemmed from the belief that the original presentation of the Hohokam sequence in the Snaketown report (Gladwin and others 1937: 212–29, 247–69) was essentially correct and that various later attempts to revise this sequence were not based on sufficient relevant data. Consequently, the materials collected were viewed in this frame of reference, and they were critically examined from the standpoint of the degree to which the evidence supported, or did not support, the Snaketown sequence.

A second bias derives from a current interest in Southwestern archaeology in the problem of contacts with Mesoamerica. The extent of these contacts may have been greater than had previously been indicated, and an attempt has been made to collect and present data in support of this idea.

A third bias assumes more importance than usually would be accorded it because it is in conflict with one which has influenced the interpretation of other work in the Gila Bend area. From the very beginning we have viewed the archaeology of the Painted Rocks Reservoir from the standpoint of what is known about the Hohokam culture in the Gila-Salt basin, and particularly at Snaketown. Schroeder's interpretation of the preliminary survey of the area (1961: 1–28), on the other hand, is based to a large extent upon what is known about the cultures of the lower Gila River. Hohokam archaeology is known from surface reconnaissance and from excavation, while the cultures of the lower Gila River are known from surface reconnaissance and from what may be learned through ethnohistoric and ethnographic studies.

We trust that these biases have not influenced to any great extent the gathering and presentation of basic data. On the other hand, our interpretations have naturally been influenced by the biases, and for this reason we have tried to make a clear separation between the basic data and the interpretive and theoretical sections of this report.

ACKNOWLEDGEMENTS

All phases of the archaeology of the Painted Rocks Reservoir project, from the initial field work through the analysis of specimens, the preparation of illustrations, and the writing of the reports, were facilitated by the assistance and guidance of a number of individuals. We gratefully acknowledge the help of all of these people.

Norton Allen, an outstanding amateur archaeologist, has wintered in the Gila Bend area for many years and has become thoroughly acquainted with the archaeology of the region. Several statements in the following report are the result of discussions with Allen, and we are grateful for his comments and descriptions of sites which were destroyed in the process of recent agricultural expansion before we came on the scene. A particularly welcome addition to this report is a section illustrating documented pottery and artifact associations which Mr. and Mrs. Norton Allen and Allen's father, Mr. Ernest G. Allen, have collected from the region (Appendix A).

Field work in the Gila Bend area was made more pleasant and profitable through association with and the cooperation of a number of local residents including H. K. Conrad, Lynn Cool, Robert W. Crichton, the Cole Gatlins and J. E. Gatlin, Ward Gilbert, Edwin Hunt, James Robertson, Thearl Tibbetts, and Richard Wright.

Field assistance was provided during the first season by Frank W. Eddy and Michael Hoffman, during the second season by J. Anthony Pomeroy, and during the third season by Fred Bohannan.

Laboratory analysis of the artifacts and the preparation of portions of the manuscript were facilitated through the work of a number of students in Raymond H. Thompson's class in Southwestern Archaeology at the University of Arizona. As a laboratory exercise for the class, the following students analyzed the artifacts from several of the excavated sites: Jeffrey S. Dean, Philip M. Hobler, Roger E. Kelly, Leif C. Landberg, and Donna Thatcher.

Lyndon L. Hargrave of the National Park Service Southwest Archeological Center in Globe, Arizona, supplied identification of bird bones. Marine shells were identified by Johnson working from a type collection supplied by Leo G. Hertlein of the California Academy of Science. Hertlein also made identifications of specimens not represented in the type collection. Botanical remains were identified by Hugh C. Cutler of the Missouri Botanical Garden whose report is included as Appendix B of this study. Fragments of charred basketry, sandals, and fabrics, many of which are in the Norton Allen collection, are described in Appendix C by Mary Elizabeth King of the Textile Museum, Washington, D. C.

Calvin Cummings, Ernest E. Leavitt, and William R. Krueger prepared the line drawings. Leavitt also assisted with the reconstruction of pottery vessels. Photographic illustrations were prepared by Gilbert Bartell, Hobler, and Bruce D. Lindsay, staff photographers for the Arizona State Museum, and by Norton Allen. Emil W. Haury, Edwin N. Ferdon, Jr., and Raymond H. Thompson read the manuscript and made numerous suggestions for improvement.

November, 1963

William W. Wasley

Alfred E. Johnson

ABSTRACT

Under contracts with the National Park Service, the Arizona State Museum conducted archaeological salvage excavations in the Painted Rocks Reservoir area of western Arizona during three field seasons beginning late in 1958 and ending early in 1961. The results of the first season's work primarily devoted to the excavation of a platform mound at the Gatlin site (Arizona Z:2:1) have been summarized by Wasley (1960b). The present volume contains additional data collected during the first season, as well as reports on information gathered during the second and third seasons. Most of this salvage work was conducted in sites of the Hohokam culture. Hohokam sites ranging from the Gila Butte phase through the Classic period were excavated. Some excavation was also undertaken in Lower Colorado buffware sites.

A rock-ridged ball court assigned to the Gila Butte phase was completely excavated. One court originally constructed during the Santa Cruz phase and rebuilt during the Sacaton phase was extensively tested. In addition, four other ball courts of the Sacaton phase were tested. Hohokam houses of the Gila Butte and Sacaton phases and one built during the Classic period were excavated. A prehistoric irrigation canal near the Gatlin site was tested. At the Citrus site (Arizona T:13:2) there was evidence of houses grouped around a plaza with a raised caliche floor. New data on burial practices during the Classic period were obtained. Some data on petroglyphs are presented.

Following the excavation reports is a series of discussions on specific topics: 1) the Hohokam phase sequence, 2) settlement patterns, 3) ball courts, 4) burial practices, 5) pottery and artifacts, and 6) Mesoamerican influences.

Appendices include 1) an illustrated presentation of materials from the Gila Bend area in the Norton Allen collection, 2) a description of the prehistoric plant remains by Hugh C. Cutler, and 3) a description of the prehistoric textiles by Mary Elizabeth King.

CONTENTS

FIGURES

INTRODUCTION

Painted Rocks Dam is about 20 air miles northwest of the present town of Gila Bend in western Arizona (Fig. 1). The ultimate derivation of the name is from an extensive series of petroglyphs pecked into a boulder outcrop on the desert floor about four air miles southwest of the dam. A description of this group of petroglyphs, most of which are prehistoric, is presented in this report.

The dam was completed under the direction of the U. S. Army Corps of Engineers in March of 1959. It extends across the Gila River Canyon which is formed by the proximity, in this area, of the Gila Bend Mountains on the north and the Painted Rocks Mountains on the south. The dam and reservoir behind it are a flood-control project, intended to impound water of the Gila River for a maximum holding period of 48 hours. If the maximum pool level of 661 feet above sea level is attained, water will be backed up along the Gila River to a point about 10 miles north of Gila Bend. In terms of possible danger to archaeological remains within the reservoir area, water washing back and forth over the sites as a result of alternate filling and emptying of the reservoir poses a more serious threat than in other reservoir areas where the water is to be held at a high level and will therefore constantly cover most of the sites.

The region of Gila Bend, including the Painted Rocks Reservoir, is in the Sonoran biotic province which covers much of the northwestern part of the Mexican state of Sonora, southwestern Arizona, and the neighboring portions of southeastern California and northeastern Baja California, which is also a state in Mexico. This biotic province is characterized by basin-and-range topography and an arid environment (Dice 1943: 51–52).

The Gila River and its tributaries form one of the major drainage systems of the Sonoran province. The Gila River rises in the mountainous country of New Mexico and flows in a generally westward direction until it joins the Colorado River at Yuma, Arizona. Major tributaries of the Gila entering from the north are the San Francisco, the San Carlos, the Salt, the Agua Fria, and the Hassayampa rivers. Southern tributaries of significance are San Simon Creek, the San Pedro River, and the Santa Cruz River.

The single major deviation in the course of the Gila River occurs in the vicinity of Gila Bend (Fig. 1) where the river abruptly changes its course and flows southward, paralleling the east side of the Gila Bend Mountains. At the southeastern corner of the mountains, opposite the town of Gila Bend, the river even more abruptly resumes its westerly course. Both the mountains and the present community of Gila Bend derive their names from this change in the river's course.

The town of Gila Bend is situated at an elevation of 737 feet above sea level, and the surrounding countryside along the Gila River is approximately the same elevation. To the northwest the Gila Bend Mountains rise abruptly to an elevation of 3200 feet, and an elevation of 4000 feet is attained in the Sand Tank Mountains several miles to the southeast. Precipitation ranges from 2.12 to 13.21 inches a year and averages 5.69 inches. About 344 days out of every year are frost free. Principal vegetation types along the Gila River and on the desert floor are saltbush, creosote bush, and mesquite (Sellers 1960). The saltcedar shrub, introduced into Arizona in the early part of this century (Dodge 1958: 71), grows in large stands in the river bottoms, actually delimiting the river channels in many cases. At elevations above 1000 feet in the surrounding mountains, palo verde, cacti, and burr sage are common (Sellers 1960).

In the vicinity of Gila Bend the Gila River is marked by a wide floodplain with low banks. The entire floodplain is covered with a dense growth of brush where it has not been cleared and leveled by recent agricultural developments. The only water to be seen in the river channels today is the result of irrigation runoff, except after heavy rains. A series of upstream dams along the Gila and its major tributaries has effectively cut off the flow of water to this downriver section.

Some idea of the former condition of the Gila

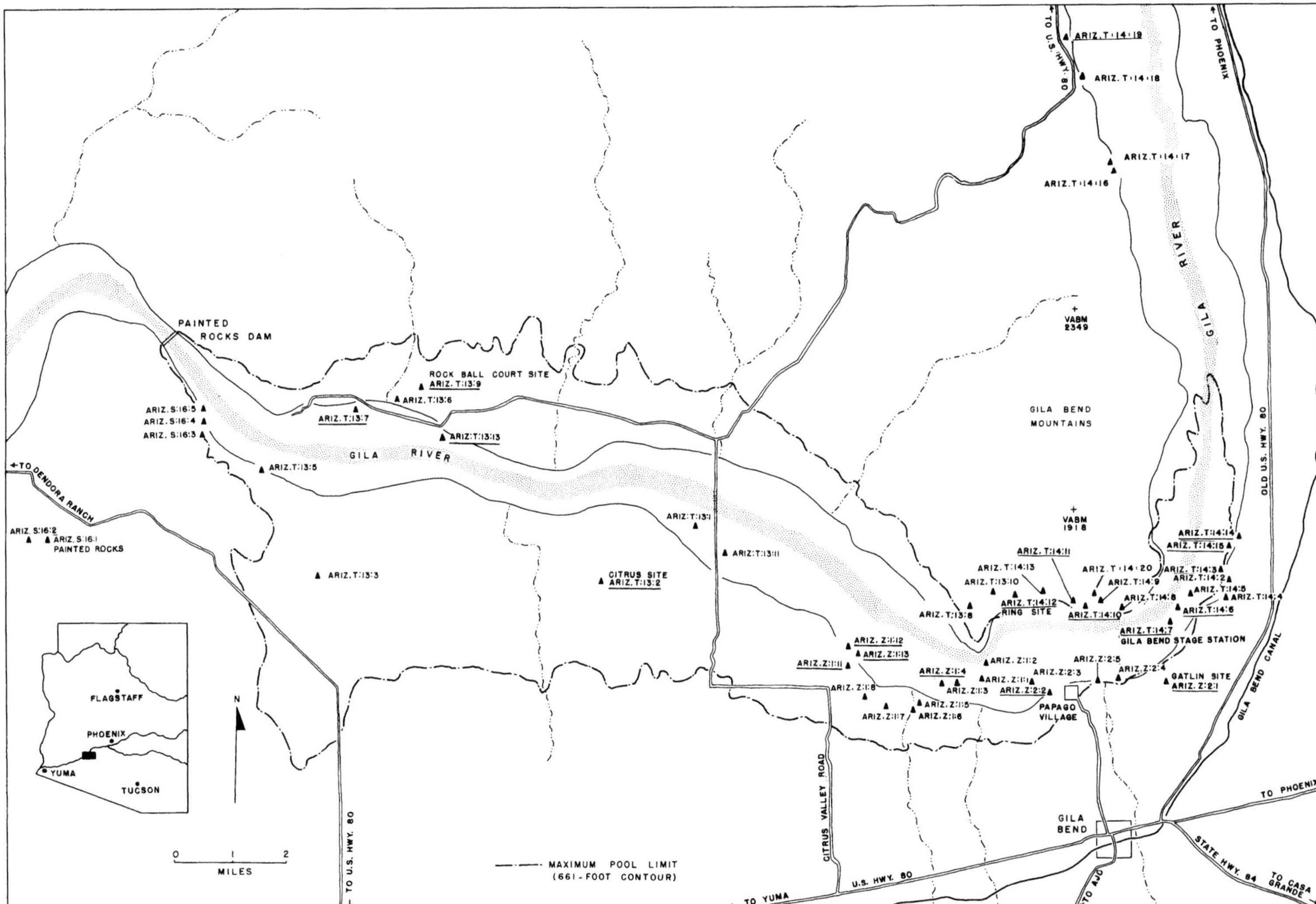

Fig. 1. The Gila Bend area showing sites located. Excavated sites underlined.

River can be gleaned from the accounts of early visitors to southern Arizona. Captain Juan Mateo Manje (1954: 84) commented during a trip he made in November, 1697, that there was sufficient water in the Gila up as far as the mouth of the San Pedro River to navigate a ship. Reports made during the 1800's indicate similar conditions. James Ohio Pattie in 1826 was a member of a party trapping beaver on the Gila and its tributaries. At one point it was necessary to construct a canoe to cross the river, since it was too deep and wide to be fordable by horse (Thwaites 1905: 184). Emory (1848: 91–92) noted that the Gila River east of Gila Bend was spread over an area about 100 yards in width, flowing gently along over a sandy bottom, the banks fringed with cane, willow, and myrtle. Writing about 1876, Hinton (1954: 281–82) described the river from Oatman's Flat, just west of Gila Bend, to Mohawk Station as being 600 feet in width and three to five feet in depth.

From these accounts it would appear that the valley of the Gila River in the vicinity of Gila Bend constituted a desirable region for prehistoric habitation. The archaeology of the Gila Bend area tends to support this view, indicating that it was more-or-less intensively occupied for several hundred years prior to the coming of the white man. Chief among these early inhabitants of the area were the agriculturally-minded Hohokam culture bearers who practiced extensive canal irrigation.

Prior to the Painted Rocks project, published archaeological work in the Gila Bend area was limited to a survey conducted by Gila Pueblo (Gladwin and Gladwin 1930). The initial phase of the salvage project consisted of a more intensive survey conducted during December, 1957, for the National Park Service by Albert H. Schroeder (1961) and Paul H. Ezell (1963a). As a result of this survey an excavation program was developed. This report concerns the results of the archaeological excavations carried out during three winter seasons by the Arizona State Museum, through contracts with the National Park Service, as a part of the Inter-Agency Archeological Salvage Program. The first season, extending from November 12, 1958, to February 28, 1959, was devoted primarily to the excavation of a Hohokam platform mound at the Gatlin site, Arizona Z:2:1 (Wasley 1960). All of the prehistoric sites excavated during the second season, from January 5, 1960, to March 4, 1960, and the third season from November 14, 1960, to February 3, 1961, are reported herein. Pottery and artifact provenience data from all three seasons have been made available in microcard form (Johnson and Wasley 1961). The results of the excavation of two historic sites, the old Gila Bend Stage Station and a Papago village, are planned for separate publication.

Schroeder and Ezell located 28 sites of archaeological and historical interest in the Painted Rocks Reservoir during the course of their survey. As a result of further survey work by the Arizona State Museum, an additional 26 sites were located, bringing the total for the reservoir and immediately surrounding areas to 54 (Fig. 1). This figure probably represents only about one half of the archaeological sites originally occupying the area, the remainder having been destroyed by recent agricultural expansion. In an attempt to determine as much about the local archaeological picture as was possible, 18 sites were selected for excavation. These were judged, on the basis of surface remains, to be the least disturbed sites, in which all of the cultural manifestations and most of the temporal periods in the reservoir area were represented. Although Pioneer-period Hohokam sites are known from the Gila Bend area, no excavations were made in sites of this period.

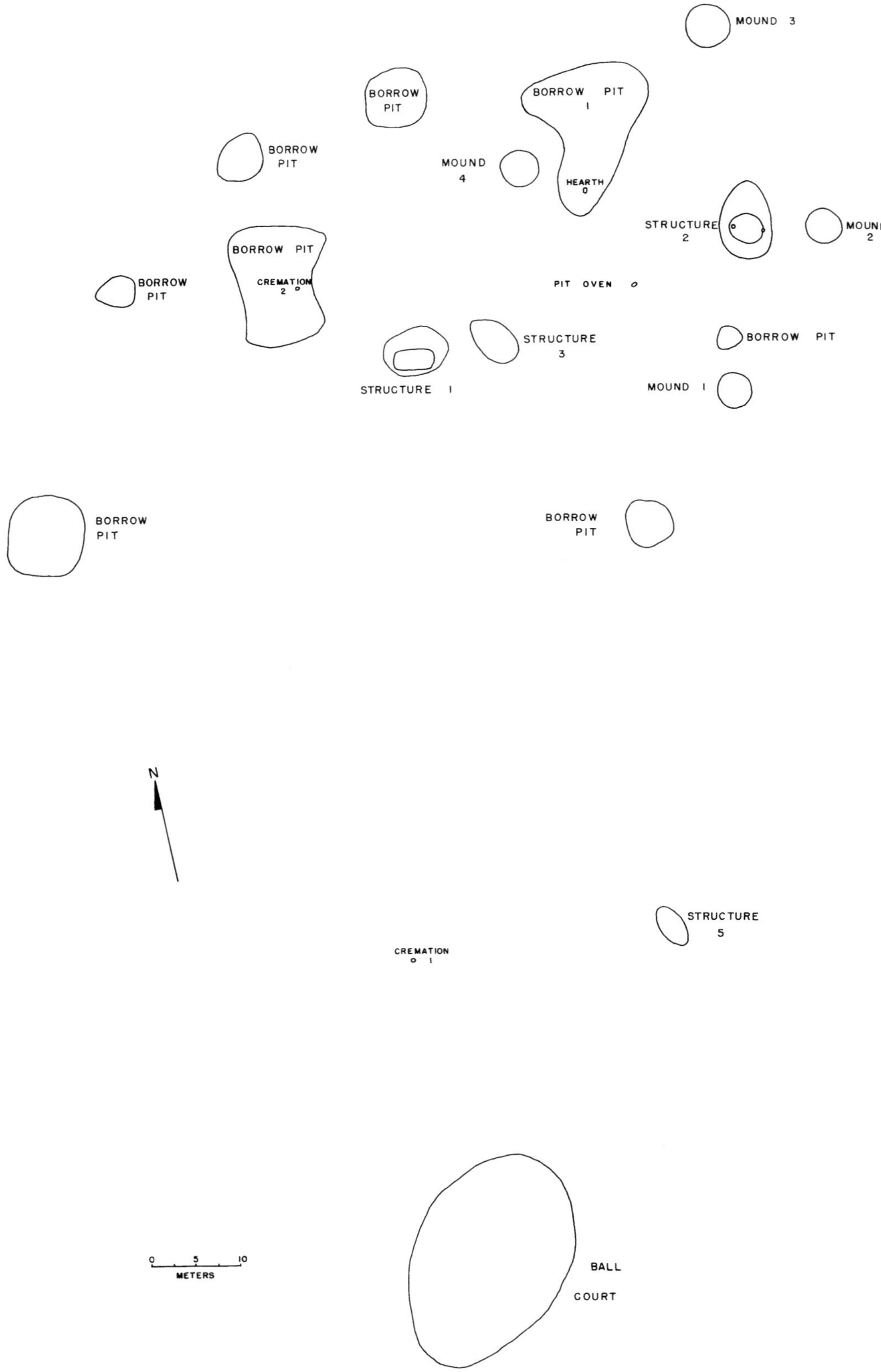

Fig. 2. The Rock Ball Court site, Arizona T:13:9. Structure 4 too far northwest to be shown.

THE COLONIAL PERIOD

In the original report on the excavations at Snaketown (Gladwin and others 1937), the Colonial period of the Hohokam sequence was subdivided into two sequent phases. The earlier phase, Gila Butte, was assigned dates of A.D. 500 to 700, and the later Santa Cruz phase was believed to cover the period from 700 to 900. Data obtained from the excavations in the Painted Rocks Reservoir indicate that the same sequence of phases pertains in this area.

The earliest material obtained in the reservoir area can be assigned to the Gila Butte phase. The Rock Ball Court site, Ariz. T:13:9, is the only excavated site with a Gila Butte-phase component, although there are at least three others in the vicinity of Gila Bend according to surface indications.

Unfortunately, due to the destruction wrought by recent agricultural expansion (Norton Allen, personal communication), little information was obtained on the Santa Cruz-phase occupation in the Gila Bend area. Some information was gained from the Rock Ball Court site, which continued to be occupied into the early part of the Santa Cruz phase, and from the Gatlin site which was first occupied during this phase. One site, which might possibly have yielded a fully-developed Santa Cruz-phase occupation, and which had been largely destroyed prior to excavation, Ariz. Z:2:2, is described below.

GILA BUTTE PHASE

THE ROCK BALL COURT SITE

The Rock Ball Court site (Ariz. T:13:9) is situated 15 airline miles northwest of Gila Bend and 5 miles east of the Painted Rocks Dam (Fig. 1). The site is on a malpais terrace overlooking the Gila River bottoms which are immediately below the terrace to the south. Much of the surface of the site is covered with desert-varnished gravel and basalt boulders. A few saguaros are present, but the most common form of the sparse vegetation at the site is the saltbush.

Surface indications of archaeological features were not prominent, with the exception of the ball court (Fig. 2). Several small trash mounds could be discerned, and a few unusual areas not littered with basalt boulders were noticed. The ball court was quite distinctive, as it was marked by two, long, semicircular ridges of rock. It is from this feature that the site derives its name.

Initial excavations took the form of a number of test trenches scattered at random over the north end of the site. It soon became obvious that the archaeological features were to be found in the areas not littered with basalt boulders, and that there was no further need to test areas covered by boulders. In other words, these cleared areas were the result of intentional clearing, and were not natural features.

Most of the month of December, 1960, was devoted to the excavation of the site. During this period five structures, two cremations, a pit oven, and the ball court were completely excavated. In addition, four trash mounds and seven borrow pits were tested. Numerous trenches were dug to determine the nature of the subsurface conditions at the site (Fig. 2).

Structures

Native soil at the site consisted of gravel and rocks cemented together with caliche. This was overlain by a layer of from 15 to 25 cm. of sandy soil, probably wind- and water-deposited material, rocks, and gravel. Test trenches dug to locate subsurface features were excavated through the upper sandy deposit to the underlying caliche. Features were marked by a break in the relatively-level caliche surface, where a pit had been dug into the ground.

Structure 1

Structure 1 (Figs. 3, 4) was located by excavating a trench along the caliche surface until one of these breaks was located. The trench was extended across the depression until an edge was reached at the opposite side. A narrow trench was then dug entirely around the depression, outlining an irregular but roughly oval pit, which had been excavated into the native caliche. The pit was 8.4 m. long, 6.5 m. wide, and 85 cm. deep. It was oriented in a general east-west direction.

The first trench which extended across the pit had encountered a floor level, so the next project was the removal of the fill overlying the floor. This was done in two steps, the removal of a fill level and a floor level, the latter consisting of the material from 10 cm. above to the floor. This uncovered an oval floor, oriented east-west, and measuring 5.5 m. in length and 3.25 m. in width. The floor did not extend to the edges of the pit, but was separated from the edges by from 1 m. to 3 m. of trashy fill. In addition, the floor was not constructed on the bottom of the pit, but rested on a 10 cm. layer of trash above the bottom.

It is apparent, therefore, that initially a large, roughly oval pit was dug into the native caliche, in which a house was to be constructed. Due to the problem of leveling the bottom of the pit, through which a number of large rocks extended, the alternative of depositing a layer of trash over the pit bottom, which could easily be leveled, was selected. A reason for the construction of the house in the center of the pit, without utilizing the limits of the pit as the edges of the house, is difficult to determine. It was undoubtedly necessary to fill the pit level with the surface of the ground around the house, since rain water would have collected in the pit and made the area unliveable. It should be noted that houses-in-pits are typical of the Hohokam (Gladwin and others 1937: 59).

The house floor was not of caliche, but of a gray-colored clay. A definite post pattern could not be determined, for only a single hole was found in the floor of the house. Four post holes were present outside the floor on the north side of the house. A narrow trench, 10 cm. in width and 15 cm. in depth, could be traced part way along the south side of the floor. This perhaps functioned to hold posts and reeds used in wall construction. A formal hearth was not present, only

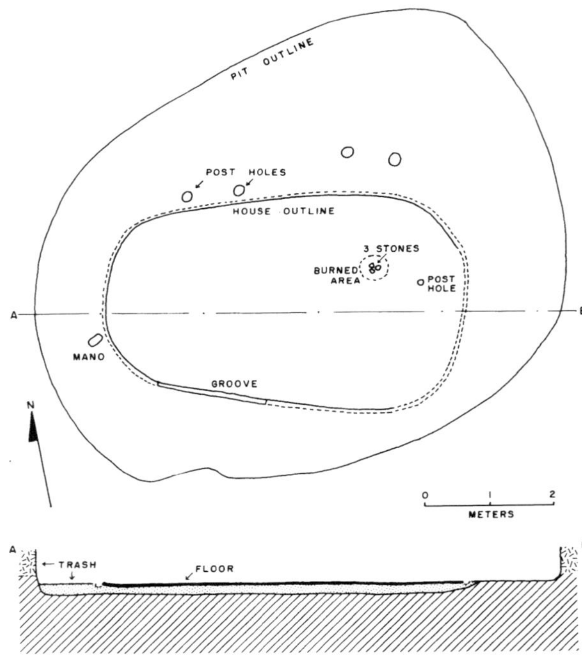

Fig. 3. Plan and section, Structure 1, Rock Ball Court site.

Fig. 4. Structure 1, Rock Ball Court site. Floor edge shown by dotted line where not readily visible.

a roughly circular burned area on the floor near the northeast corner. Three rocks, probably supports for cooking utensils, were present in the center of the burned area. An entrance was not located. Final excavations in connection with Structure 1 consisted in the removal of the east half of the floor, and the underlying trash, which presumably predated the construction of the house.

The only locally-made painted sherds found on the floor of Structure 1 are Gila Butte Red-on-buff, indicating that the house can be assigned to this phase. In addition, the trash layer beneath the floor contained no sherds earlier or later than Gila Butte Red-on-buff. This is an indication that the Rock Ball Court site was occupied for a period of time prior to the construction of Structure 1. During this period, sufficient trash accumulated to allow the deposition of a layer over the bottom of the pit in which Structure 1 was built. Painted sherds from the fill of the house were primarily Gila Butte Red-on-buff, so that most of the trash in the fill was deposited during the Gila Butte phase. A few Santa Cruz Red-on-buff sherds found in the fill indicate the abandoned house area was used for the deposition of trash during the Santa Cruz phase also.

Structure 2

Structure 2 was generally similar to Structure 1. The house was constructed in an oval pit cut into the native caliche-cemented rock and gravel. The pit was 9 m. in length, 6.5 m. in width, and 50 cm. in depth. The floor, which was separated from the edges of the pit by a distance of from 1 m. to 3.5 m., was oval in outline. The long axis, measuring 4.4 m., was oriented east-west. The shorter dimension was 3.4 m. The floor, a clay and caliche mixture about 5 cm. in thickness, was laid on a layer of sterile fill which covered the bottom of the pit to a depth of 10 cm. Four post holes were found in the floor of the structure, but they did not form a regular pattern. Two were at the southeast edge. Two hearths were found, both shallow basins marked by accumulations of burned earth and ash.

Structure 2 was poorly preserved and as a consequence difficult to define. Problems involved in excavating the house were considered difficult enough without compounding them by attempting to maintain strict level digging. As a consequence, some information on the exact temporal placement of the house was lost. This was sacrificed to obtain data on the type of construction.

All of the sherds from the fill and floor of the house were lumped as coming from the general excavation. In the field it was assumed that Structure 2 was an early house, since the fill beneath the floor was sterile. It was felt that the house might have been constructed before enough trash had accumulated to allow the use of this material for leveling the bottom of the pit.

This interpretation is brought into question, however, by the sherd counts from the structure. Only a small amount of locally-made red-on-buff pottery was found, but the sample is about equally distributed between Gila Butte and Santa Cruz Red-on-buff.

Although an exact temporal placement cannot be given, this is not a serious loss. The important fact is that the house corresponds closely in form to the other houses at the site which have been placed in phases, indicating that the house was built by the same people in the same tradition.

Structure 3

Structure 3 was another house-in-a-pit. The pit measured 7 m. in length, 5.5 m. in width, and 70 cm. in depth. The floor, of which only a small section was preserved, was laid on 15 cm. of trash used to level the bottom of the pit. The small triangular section which remained intact was composed of gray-colored clay. The pit was filled with trash, indicating that the site was not abandoned at the time the house fell into disuse.

The house can be assigned to the Gila Butte phase on the basis of the presence of only Gila Butte Red-on-buff sherds on the floor. The trash layer below the floor also dated to this phase. With the exception of a single Santa Cruz sherd, all of the locally-made painted pottery from the trash fill of the house is Gila Butte Red-on-buff. The single later sherd may have been a fortuitous occurrence. The house was probably constructed, abandoned, and the pit filled with trash during the Gila Butte phase.

Structure 4

Structure 4 (Fig. 5) differed considerably from the three just described. It consisted of an oval ring of basalt boulders which were apparent on the surface of the ground. The oval, which was 8.5 m. long and 3.5 m. wide, was oriented northeast-southwest. The caliche floor was extremely irregular, and only 15 cm. below the surface of the ground. A hearth and entrance were not found, nor were post holes present. The smaller oval representing the structure was partially enclosed by a larger oval ring of rocks. There was no evidence of a floor between the outer and inner rings. Considering the obvious differences between Structure 4, and Structures 1, 2, and 3, a different function is suggested. Structure 4 is perhaps a storage unit, and was not used for habitation. This is suggested by the absence of post holes and hearth. The structure could have been roofed by

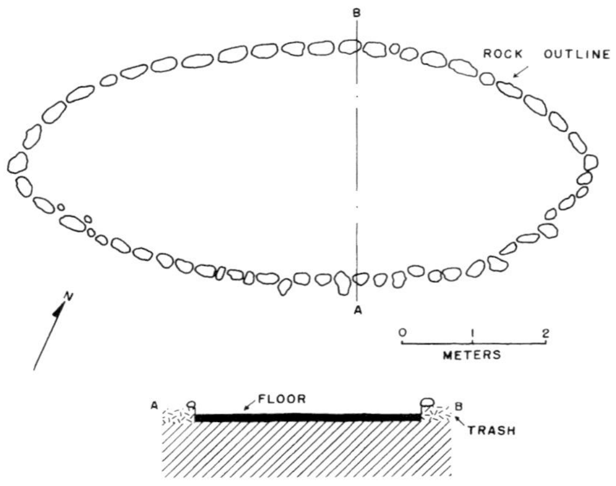

Fig. 5. Plan and section, Structure 4, Rock Ball Court site.

wedging brush between the stones at the edge and bending it together at the center.

Only four sherds were recovered from the excavation of Structure 4. Two of these were Gila Butte Red-on-buff, indicating the likelihood of a Gila Butte-phase construction. The other sherds bore buff slips, but no traces of paint were present.

Structure 5

In most respects, Structure 5 was similar to Structure 4. It was an oval outline of rocks 5 m. in length and 3 m. in width. A floor could not be defined, nor were there any evidences of post holes or a hearth. The smaller oval of rock was not inside a larger area, as was the case for Structure 4. No sherds were found in the structure, and therefore a phase assignment cannot be suggested.

Ball Court

As noted above, the ball court at Ariz. T:13:9 was the most prominent feature at the site. It was marked by two long, semicircular ridges of basalt boulders surrounding an oval depression oriented in a general northeast-southwest direction. The entire court was excavated (Figs. 6, 7).

In the following discussion of the court, an attempt will be made to identify the various stages involved in the construction. The initial step was to clear the area designated for the court of large basalt boulders which littered the surface. These were carried to the sides of the court, and piled in semicircular ridges.

Next, an excavation was made through the overlying topsoil into the native caliche. The maximum depth of the excavation, 50 cm., was in the center, and from this point it sloped upward to the edges. Caliche obtained from the excavation of the court, and perhaps additional caliche brought in from borrow pits, was used to put a smooth surface over the excavation. At the sides of the court, caliche was plastered over the remaining topsoil to form sharply-sloping edges. The edge sloped upward to the base of the rock pile. A hole, 20 cm. in diameter and 10 cm. in depth, was cut into the center of the court for a marker. At the ends of the court, the caliche floor was extended out through the break between the boulder ridges and connected to an apron of caliche which completely encircled the court outside the boulder ridges. The apron averaged 1 m. in width, and

Fig. 6. Ball court, Rock Ball Court site.

sloped downward from the point where it joined the ridges.

In summary, the ball court at the Rock Ball Court site consisted of an oval floor measuring 26 m. in length by 14.5 m. in width. The floor was bordered on each side by semicircular ridges of earth and basalt boulders, material cleared from the court during construction. The floor was connected to a caliche apron, which completely encircled the court outside the ridges. End markers were not found, but a center marker consisting of a shallow hole in the floor was present. The court was oriented 43 degrees 30 minutes east of north.

In a discussion of dates for the Rock Ball Court site in a later section, evidence is presented in support of the fact that the occupation of the site began during the Gila Butte phase, and continued to the Gila Butte-Santa Cruz transition, or into the early part of the Santa Cruz phase. The ball court could presumably date to either the Gila Butte or the Santa Cruz phase. Only a small number of locally-made painted sherds were found during the excavation of the ball court. With one exception, all were Gila Butte Red-on-buff. The

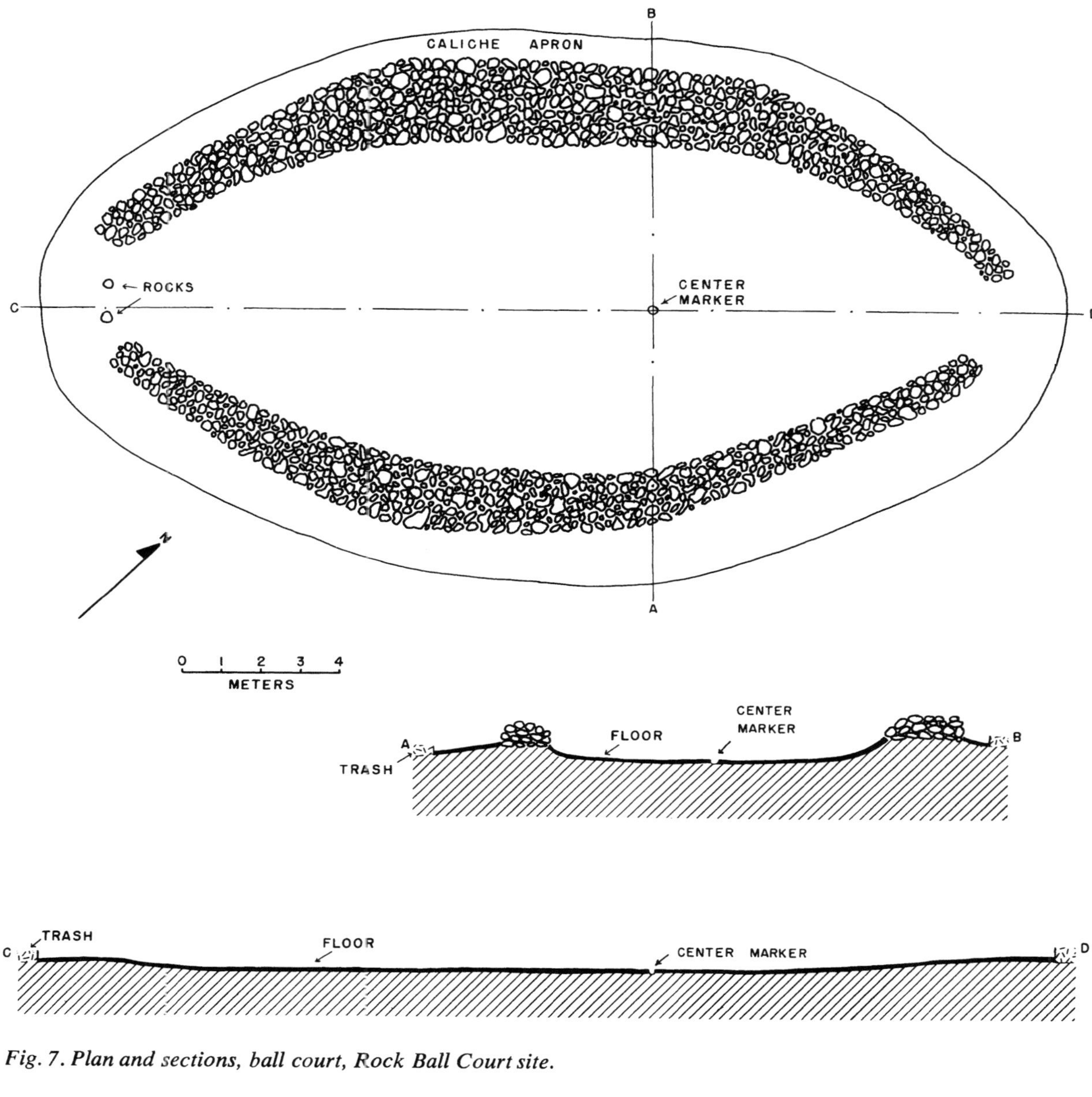

Fig. 7. Plan and sections, ball court, Rock Ball Court site.

exception was a Santa Cruz Red-on-buff sherd found in the fill at the southwest end of the court. The fact that a majority of the red-on-buff sherds were Gila Butte is an indication that the construction and use of the court can be assigned to this phase.

Material covering the floor of the court consisted of wind- and water-deposited sand and silt, as the court was filled by natural means. This is in contrast to the situation at a number of other courts in the Gila Bend area, which were found to have trash fills, indicating that they were used for the deposition of trash after the period of use as a ball court had ended. The fact that this court was filled by natural means, and that a majority of the sherds from the court were Gila Butte Red-on-buff, indicates the probability that the filling did not take place much later than the end of the Gila Butte phase. This is another indication, therefore, that the court should be assigned to this phase.

Other data collected at the site reinforce the suggested Gila Butte-phase assignment. First is the fact that excavations in other sections of the site all point to an essentially Gila Butte-phase occupation. This occupation continued to the Gila Butte-Santa Cruz transition or into the early part of the Santa Cruz phase, but material dating to this later period is extremely scarce. Although only the northern one-third of the site was tested, sherd collections obtained from the surface of the remainder of the site suggested no areas where a concentration of Santa Cruz phase material was present. The fact that the major occupation of the site was during the Gila Butte phase indicates further that the ball court should be assigned to the Gila Butte phase.

Comparative data are also in support of this conclusion. At the Gatlin site (Ariz. Z:2:1) the earliest period of construction in Ball Court 1 was found to have been during the Santa Cruz phase. This court was typical of Casa Grande-type courts known from later periods (see discussion of ball courts below), but varied somewhat from the court at the Rock Ball Court site. The major points of variance were the absence of a caliche apron from the Gatlin-site court, and the shallowness of the Rock Ball Court as compared to the court at the Gatlin site. This indicates that by the time of the Santa Cruz phase, the more typical Casa Grande-type court was established, and that the varying features found on the ball court at Ariz. T:13:9 date to an earlier period of time.

In summary, the ball court at Ariz. T:13:9 can be assigned to the Gila Butte phase for a number of reasons. First is the fact that a majority of sherds from the court were Gila Butte Red-on-buff. Second, the major period of occupation of the site was during the Gila Butte phase. Third, the court varies somewhat in construction features from typical Casa Grande-type courts, which were being constructed from the Santa Cruz phase through the Classic period.

Cremations

Cremation was the typical method of disposal of the dead among the Hohokam (Gladwin and others 1937: 91), and cremations are usually among the more common discoveries in Hohokam sites. On the other hand, at the Rock Ball Court site only two cremations were located (Fig. 2). In part this is probably due to the restricted amount of excavation accomplished and to the fact that most of this excavation was centered in the northern end of the site. Cremation areas may have been localized farther south, but if this was the case, there were no indications on the surface of the ground in the form of calcined bones brought up by rodents.

Cremation 1

Cremation 1 consisted of a small circular pit, in the native caliche-cemented rock, beneath the trash fill in one of the borrow pits. The pit was 20 cm. in diameter and could be traced to a depth of 15 cm. in the caliche. No trace of the pit outline could be found in the overlying trash. The pit contained a handful of poorly reduced human bones and a quantity of mesquite charcoal. Despite the presence of charcoal in the pit there was no evidence of burning. The charcoal was probably gathered up at the crematorium for burial with the bones. No offerings accompanied the cremation.

Cremation 2

Cremation 2, an oval pit with a length of 60 cm. and a width of 45 cm., was excavated into native soil to a depth of 20 cm. Calcined human bone and mesquite charcoal fragments were scattered throughout the pit. Apparently the body was cremated at some other spot, and some of the larger bone fragments and pieces of charcoal were gathered up and deposited in the pit. No offerings accompanied the cremation.

No artifacts were found in association with the cremations at the Rock Ball Court site, so that it is not possible to suggest phase assignments. Both are typical of the cremations of the Colonial Hohokam period (Gladwin and others 1937: 93).

Pit Oven

The pit oven was located by means of a test trench placed near the north end of the site (Fig. 2). It consisted of a roughly circular hole, 60 cm. in diameter and 30 cm. in depth, cut into the native caliche-cemented rock. The pit was filled with sand, charcoal, and ash. It may have been used to cook some form of vegetable food. No painted sherds were found, and a phase assignment cannot be given.

Trash Mounds

Several small trash mounds were scattered over the surface of the site (Fig. 2). A majority of these were near the north end, and it was on the basis of this distribution that the decision was made to concentrate excavation in this area. All of the mounds were marked by low piles of basalt boulders, representing material cleaned from areas of the site where excavations were to be made. Small quantities of trash, the residue from occupation of the site, were found in the mounds in addition to the rocks.

Excavations were made in four of the mounds which averaged 4 m. in diameter. In the case of three, trenches measuring 75 cm. in width were dug through the centers. A fourth was further tested by means of a 2-m.-square block removed to obtain a large sample of sherds. Stratigraphic controls were not maintained due to the absence of any significant depth (the mounds averaged about 25 cm. in depth), and due to the fact that the trash was mixed with large boulders making controlled excavation difficult.

Trash Mound 1 was the only mound which had no Santa Cruz Red-on-buff sherds included in the trash. This indicates that the mound accumulated during the Gila Butte phase. Trash mounds 2, 3, and 4 all contained a few Santa Cruz Red-on-buff sherds, but most of the locally-made painted pottery in these mounds was Gila Butte Red-on-buff. Most of the trash in these three mounds was apparently deposited during the Gila Butte phase, but use of the mounds continued to the Gila Butte-Santa Cruz transition or into the early part of the Santa Cruz phase.

Borrow Pits

The most common archaeological features encountered at the site were large pits which were dug into the caliche apparently to obtain construction material (Fig. 2). Seven of these were tested thoroughly enough to determine their outlines. In the case of one other pit, approximately one-half was completely excavated. Most of the borrow pits, while irregular, were generally circular in outline. They varied in diameter from 2.5 to 18 m. All had been used for the deposition of trash.

Borrow Pit 1

One-half of this borrow area was completely excavated in hopes of learning more about the function of the pits. The maximum depth, 75 cm., was in the center. From this point it sloped in all directions to the surface of the caliche. The bottom of the pit was rough and marked by many small cavities and depressions. Several large basalt boulders rested on the bottom of the pit, probably those which were too large to move. A hearth was discovered in the bottom of the pit near the south end (Fig. 2). It measured 40 cm. in diameter and 15 cm. in depth. The shallow basin was underlain by a layer of burned caliche. Little more was added to the understanding of these features by the excavation of Borrow Pit 1. The most obvious explanation would seem to be that they were borrow pits from which caliche was obtained for use in the construction of house floors, walls, and roofs.

A majority of the locally-made painted sherds from Borrow Pit 1 can be classified as Gila Butte Red-on-buff, indicating that most of the trash fill was deposited during the Gila Butte phase. A few Santa Cruz Red-on-buff sherds represent the continued use of the pit for the deposition of refuse during the Gila Butte-Santa Cruz transition, or during the early part of the Santa Cruz phase.

Pottery

A total of 5,461 sherds was collected at the Rock Ball Court site. No complete or restorable vessels were found. A majority of the sherds (4,521 or 82.9 per cent) was plainware. Painted pottery accounts for 11.5 per cent of the sample (622 sherds). The remainder of the collection is made up of several categories which occurred in minor percentages. Each of the pottery types and varieties found at the site will be considered in detail below.

Gila Butte Red-on-Buff

A single painted pottery type, Gila Butte Red-on-buff (Fig. 8), accounted for 96.0 per cent of the painted pottery found at the site. The type was only found in sherd form. Despite the disadvantage of having no complete vessels for comparative study, it is noteworthy that no differences could be discerned between the sherds from Ariz. T:13:9 and those from Snaketown (Gladwin and others 1937: 185–89). Gila Butte Red-on-buff is diagnostic of the Gila Butte phase, and the preponderance of the type at the Rock Ball Court site indicates that the major occupation of the site can be assigned to this phase.

Santa Cruz Red-on-Buff

Santa Cruz Red-on-buff (Fig. 13) was the only other locally-made painted pottery type found at the site. It constitutes 3.5 per cent of the painted sherds. The discovery of this type is important, for it demonstrates a later use of the site.

Unclassified Red-on-Buff

Included in this category are a number of locally-made painted sherds which could not be classified, for various reasons. Most of the sherds were small, and in addition lacked sufficient paint or diagnostic design elements which would have allowed classification into types.

Unpainted Grooved

Grouped together under this heading are sherds with grooved decoration, but with no traces of paint. All are probably Gila Butte Red-on-buff sherds which have been worn and eroded to the point where no paint remains. They were grouped under this heading, however, because the possibility remains that they could represent other types.

Hohokam Buff

Another miscellaneous category contains all of the buff-slipped sherds which have no traces of paint. These sherds could represent eroded examples, or sherds broken from sections of vessels where paint was not present. Probably both Gila Butte and Santa Cruz Red-on-buff are represented in this group.

Fig. 8. Gila Butte Red-on-buff sherds, Rock Ball Court site.

Gila Plain

A total of 1,193 sherds (25.4 per cent of the plainware) can be classified according to the published definition of Gila Plain (Gladwin and others 1937: 205–207). This type grades imperceptibly into Gila Plain, Gila Bend Variety.

Gila Plain, Gila Bend Variety

Gila Plain, Gila Bend Variety has not previously been described in the literature. It accounts for the bulk of the plainware found at the Rock Ball Court site (74.6 per cent). The assignment of varietal status to the sherds in this group is in recognition of the fact that local materials were used in their manufacture. As a consequence, the sherds have a significant geographical distribution, one of the criteria on which pottery varieties are based (Wheat, Gifford, and Wasley 1958: 36).

Problems arise, however, when an attempt is made to distinguish this variety from the already-established type, Gila Plain. In the following discussion, comparisons are made with Gila Plain as it is known from Snaketown (Gladwin and others 1937: 205–207). The presence of quantities of mica in the paste of Gila Plain is its major diagnostic feature. The local Gila Bend Variety of Gila Plain is distinguished from Gila Plain by the fact that it has little or no mica as a component of the paste. This is essentially a negative distinction, but the only one which can be offered at the present time. If in the future detailed microscopic and petrographic analyses are made of Hohokam plainware, it may be possible to define valid distinctions on the basis of differing mineral constituents in the paste of the various local varieties.

It was noted above that Gila Plain corresponding to the original definition of the type (Gladwin and others 1937: 205–207) is present at the Rock Ball Court site. Two alternative explanations of this information are possible. First of all, Gila Plain from the Rock Ball Court site may represent the results of trade with Hohokam sites farther east, such as Snaketown. Second, it may represent the local production of pottery from sources of material closely similar to the materials available to Hohokam potters farther east. The second alternative is favored for several reasons.

It is doubtful that trade in utility pottery was extensive enough to account for the quantity of Gila Plain which was found at Ariz. T:13:9. Utility pottery was produced in quantity, and used in everyday preparation of food for storage. Judging from the quantity of sherds found in refuse deposits, breakage must have taken place at a rapid rate. It is doubtful, therefore, that a reliance was placed on trade for the supply of utility pottery. Some trade may have occurred, but not to a degree that would account for one-fourth of the plainware.

Further support for the inference that Gila Plain found in the Gila Bend area was made from local materials similar to those used at Snaketown comes from the knowledge that Gila Plain, Gila Bend Variety, grades into Gila Plain. Although most sherds of Gila Plain, Gila Bend Variety, can be distinguished from Gila Plain there are cases in which the separation is difficult. This would seem to indicate that materials available in the Gila Bend area for the production of pottery graded from those in which quantities of mica were present to those with absolutely no mica. Another possibility is that Hohokam potters in the Gila Bend area attempted to duplicate Gila Plain by adding quantities of mica to the paste. Usually, however, less mica was incorporated, and Gila Plain, Gila Bend Variety, was the result.

Despite these difficulties, it is known that a local variety of Gila Plain was produced in the Gila Bend area, from local sources of materials. The earliest occurrence of Gila Plain, Gila Bend Variety, is dated to the Gila Butte phase, as no earlier sites were dug in the Painted Rocks Reservoir. It is worthy of note that Gila Plain and the Gila Bend Variety are found in all of the later phases encountered in the Gila Bend area.

Intrusive Pottery

When work was begun at the Rock Ball Court site, it was hoped that intrusive sherds would be found which would assist in dating the Gila Butte phase. Unfortunately, this was not the case, and only three intrusive sherds were collected at the site. All of the sherds are probably from a single Rillito Red-on-brown bowl. Rillito Red-on-brown is a Hohokam type from the Tucson area which is equated in time with Santa Cruz Red-on-buff from the Gila Basin. The sherd probably dates to the Santa Cruz-phase occupation of Ariz. T:13:9.

It came as a surprise that no sherds of Lower Colorado buffware were recovered from the site. This ware is of common occurrence in sites in the reservoir from the Sacaton phase through the Classic period. The fact that none were recovered from the Rock Ball Court site indicates that contact had not yet taken place between the groups of the Lower Colorado and the Hohokam of the Gila Bend area.

Discussion

A majority of the locally-made painted pottery collected at the Rock Ball Court site can be classified as Gila Butte Red-on-buff. This indicates that the major period of occupation at the site was during the Gila Butte phase, which has been assigned dates of A.D. 500–700 (Gladwin and others 1937, Fig. 106).

Santa Cruz Red-on-buff sherds were also found at the site, but in minor quantities. They were scattered indiscriminately, and were not found in clear-cut stratigraphic situations which would demonstrate their relationship to Gila Butte Red-on-buff. No archaeological features were found in which Santa Cruz Red-on-buff predominated. The occupation of the site may have been continuous from the Gila Butte phase into the Santa Cruz phase, although it is equally possible that the Santa Cruz sherds represent a later sporadic reuse of the site for the mining of caliche.

Artifacts

The collection of artifacts from the Rock Ball Court site is not large. This is due in part to the restricted amount of excavation which was carried on, and apparently in part to the fact that artifacts were not as common at this site as they were at other sites in the Gila Bend area. Those which were found indicate a well-developed technical knowledge and a realization of the potentialities of the local resources.

Ceramic Artifacts

Figurines. Two fragmentary figurines were collected. Both are crude representations, modeled from a coarse paste. One is a human form, although only the torso remains. Arms are represented by short stubs of clay pinched out from the body. The sex is not indicated. Dimensions: length, 3 cm.; width, 1.5 cm.; thickness, 1.2 cm.

The second figurine, which is more fragmentary, is probably a human form. A section of an arm remains, which was added to the body as a separate lump of clay. A breast is indicated by a small hole punched into the body. Dimensions: length, 7 cm.; width, 3.5 cm.

Sherd Discs. Six perforated or partially-perforated discs manufactured from sherds were found. The edges of all the discs were ground until a circular shape was attained. Three of the discs are of Gila Plain, one is of Gila Plain, Gila Bend Variety, one is formed from an unpainted grooved sherd, and the last is made from an unclassified red-on-buff sherd. Dimensions: diameter, 4.2 to 8.5 cm.

Two unperforated sherd discs were manufactured from Gila Plain, Gila Bend Variety sherds. Dimensions: diameter, 4 to 5 cm.

Miscellaneous Ceramic Objects. Grouped under this heading are three small ceramic fragments, which defy exact identification and classification. All have been modeled, and it is possible that they are sections broken from figurines.

Stone Artifacts

Choppers. Three artifacts fashioned from water-worn cobbles are classifiable as choppers. In all three cases, the only modification of the original

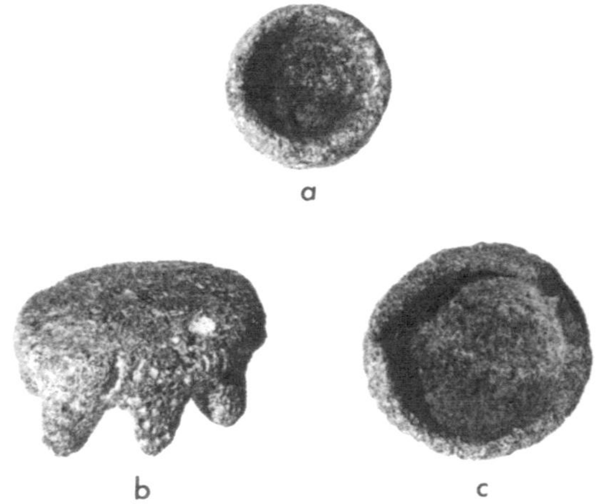

Fig. 9. Ground stone artifacts, Rock Ball Court site: a, c, *stone vessels;* b, *footed table, diam. 8.2 cm.*

cobble has been the removal of several large flakes from one surface, thereby forming chisel-shaped cutting edges. Flakes were removed by the percussion technique. The hand-hold is the unmodified cobble surface. In two cases, the cutting edge has been battered and rounded. Dimensions: length, 7.8 to 11.3 cm.; width, 3.8 to 8.4 cm.; thickness, 1.3 to 4.5 cm.

Stone Vessels. The three stone vessels collected from the site are manufactured from vesicular basalt. One is a simple form, with a circular outline, slightly outcurved walls, and a convex base (Fig. 9*b*). The rim is rounded, and the walls of the central basin slope in from the rim to a curved bottom. Dimensions: diameter, 5 cm.; height, 4 cm.

The second vessel (Fig. 9*a*) is also circular in outline. A deep groove encircles the circumference, and the bottom is flat. The rounded rim slopes gradually into a central concave basin. Dimensions: diameter, 7.5 cm.; height, 7.5 cm.

The third vessel is circular in outline, but differs from the other two in that it is in the form of a small table supported by six pointed legs (Fig. 9*c*). The legs vary in length and slope slightly outward. Traces of grinding are present on the flat surface. Dimensions: diameter, 8 cm.; height, 3.5 cm.

Manos. A sample of five manos was gathered from the site. All are roughly rectangular in outline. They were manufactured for use with both hands. Three examples exhibit unifacial wear, and the other two were used on both faces. All of the manos have ground ends indicating that they were used in trough metates. Two of the specimens were manufactured from vesicular basalt, two from quartzite, and one from granite. In two cases the manos are modified water-worn cobbles. Dimensions: length, 18 to 22 cm.; width, 10 to 11 cm.; thickness, 3.5 to 6 cm.

Pestle. The single pestle recovered is circular in cross section, has a roughly conical outline, and is made from vesicular basalt. The grinding end is flat to slightly concave and the edges are battered indicating that the pestle was probably used in a stone mortar (Haury 1950: 321). Dimensions: length, 13.5 cm.; diameter, 7 cm.

Abrading Stones. Two small abrading stones were found at the site. One is a fine-grained water-worn pebble with traces of grinding on both faces, and the other is a flat plate of stone with similar marks of use.

Miscellaneous Ground Stone Fragments. Included in this category are two ground fragments of vesicular basalt, which cannot be definitely categorized. Both may originally have been sections of stone vessels.

Shell Artifacts

Shell species in the collection include *Glycymeris maculatus, Cardium elatum,* and *Turitella leucostoma.* All are from the Gulf of California.

Plain Glycymeris Bracelets. The most common artifacts of shell from the site are bracelets manufactured from *Glycymeris* valves. A total of 38 uncarved examples were collected. Twenty-nine of these are of the medium-width-band type (band width between 5 and 10 mm.). Four of the 29 retain the umbo, which has been modified in every case by its reduction to a small rounded projection. None have perforated umbos. The other nine are plain bracelets with thin bands (band width less than 5 mm.). Five of these retain umbos, modified in the same fashion. Again, none are perforated.

Carved Glycymeris bracelets are represented by two fragments. One is a small shell frog which was broken from a bracelet, and the other is a bracelet which retains a small section of a carved frog. In both cases, the frog representation was carved from the umbo.

Miscellaneous Fragments. A single fragment of a *Cardium* shell retains a section of a V-shaped cut along one edge. This is probably a reject piece, cut from a shell which was being fashioned into an ornament.

SANTA CRUZ PHASE

THE ROCK BALL COURT SITE

It has been noted in the foregoing description of the Rock Ball Court site (Ariz. T:13:9) that some use of the site was apparently made during the Santa Cruz phase (A.D. 700–900). The absence of architectural features assignable to this phase and the general scattering of Santa Cruz Red-on-buff sherds in relatively small quantities suggest a possible intermittent use of the site during this period, perhaps for the purpose of obtaining caliche for use in sites down on the floodplain where there were no local caliche deposits.

THE GATLIN SITE

Excavations at the Gatlin site (Ariz. Z:2:1) are described in the section dealing with the Sedentary Period. Here it will suffice to report only the evidence pointing to a Santa Cruz-phase occupation of the site.

In Trash Mound 3 the lower two levels contained Santa Cruz Red-on-buff as the only locally-made painted pottery. Sherds from the layer of trash between the two main construction periods in Ball Court 1 indicate that the trash was deposited during the Santa Cruz-Sacaton transition. This indicates that the first period of ball-court construction at the Gatlin site probably took place during the Santa Cruz phase, and the evidence suggests that the initial occupation of this site was during the Santa Cruz phase.

ARIZONA Z:2:2

A site which might possibly have yielded a fully-developed Santa Cruz-phase occupation for the Gila Bend area was Ariz. Z:2:2 (Fig. 1). Unfortunately, between the time of the original survey in 1957 (Schroeder 1961) and the test excavations in 1961, the site was almost completely destroyed by construction activities. During the winter of 1958–59, a large dike was constructed around the cemetery for the Papago village situated two and one-half miles north of Gila Bend. The dike, for the protection of the cemetery against water in the Painted Rocks Reservoir, had incorporated in its fill most of Ariz. Z:2:2. During the initial survey of the site in 1957, three areas were delimited. Area A was primarily Hohokam of the Colonial and Sedentary periods. Areas B and C both had historic Papago material.

The section in which excavations were made was a small remaining portion of Area A. It was tested by means of 11 trenches, none of which succeeded in locating prehistoric architectural features.

Pottery

Hohokam red-on-buff sherds were found in a ratio of about three Santa Cruz sherds to one Sacaton sherd, indicating the possibility of a fully-developed Santa Cruz-phase occupation. As was the case for other Hohokam sites in the reservoir, plainware accounted for most of the ceramic inventory. In the case of Ariz. Z:2:2, 577 sherds out of a total of 780 were Gila Plain, Gila Bend Variety. The single intrusive sherd is Lower Colorado buffware. One sherd of Papago Red-on-buff is probably a float specimen from either Area B or C.

Artifacts

A small collection of artifacts found during the test excavation of this site seems to belong to the prehistoric Hohokam occupation.

Ceramic Artifacts

Sherd Discs. Three fragmentary sherd discs, all with central biconical perforations, were collected at the site. One is made from a Gila Plain sherd, another from a Gila Bend Variety sherd, and the third from a sherd of Hohokam buffware.

Stone Artifacts

Chopper. The single chopper was manufactured from a water-worn cobble by the removal of a number of flakes from one face. This has formed a chisel-shaped cutting edge. The hand-hold is the natural surface of the cobble. Dimensions: length, 8.1 cm.; width, 4.1 cm.; thickness, 3.1 cm.

Pitted Stone. One irregularly-shaped stone with concave pits in each face was found. Dimensions: diameter, 5.3 cm.; thickness, 3.4 cm.

Shell Artifacts

Plain Glycymeris Bracelets. Two fragmentary bracelets made from *Glycymeris* valves were found at the site. Neither is ornamented, and both lack the umbo. One of the bracelets is of the medium-band type, and the other has a wide band.

Carved Glycymeris Bracelet. The only other shell artifact found at the site is a fragment of *Glycymeris* bearing three U-shaped notches on one edge. This may be a fragment of a bracelet.

DISCUSSION

Excavation in Colonial-period sites of the Painted Rocks Reservoir area was not extensive, but at the Rock Ball Court site (Ariz. T:13:9) significant new information about the Gila Butte phase was gathered. These new data concern primarily the ball court and the nature of the domestic structures, but they also include caliche borrow pits and the methods of disposing of refuse.

The ball court, small and oriented northeast-southwest, can be classified as a Casa Grande-type of Southwestern ball court. However, it is the earliest yet excavated by about two hundred years. The most unusual feature about this court, perhaps a unique characteristic, is the caliche apron built outside the rock ridges and connected to the court floor through the end units. This feature, together with the rock ridges, the unusual shallowness of the court, the fact that it is not oriented north-south much more than it is oriented east-west, and the early date (Gila Butte phase)—all may combine to suggest to some that perhaps it should not be called a Casa Grande type of court. Our reasons for calling it this are presented in the section in which the classification of Southwestern ball courts is discussed in some detail (p. 81).

Characteristic pre-Classic-period houses of the Hohokam are described as houses built completely within pits. These pits are usually fairly shallow and not much larger than the houses built in them (Gladwin and others 1937: 79–80). The

Rock Ball Court-site houses are somewhat at variance with this pattern, since they were built in relatively large, deep, and irregularly-shaped pits. Possibly these houses were built in the pits as an afterthought, after the pits were developed as caliche was mined from them. Equally possible is the suggestion that this local pattern represents a regional exaggeration of the normal Hohokam house tradition. Not previously reported for the Colonial period of the Hohokam are surface structures similar to those encountered at the Rock Ball Court site, which were probably used for storage. Whether this is a local development or merely a common Hohokam architectural feature not previously recognized archaeologically is a question which cannot be answered without more work in other areas.

While there may be some question about whether the house pits were originally dug in order to obtain caliche, there seems to be little doubt about the fact that pits were dug for this purpose at the Rock Ball Court site. Caliche was not directly at hand for those Hohokam living down on the first terrace of the Gila River or on the floodplain, and yet caliche constituted a traditional building material for the Hohokam and was used by them in the Painted Rocks Reservoir area. The high dissected terrace on which the Rock Ball Court site was built provided a source of caliche not far from several of the lower villages.

Because of these caliche borrow pits near their houses on this malpais terrace, the inhabitants of the Rock Ball Court site were presented with an alternative method of disposing of their garbage. Traditionally, the Hohokam heaped their refuse into mounds that often became quite large. At the Rock Ball Court site this practice was not abandoned altogether, but there seems to have been a strong preference for the ready-made garbage pits.

Hohokam painted pottery in Colonial-period sites of the Gila Bend area is virtually indistinguishable from that at Snaketown. The Hohokam sequence for this period was supported at the Rock Ball Court site by the occurrence of Gila Butte Red-on-buff stratigraphically earlier than Santa Cruz Red-on-buff (Structure 3) and at the Gatlin site by the occurrence of Santa Cruz Red-on-buff stratigraphically earlier than Sacaton Red-on-buff (Ball Court 1 and Trash Mound 3).

THE SEDENTARY PERIOD

The most elaborate development of Hohokam culture in the Gila Bend area occurred during the Sedentary period, A.D. 900–1100. Although this period was originally subdivided into two sequent phases (Gladwin and others 1937: 260–64), additional work has failed to substantiate the Santan phase as more than a very local development in the Phoenix area, and consequently it has been dropped from the sequence. The Sacaton phase remains the single classificatory unit in the Sedentary period.

In the reservoir area four sites with Sacaton-phase components were excavated. Most of the work during the first season was devoted to the excavation of a platform mound at the Gatlin site (Wasley 1960b). Excavations were resumed at the Gatlin site in the second season, and in addition the field program was extended to include the Sacaton-phase Citrus site. During the third season Sedentary-period ball courts were excavated at Ariz. T:14:14 and Ariz. T:14:15, and comparative data were collected from a Sacaton-phase site, Ariz. T:14:19, which lies outside the reservoir area.

SACATON PHASE

GATLIN SITE

A detailed report on the excavation of a Sacaton-phase platform mound, which was dug during the first season at the Gatlin site, has been published (Wasley 1960b). This artificial mound was rebuilt, modified, and repaired through six major stages of construction. Typically, the platform mound in use at any given stage was flat-topped and slope-sided with rounded corners and an irregular squarish or subrectangular outline. The platforms were made of a caliche plaster, and the sides were faced with a plaster of mixed caliche and adobe, placed directly over the earth core. Three small outlying mounds were connected to the main platform mound by means of narrow radial walls. These were eventually covered up during the later enlargements of the platform mound. In its final and largest stage the platform mound was about 95 feet long and 70 feet wide at the base and probably rose to a height of about 12 feet above the plaza surface on which it was built. Evidence of pre-mound occupation of the immediate area was encountered underneath the platform mound and in an excavated pit house (Structure 1) near the southeast corner of the mound. Cremation 1 was found in the fill of the pit house (Wasley 1960b: 258).

During the second season, work at the Gatlin site focused on an attempt to obtain a fuller story of the occupation of the site than was gained from the excavation of the platform mound during the first season. Consequently, excavations were made in obvious features of the site such as trash mounds and ball courts, while numerous test trenches were dug and stripping with a bulldozer was undertaken to discover features not apparent on the surface. Data obtained during the second season are presented below.

Trash Mounds

Next to the platform mound, the most conspicuous features of the Gatlin site are 22 trash mounds scattered over the surface (Fig. 10). The mounds are low and rounded, with average diameters of about 15 meters, and average heights above the present ground surface of about 1 m. The surfaces of all the mounds are covered with sherds, broken rock, shell waste, and occasional bones. Amateur excavations are present in nearly every one. With one exception, the mounds do not seem to have any relation to one another, or to any of the other features at the site. The exception is a group of trash mounds situated approximately 120 m. northeast of the pyramid. These

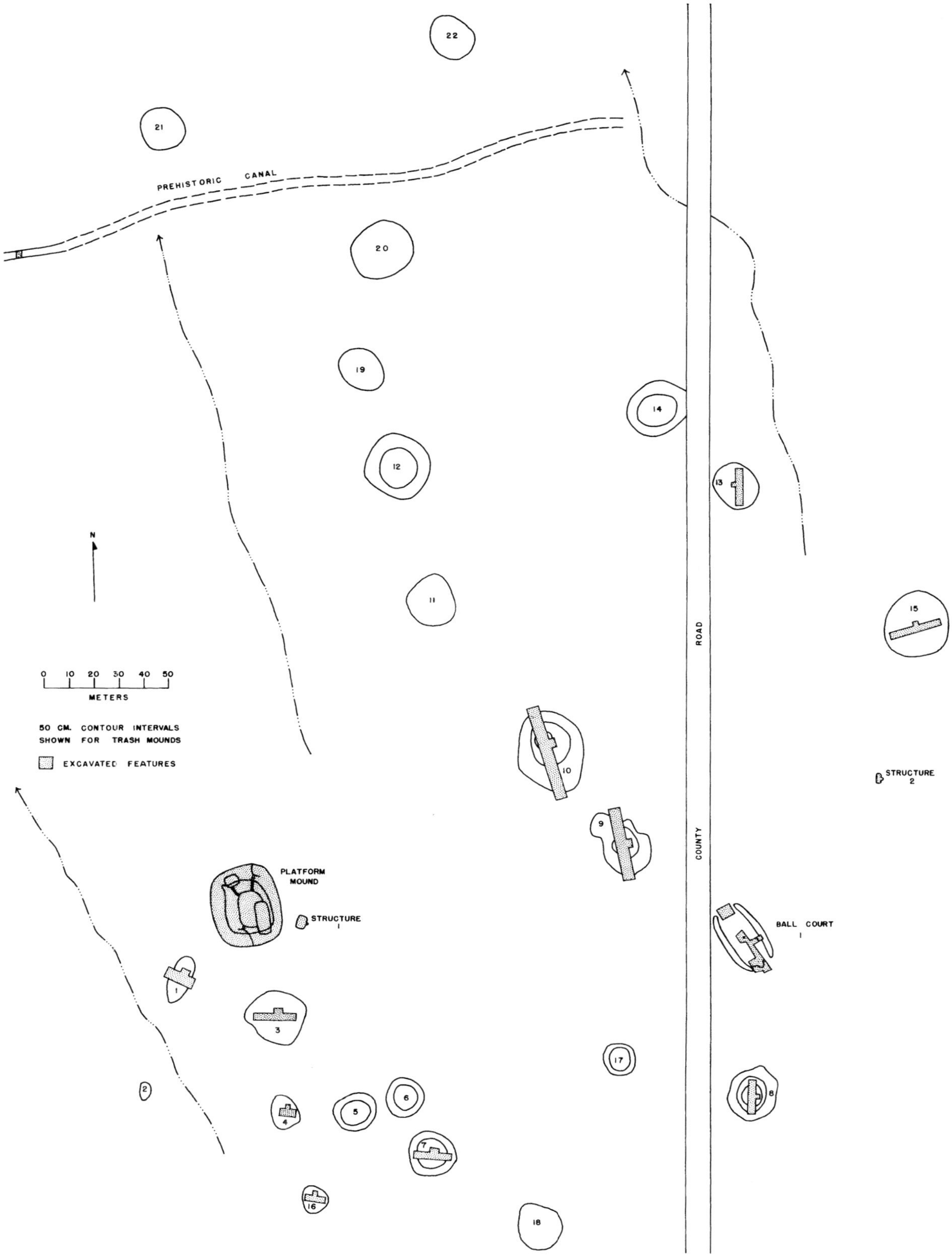

Fig. 10. The Gatlin site, Arizona Z: 2:1. Numbered areas are trash mounds.

mounds, numbers 9, 10, 11, 12, 19, and 20, are arranged in a long shallow semicircle, perhaps intentionally (Fig. 10).

Excavations were made in ten of the trash mounds, numbers 1, 3, 4, 7, 8, 9, 10, 13, 15, and 16. The general procedure followed in the excavation of the trash mounds was first to cut a long narrow trench through the mound. In the case of the largest mounds, 1, 9, and 10, the initial trench was made by a bulldozer, those of the other excavated mounds being hand dug. On completion of the excavation of the trench, which was carried into the sterile native soil below the mound, one face was straightened and carefully cleaned in an attempt to discover physical stratigraphy. In no case could any definitely separable levels be discerned. The fill of the mounds consisted of an unconsolidated mass of mixed earth, varying from mound to mound in the quantity of trash included.

The next step in the excavation of the trash mounds was to remove one or two 2-m. columns from one side of the initial cross trench. All of the artifacts from these columns and from the trench were combined and labeled as coming from the general excavation of the mound. In the case of Mounds 1, 3, 7, 9, and 10, a second set of 2-m.-square columns was removed in 20-cm. arbitrary levels. Artifacts from each level were kept separate in an attempt to pick up artifact differences from the various levels. The greatest depth of deposit in the mounds was 1.4 m., which was found in Trash Mounds 1 and 9. The other mounds averaged about 1 m. in depth.

One special feature noted in the excavation of these mounds was a difference in the quantity of trash which they contained. In the case of Mounds 1 and 3, the mound fill contained large quantities of charcoal and ash and in general had a very trashy appearance. The other excavated mounds had much cleaner fills, with lenses of sterile sand often included. The trashy nature of Mounds 1 and 3 is further demonstrated by the greater quantity of animal bone which these mounds contained. No quantitative expression of this difference can be given, but it was apparent while working these mounds in the field that the trashier mounds were producing more animal bone than those with cleaner fill. This distinction does not appear in differences in sherd quantities. Trash Mound 3 definitely had a much larger quantity of sherds than any of the other mounds, but the quantity of sherds from Trash Mound 1 is comparable to that from a number of the other mounds. The fill of the mounds with less trash closely resembled the fill in the cores of the platform mound excavated the first season (Wasley 1960b).

Ball Courts

Excavations were made in two ball courts at the Gatlin site during the second field season. Both of these were small courts of the Casa Grande type, and both were oriented northwest-southeast. Before excavation the courts were marked by shallow depressions, bordered on the northeast and southwest sides by low semi-lunar ridges of earth.

Ball Court 1

This court, situated approximately one-eighth of a mile east of the pyramid and just east of the county road which cuts through the site (Fig. 10), was the more intensively studied of the two courts. Initial excavation in Ball Court 1 consisted of a trench 9 m. in length and 1 m. in width, beginning outside of the earth ridge on the northeast side of the court. It was carried through the ridge to the estimated midline of the court. Inside the earth ridge a caliche floor was encountered. Right-angle extensions of the initial trench measuring 1.3 m. in width were made along the estimated midline of the court, and these extensions were carried into the southeast end of the court and into the center. When the end was reached, and the center located, it was discovered that the trench along the estimated midline was at an angle to the long axis of the court, so it was necessary to widen the trench at each end to work out details of construction. One further excavation was made at the northwest end of the court. It soon became apparent that this end had been almost entirely removed by erosion, and therefore little time was spent in trying to work out the remaining features.

Ball Court 1 consisted of a playing floor measuring 33 m. in length by 11.2 m. in width. The floor had a maximum depth of 1.45 m. below the present surface of the ground, and a maximum depth of approximately 1.0 m. below the level of the surface of the ground when the court was constructed. The orientation of the court was 28 degrees west of north. Two major construction periods separated by a layer of sand and trash

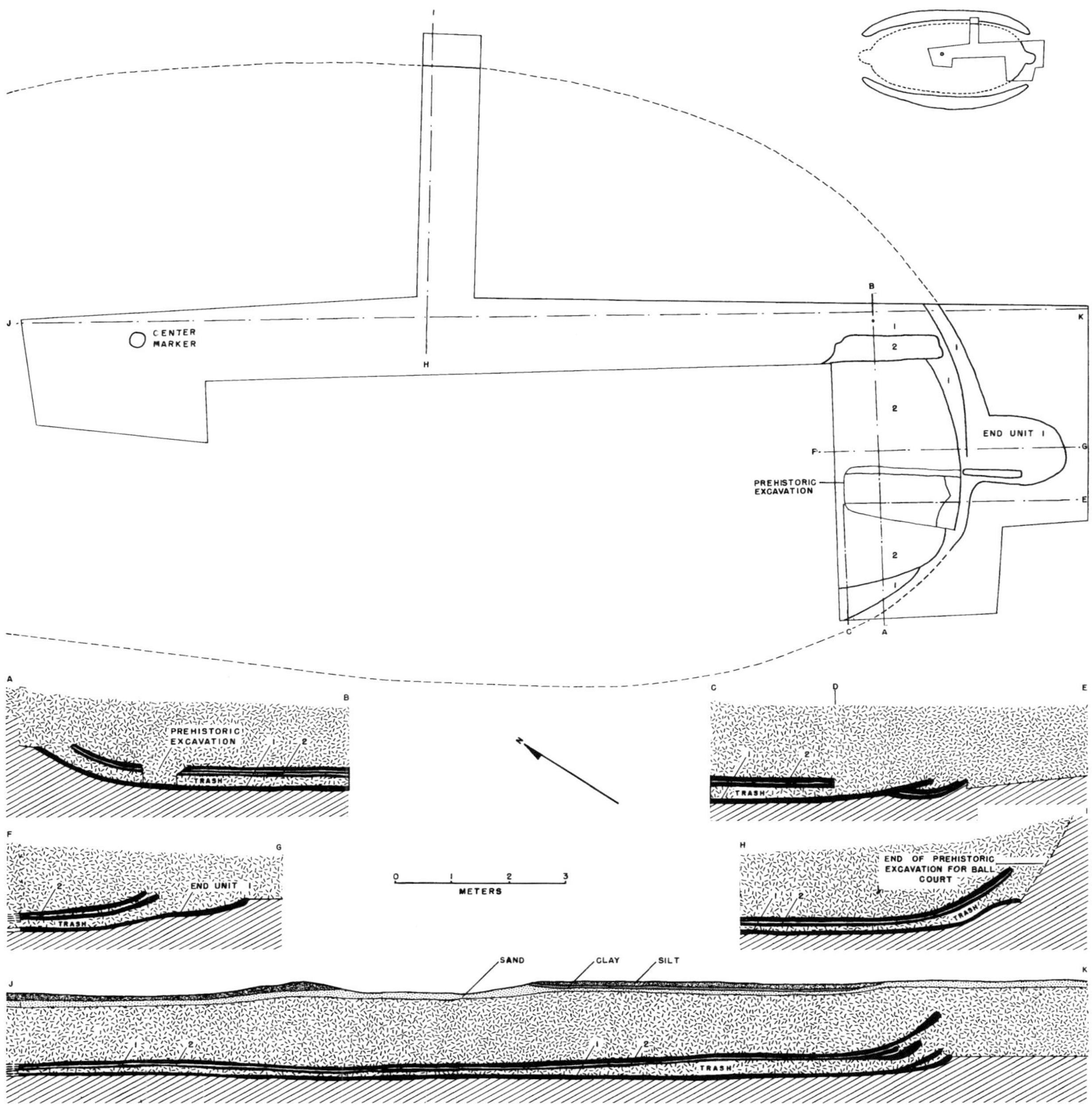

Fig. 11. Plan and sections, Ball Court 1, Gatlin site. Numbers refer to the two major construction periods. Insert shows reconstruction of entire court.

were in evidence. In addition to the two major periods of construction, there was evidence, at the southeast end of the court, of a number of remodelings (Fig. 11).

The initial phase of the construction of this ball court was apparently the excavation of a large oval pit, which sloped inward from the edges and ends to the center. Earth removed from the excavation was piled along the sides forming ridges. The floor of the pit was then smoothed and covered with a layer of caliche 7 or 8 cm. in thickness. At the ends and edges this floor sloped up slightly following the contours of the pit. End units consisted of U-shaped caliche extensions from the rounded ends of the court. The single remaining end unit measured 1.6 m. in length by 1.2 m. in width. It had a concave cross section in both directions. In the center of the court a small hole, some 35 cm. in diameter, was dug to serve as a center marker. Its depth could not be determined. No end markers were found.

After the court had been used for some time, it was found necessary to remodel at least the southeast end. This was done by laying another caliche surface over the end of the court. This layer was placed directly on the original floor, and so well blended that it could be differentiated in only a few spots. It is possible that the entire floor was resurfaced with a thin coat of caliche during all of these remodelings, but if this were the case the new surfaces could not be distinguished. The original center marker and remaining end unit continued in use with no modifications. A second remodeling of this end of the court is indicated by the presence of another layer of caliche. In this case, a layer of sand and gravel was placed between the two remodelings, and the angle of the sloping end increased somewhat. No changes were made in the shape of the end unit or the center marker.

Following the second remodeling of the southeast end, Ball Court 1 apparently fell into disuse. A layer of sand and some trash, about 30 cm. in depth, accumulated over the floor. An entirely new floor of caliche was then constructed on this sand layer. The new floor was slightly thinner than that of the first construction period, measuring only about 5 cm. in thickness. A new center marker and new end units were constructed. The center marker was placed directly over the old one, and was again a basin-shaped hole of about the same diameter and depth. The end unit associated with this period of construction was badly damaged by post-court activity, and a description of its shape cannot be given. Again, probably after a period of use, the end of the court was remodeled by adding another layer of caliche. The new layer was separated from the old by a thin deposit of sand. Finally, the entire court was resurfaced with another layer of caliche placed directly over the last. During this final period of modification, the center marker was remodeled. This was done by constructing a square box of caliche plaster inside the old circular marker. There possibly was one further period of construction in the court, but the floor associated with this period is very tenuous, and it seems better to consider that there were two major construction periods, each with two later remodelings.

Following the final abandonment of Ball Court 1 a number of events took place which are worthy of note. First, a trench was dug through the various remodelings of the southeast end of the court down to the original floor. That the trench was cut aboriginally is indicated by the fact that it was filled with sand, gravel, and earth containing red-on-buff sherds. Perhaps the trench was cut to obtain caliche for reuse elsewhere. Caliche does not occur at the site, but can be obtained about one mile south. The problem of carrying it this distance may have made the reuse of caliche worthwhile.

Second, the entire court was apparently used as a trash dump, after the final abandonment, since large quantities of sherds were found in the fill over the last remodeling. During this period of use for trash disposal, a human cranium was placed in the trash at the southeast end of the court. Finally, and probably in recent years as a result of irrigation farming in fields to the south, water flowed into the depression of the court. This water carried quantities of sand and clay which were deposited in bands over the aboriginal trash deposit. At the northwest end of the court a large sump was present, perhaps formed by the irrigation water. The sump was filled with large quantities of clay and sand. It is possible that the irrigation water flowed through the court and carved out this sump, removing this end of the court in the process.

Before presenting information on the dates of Ball Court 1, a problem in dating all ball courts should be mentioned. If the excavation for a ball court cuts through an already-present trash deposit, sherds included in this trash will be incorporated in the earth banks at the sides of the court. Since the banks are high and subject to rapid erosion, the first material deposited when a court fills may be from the banks. Consequently, any trash in the banks which pre-dates the actual construction of the court may be the first material to be deposited on the floor, and will appear to give an earlier date to the court than is actually the case. It is not felt that this is the situation in the case of

Ball Court 1 at the Gatlin site since tests in the area surrounding the court yielded no sherds of the same time period as the earliest construction of the court. It does not appear, therefore, that the court was excavated through earlier trash.

An analysis of the sherds from Ball Court 1 indicates that the first period of construction may have been during the Santa Cruz phase, or in a transitional period between the Santa Cruz and Sacaton phases. Sherds from the sand-and-trash layer between the two major construction periods (Level 2) are predominantly Santa Cruz Red-on-buff, although Sacaton Red-on-buff sherds occur. Unfortunately, the number of painted sherds from this deposit is small, and they can be offered only as tentative indications of the time of first construction. The painted sherds in the trash deposit over the last remodeling (Level 1) consisted of a large majority of Sacaton Red-on-buff sherds, although a few Santa Cruz Red-on-buff sherds were present. This indicates that the court was probably abandoned during the Sacaton phase.

Ball Court 2

The second ball court at the Gatlin site is situated about one-half mile northeast of the pyramid across a large wash which runs through the site. The surface indications of this court were quite similar to those of Ball Court 1; an oval depression bordered on the northeast and southwest sides by ridges of earth. The ridges were somewhat lower in this case than for Ball Court 1. The orientation was approximately the same as for Court 1.

Excavation consisted of three trenches, one at the northwest end, one in the center, and one at the southeast end. All of the trenches were excavated to depths below the level at which the floor was encountered in the first court, and in none of the trenches was a floor found. Careful examination of the trench walls showed the presence of a soil line some 75 cm. below the present surface of the ground. This soil line could be seen in all of the trenches excavated in the court, and was also found in test excavations beyond the edges of the court. The soil line indicates that the court could not have been dug below this level, or the excavation would have cut through it. Consequently, it appears that the excavation for Ball Court 2 was quite shallow, and that the court was not floored with caliche. In addition, no traces of end markers or center markers were found.

Probably then, Ball Court 2 represents an unfinished court, one which was abandoned before the excavation was completed and the floor laid. An alternative explanation is that Ball Court 2 represents a practice court, which was never elaborated on, but left rough for hard use. A distant parallel may be seen in the athletic fields of today where there are often two fields, one a fully elaborated example and the second a rough field for practice.

Few sherds were obtained from Ball Court 2, but all of the painted sherds were Sacaton Red-on-buff, indicating that the court was constructed during this phase.

Crematorium

Crematorium 1 was discovered in a test trench placed a little over one-eighth of a mile east of the pyramid and just east of Ball Court 1. The test was placed in this area to determine the exact nature of the occurrence of calcined bones on an amateur excavator's back dirt. Apparently the amateur had discovered and removed a cremation overlying the crematorium. The crematorium was not disturbed.

Crematorium 1 consisted of a rectangular pit measuring 1.17 m. in length (east-west) by 92 cm. in width (north-south). The east side of the pit was slightly undercut, while the west was straight, sloping to a flat bottom. The sides could be traced to a height of 22 cm. above the floor of the pit. Probably the pit was dug from an old ground level, seen in the trench wall, some 55 cm. below the present surface of the ground. Disturbance by the amateur made it impossible to be sure, however.

The bottom of Crematorium 1 was covered with a clay lining some 1 or 2 cm. in thickness. Above this a 4-cm. layer of charcoal and ash containing some burned human bone was present. This layer probably represents the cremation fire. Another layer filling the remainder of the pit was encountered. This consisted of sandy soil mixed with some ash, charcoal, and calcined human bone. The only artifacts found in Crematorium 1 are five buff-slipped sherds, probably from an unpainted section of a red-on-buff vessel. All are burned.

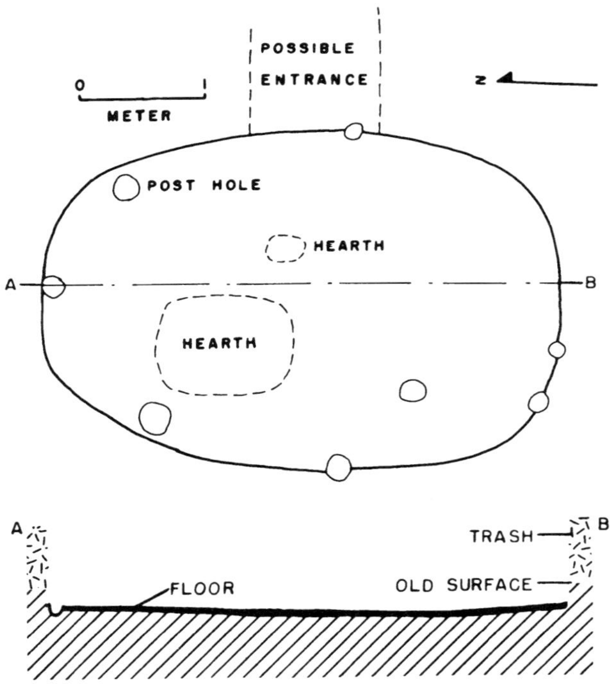

Fig. 12. Plan and section, Structure 2, Gatlin site.

Structure 2

Structure 2 was discovered in a test trench northeast of Ball Court 1 (Fig. 10). (Structure 1 at the Gatlin site is described in Wasley 1960b: 257–59.) There was absolutely nothing on the surface of the ground to indicate the presence of a structure in this area, and it was found only after several sterile tests had been dug in the vicinity.

Structure 2 (Fig. 12) is a fairly typical Hohokam house of the Sacaton phase. It is not well preserved, but enough remains to give the outline of the floor, and at least a partial post pattern. The structure has an oval outline measuring 4.1 m. in length by 2.85 m. in width. It is oriented north-south, and the entrance probably opened to the east. The entrance is very tenuous, and it is impossible to be sure about the orientation.

A cross section through the long dimension indicates that the floor, which consists of a layer of caliche 2 to 3 cm. in thickness, slopes very slightly from the edges to the center. Probably the house was supported on four main posts, but only three of these could be located. Six other post holes are present around the edges of the house. A well-demarcated fire pit was not found, but two irregularly-shaped fired areas were present on the floor in the north half of the structure. A concentrated layer of charcoal and ash rested on the floor, indicating the house was destroyed by fire. This is further supported by the fact that the caliche floor was burned a gray color.

All of the painted sherds from the structure are Sacaton Red-on-buff, indicating that the house was constructed during the Sacaton phase.

Canal

Several sections of a large prehistoric irrigation canal could be traced at the Gatlin site (Fig. 10) and in adjoining areas. These consisted of long U-shaped depressions bordered on both sides by rounded ridges of earth. The remaining sections of the canal, not destroyed by erosion or by recent farming activity, indicate that water was brought from the Gila River some five miles to the northeast of the Gatlin site. After it left the river, the canal ran south, then turned west to cut across the northern edge of the Gatlin site. The canal was cross-trenched in three places in conjunction with the University of Arizona's arid-land studies conducted by Richard B. Woodbury with Rockefeller Foundation support. Comments by Woodbury on the canal tests follow.

> Three sections were dug across the canal at approximately half-mile intervals, and all showed a channel about 3 m. wide and from 1.3 to 1.8 m. deep (the differences in depth no doubt due to minor changes in the local topography). All three cuts were dug into horizontally bedded coarse to fine sand with some fine gravel, old river-laid material. They showed many irregularities in the original canal excavation, although it conformed to a roughly U-shaped profile (in contrast to the V-shaped profile occurring at Pueblo Grande). The banks were extremely weathered, and probably never had any great height, as the canal was probably not used long enough to accumulate a great deal in the way of cleared-out deposits piled up on the banks. The fill of the canal is fine and coarse sand with some lenses of silt, and although interbedded and laminated, shows no pronounced sequence or major change in the deposits. As well as could be determined, water-laid material that would have accumulated during the use of the canal had a thickness of 80 cm. to 1.2 m., with dry-laid (post-use) material above this.

On the ground and from the air the canal can be traced for only a part of what must have been its original total extent. West of the pyramid at the Gatlin site (which is just south of the westernmost of the three cross sections) it can be followed for no more than one-fourth mile, and may never have gone much farther, as there are some large washes just west of here which would be hard to cross (or the washes could be recent and could have destroyed the last mile or so of the canal). Going east and northeast from the nearest point to the pyramid the canal can be traced for about one and one-fourth miles, and then is destroyed by modern activities. Again about a mile farther north for a short distance, and possibly once more a little farther north the canal can also be traced. The still-observable traces of it cover at the most about three miles, and its intake must have been about two miles north of the last traces now visible. This would put the intake about at the northwest corner of Section 33 (T4S, R4W) and would carry the canal close to the 660 foot contour all the way. For a distance of five miles the drop should have been only a few feet at most.

There appears to be nothing in the evidence that is incompatible with a relatively brief use of the canal during the occupation (or use) of the Gatlin site.

Test Trenches

In addition to the excavations described above, approximately two-thirds of the site was quite thoroughly tested for other structures, cremations, and miscellaneous features. The testing was accomplished by hand excavation, soil-auger examinations, and D7 bulldozer trenches. In all, 64 trenches were excavated by hand. These trenches were usually 75 cm. in width, and varied in length from 2 m. to 10 or 15 m. They were scattered over the site, but concentrated in those areas which seemed to hold the greatest promise of finding something under the surface. Soil-auger tests were used in addition to the hand-dug trenches to examine subsurface conditions in areas not trenched. Dozens of these tests were made at various spots over the site. A D7 tractor with bulldozer blade worked at the site for a week, scraping some 36,000 square feet of soil from the surface.

In all of this digging, no other houses, cremations, crematoriums, or any of the other features known to occur in Hohokam sites were located. It should be pointed out, however, in relation to the cremations, that most of them have been removed by relic collectors. Abundant evidence of this unauthorized type of excavation is present at the site. Numerous back-dirt piles with calcined bones on them are present, and probe holes were omnipresent discoveries in the current excavations.

Pottery

In the course of field work at the Gatlin site (Ariz. Z:2:1) during the second season, one complete bowl, one restorable jar, and 32,442 sherds were collected. A majority of the sherds (21,271) came from excavations in 10 trash mounds. The remainder are from excavations in two ball courts, from Structure 2, from Crematorium 1, and from over 50 test trenches scattered over the site. Of the 32,442 sherds, 97.6 per cent were probably locally made. The remaining 2.4 per cent were traded in from various regions of Arizona.

The locally-made pottery may be assigned to types which have been previously described, primarily in the report on Snaketown (Gladwin and others 1937: 168–229). One of the striking features of the pottery from the Gatlin site is its very close similarity to the Snaketown ceramics. The various types from the two sites are practically indistinguishable, although they are spatially separated by some 40 miles. This very close similarity argues well for the strength of cultural tradition in the manufacture of Hohokam pottery.

Santa Cruz Red-on-Buff

The two locally-made painted pottery types which occur at the Gatlin site are Santa Cruz Red-on-buff (Fig. 13) and Sacaton Red-on-buff (Fig. 14). At Snaketown (Gladwin and others 1937: 25–34) Santa Cruz Red-on-buff was demonstrated to be stratigraphically earlier than Sacaton Red-on-buff, the latter type developing out of the former. Santa Cruz Red-on-buff is the major diagnostic type of the Santa Cruz phase, while Sacaton Red-on-buff holds the same position in relation to the Sacaton phase. The discovery of Santa Cruz Red-on-buff at the Gatlin site would then indicate a first occupation of the site during the Santa Cruz phase. The presence of Sacaton Red-on-buff points to a continuation of the occupation into the Sacaton phase. Data collected from the excavation of Trash Mound 3 tend to support this inference. In Trash Mound 3, the lower levels

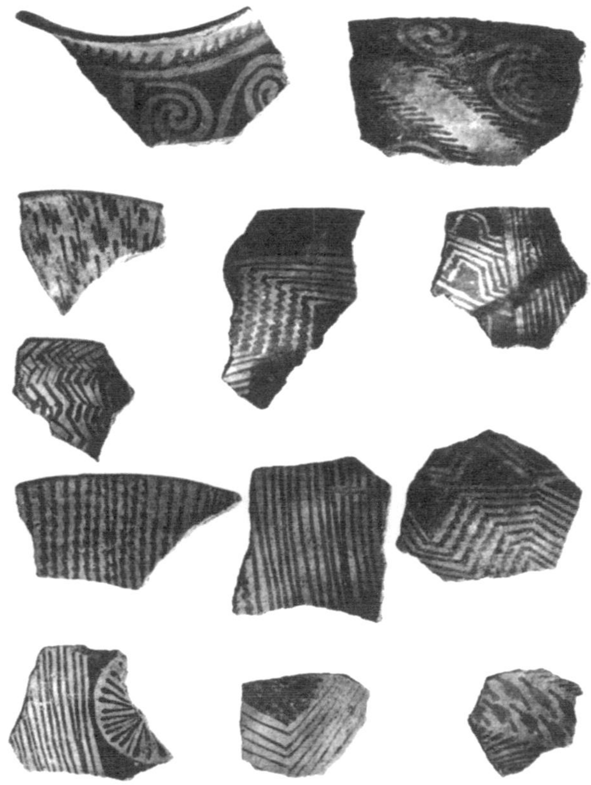

Fig. 13. Santa Cruz Red-on-buff sherds, Gatlin site.

Fig. 14. Sacaton Red-on-buff sherds, Gatlin site.

have Santa Cruz Red-on-buff as the only locally-made painted type. In the upper three levels of this mound, Santa Cruz Red-on-buff is found in association with Sacaton Red-on-buff, indicating a probable transitional period between the two phases.

The only other excavation unit in which Santa Cruz Red-on-buff is found as a predominant painted type is the trash layer between the two main construction periods of Ball Court 1 (Level 2). In this unit, while the percentage differences are not great enough to be really significant (4.3 per cent Santa Cruz Red-on-buff as opposed to 2.8 per cent Sacaton Red-on-buff), there is an indication that the first construction of Ball Court 1 may have occurred during the Santa Cruz phase or during a transitional period between the Santa Cruz and Sacaton phases. Other occurrences of Santa Cruz Red-on-buff are scattered at random over the site, and are in all cases of a minor frequency. They add little more to the picture than further support of the Santa Cruz-phase occupation. Santa Cruz Red-on-buff accounts for 2.8 per cent of the locally-made sherds at the site, and for about 25 per cent of the sherds made locally during the Santa Cruz-phase occupation.

Sacaton Red-on-Buff

The most common locally-made painted pottery type at the Gatlin site is Sacaton Red-on-buff (Fig. 14), indicating that the principal occupation of the site was during the Sacaton phase. Evidence for a continuous occupation from the Santa Cruz phase into the Sacaton phase was presented above in the discussion of Trash Mound 3. The upper three levels of Trash Mound 3 seem to represent a transitional period between the Santa Cruz and the Sacaton phases.

Trash Mounds 1, 8, and 13 contained Sacaton Red-on-buff as the only locally-made painted type, indicating an occupation during a full-blown Sacaton phase. Stratigraphic evidence from Snaketown (Gladwin and others 1937, Pl. 151) showed a tendency for rectilinear design elements to occur more frequently in the latter part of the Sacaton phase. Similar elements occasionally occur on the sherds recovered from the Gatlin site suggesting that the occupation of this site probably continued until late in the Sacaton phase. This is supported by the presence of a minor quantity of locally-made red-slipped pottery, another characteristic of the late Sacaton phase (Gladwin and others 1937, Fig. 107).

Sacaton Red-on-buff accounts for about 10 per cent of the local pottery made during the Sacaton-phase occupation of the Gatlin site. This is one of the major differences between the ceramics of the Gatlin site and those of Snaketown. During the Sacaton phase at the latter site Sacaton Red-on-buff accounted for approximately 40 per cent of the total (Gladwin and others 1937: 177–78).

Schroeder (1940: 119–20) has demonstrated a definite trend towards diminishing quantities of painted pottery in the later periods of the Salt River Valley. During the Sacaton phase in this region 30.2 per cent of the locally-made pottery was red-on-buff. The percentage of red-on-buff in the following Soho phase was only 11, while red-on-buff dropped to 2.7 per cent during the Civano phase. The apparent reason for this shift was an increasing popularity of red wares, the manufacture of which replaced that of red-on-buff.

In relation to the Gatlin site, two explanations of the presence of such a small proportion of Sacaton Red-on-buff may be offered. On the one hand it is possible that the major part of the occupation was during the latter part of the Sacaton phase, and the quantity of red-on-buff being manufactured was somewhat less than earlier in the phase, a situation parallel to that described by Schroeder for the Salt River Valley. On the other hand, perhaps red-on-buff never gained the popularity in the Gila Bend area which it did farther to the east. Since the Gatlin site is apparently near the western periphery of the distribution of Hohokam sites, some differences between Hohokam culture in this area and those farther east might be expected. It is worth pointing out again in this regard, however, that the striking thing about the pottery of the Gatlin site is its close similarity, except in frequency, to that of the regions farther east.

Santa Cruz-Sacaton Red-on-Buff

This is admittedly a catch-all category devised to account for all of those sherds which lacked sufficient paint to allow them to be classified in one or the other of the two locally-made painted types. In the excavation units which contained only Sacaton Red-on-buff, sherds bearing only a trace of paint were grouped with the others which were definitely Sacaton Red-on-buff.

Sacaton Red

Sacaton Red (Gladwin and others 1937: 202–204) is a locally-made type significant mainly for the fact that it offers further support for the occupation of the Gatlin site in the late part of the Sacaton phase. Sacaton Red was widely distributed over the site, but in very minor quantities. It accounts for only .1 per cent of the locally-made sherds.

Gila Plain

By far the most commonly occurring locally-made type at the Gatlin site is Gila Plain (Gila Plain, Gila Bend Variety, was not separated from Gila Plain during the analysis of the materials from the first two seasons). This type alone accounts for 76.7 per cent of the locally-made pottery. One interesting feature of the occurrence of Gila Plain is its consistent frequency of approximately 75 per cent in all of the excavation units. This emphasizes the popularity of the type, which was apparently the primary ware of the Hohokam from the Estrella phase until the end of the Hohokam sequence (Gladwin and others 1937: 205–11).

One of the difficulties of working with this type, as it is known in the Gila Bend area, is the fact that it grades imperceptibly into Wingfield Plain. Wingfield Plain (Colton 1941: 46) is supposedly distinguished from Gila Plain on the basis of mica-schist tempering in the former type and its absence in the latter which has instead quantities of mica in the paste (Gladwin and Gladwin 1933: 26). Many of the Gila Plain sherds from the Gila Bend area have mica-schist as a component of the temper. Distinguishing the two types then becomes a problem of quantitative differences in the amount of mica-schist in the tempering material. In most cases, it is impossible to tell whether a given sherd belongs to one or the other type. For this analysis, questionable sherds were lumped with Gila Plain, the older and better established type.

Sacaton Buff

It is possible that some of the sherds collected at the Gatlin site belong to this type. With no complete vessels or large sherds represented in the collections, it is not possible to be sure, however. A large number of sherds (2,416) were collected which bore a buff slip, and which lacked paint. It is probable that most of these represent unpainted sections of Santa Cruz or Sacaton Red-on-buff vessels, or are sherds weathered to the point where paint is no longer visible.

Sacaton Smudged

The remaining sherds of locally-made vessels all belong to a type which has never been described in print. In essence these are sherds from Gila Plain bowls which have been smudged on the interior and occasionally fairly highly polished. The four sherds of this type occurring at the Gatlin site are not enough on which to base a type description. This will have to wait excavation of a site where the type occurs in quantity.

Intrusive Pottery

In addition to the large quantity of pottery which was made locally at the Gatlin site, a small amount found its way to the site from other parts of Arizona. These sherds indicate that trade was maintained with groups living to the north, south, east, and west. No intrusive sherds were found in contexts where they could definitely be associated with the Santa Cruz phase. It is inferred from this that most of the trade at the Gatlin site took place during the Sacaton phase, the major period of occupation.

The closest contact seems to have been with the people who manufactured Lower Colorado buffware, since by far the greatest number of intrusive sherds are of this ware (Schroeder 1952a: 16–17). In all some 704 sherds of this group were collected, representing 97.6 per cent of the intrusives which found their way to the Gatlin site. No attempt was made to divide this group of sherds into types, as for the most part they are practically indistinguishable. It should be noted that no sherds with a stucco finish occurred in the group of Lower Colorado buffware sherds, indicating a later date for this technique. This is supported by the discovery of stucco-finished sherds at later sites in the Gila Bend area.

Contact with areas to the north is indicated by the recovery of occasional black-on-white and black-on-red sherds. These included (with approximate dates following): Black Mesa Black-on-white, about 900–1100 (Colton 1946: 251); Red Mesa Black-on-white, about 900–1000 (Gladwin 1945: 56); Sosi Black-on-white, about 1050–1150 (Colton and Hargrave 1937: 211–13); Puerco Black-on-white, about 950–1150 (Colton 1941: 58–59); and Tusayan Black-on-red, about 1050–1150 (Colton 1946: 252).

On the basis of trade sherds found at Snaketown, the Sacaton phase at this site was assigned dates of 900–1100 (Gladwin and others 1937, Fig. 106). The few dated intrusives from the Gatlin site support this dating.

Evidence was presented above in support of a continuation of the occupation of the Gatlin site into late Sacaton times. There is an indication from the dates listed above for the intrusive sherds that this occupation may have lasted as late as 1150. The presence of three types – Sosi Black-on-white, Tusayan Black-on-red, and Puerco Black-on-white, all of which were still being made during the first half of the twelfth century – indicates that this may have been the case.

Contact with the Papagueria is indicated by the presence of a few sherds of Valshni Red. This type, which occurs in both Vamori and Topawa phases, has been assigned dates of 800–1250 (Withers 1941: 35–36; Haury 1950: 9–13).

In addition, a minor amount of trade seems to have taken place with the Mogollon culture to the east. This is represented by the presence of a single sherd of Mangas Black-on-white dating about 950–1050 (Haury 1936a: 22–27).

Two other intrusive types remain to be taken into account. The first of these, Wingfield Plain, was mentioned in the discussion of Gila Plain as being difficult to distinguish from the latter type in the Gila Bend area. As a consequence, only 7 sherds could be separated out which seem definitely to fit into this type. The other type, represented by a single intrusive sherd, is Gila Red. This type, which is characteristic of the Soho phase of the Classic Hohokam period (Haury 1945a: 81), seems definitely out of place at the Gatlin site. It may have been dropped on the site at some later date.

Discussion

An analysis of the pottery collected at the Gatlin site during the 1960 field season indicates that the site was first occupied during the Santa Cruz phase of the Colonial period and continued to be occupied throughout the Sacaton phase. No later types are present in sufficient quantity to suggest Classic period occupation.

A majority of the intrusive sherds came from the west and are grouped together under the name

Lower Colorado buffware. Dated trade pottery from northern Arizona supports the original dates assigned to the Sacaton phase at Snaketown (900–1100). It also suggests that in the Gila Bend area the phase may have lasted until about 1150.

Artifacts

The following descriptions include all of the artifacts, other than sherds and complete pottery vessels, collected at the Gatlin site during the first and second seasons. Wasley (1960b: 259–60) included general statements on some of the artifacts from the first season's work in his report on the platform mound. For completeness, this previously published information is repeated.

Ceramic Artifacts

Miniature Vessels. In this category is a miniature Sacaton shouldered jar with an interlocking scroll design. The vessel, which contained the cremated bones of an infant or small child, was found in the fill of Structure 1 at the site. Accompanying the cremation was a large unworked *Cardium* valve, a carved stone bowl (described below), a large sherd from a Gila Plain jar, and a river cobble (Wasley 1960b: 258). Dimensions: shoulder diameter, 8.5 cm.; height, 5 cm.

The second miniature vessel is a Gila Plain jar. The body of the vessel is globular, and the rim is slightly outflared. A few irregular incised lines, made when the clay was still plastic, are present on one side. The bottom is charred. Dimensions: diameter, 7.9 cm.; height, 7.8 cm.

Thick-Walled Vessels. The three thick-walled vessels recovered are all circular in outline, but vary somewhat in details. All are typical of types manufactured during the Sacaton phase (Gladwin and others 1937, Fig. 109, Pl. 135). The complete example (Fig. 15*d*) has a flat rim, straight sides, and a slightly convex base. The inner walls are slightly undercut, and the bottom is concave. Traces of burning and cracking are present in the basin. This is a plainware vessel. Dimensions: diameter, 6.1 cm.; height, 4 cm.; wall thickness, 1.6 cm.

A second specimen, which is fragmentary, has a flat rim and base but concave sides. The inner walls are straight and the bottom concave. This is a red-on-buff vessel, but only a faint trace of the paint remains. Dimensions: diameter, 8 cm.; height, 4.7 cm.; wall thickness, 1.8 cm.

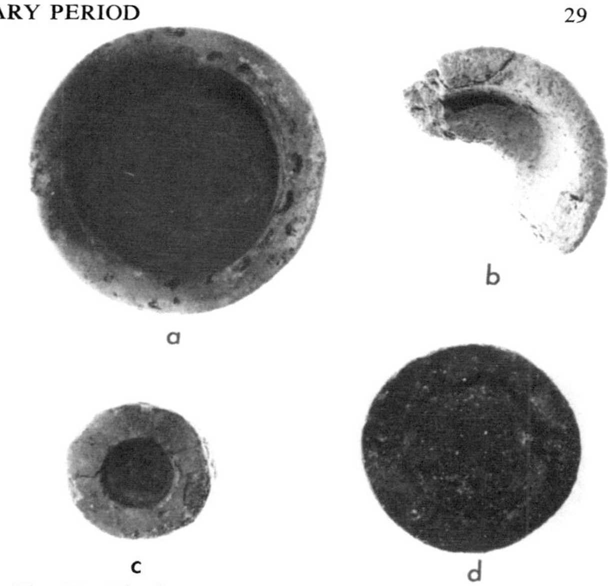

Fig. 15. Thick-walled vessels, Sedentary-period sites: a, c, *Citrus site;* b, d, *Gatlin site;* a-c, *Sacaton Red-on-buff;* d, *plainware, diam. 6 cm.*

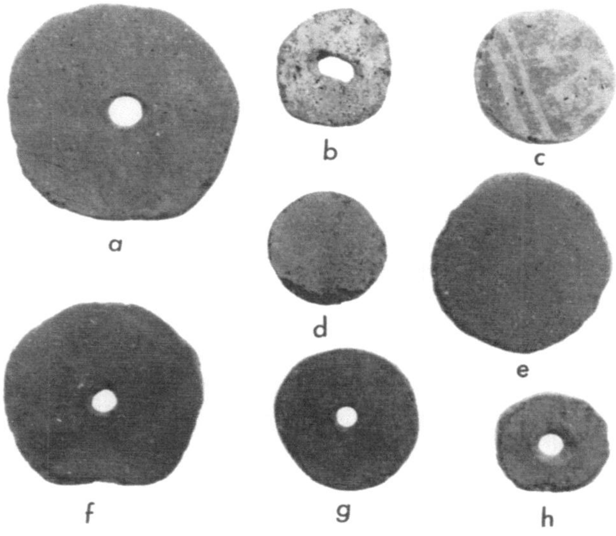

Fig. 16. Sherd discs, Sedentary-period sites: a, b, g, h, *Gatlin site;* c-f, *Citrus site;* a, b, *buff slipped;* c, *Sacaton Red-on-buff;* d-h, *plainware. Diam* h, *2.8 cm.*

The remaining fragmentary thick-walled vessel has concave sides, a rounded rim, and a concave base (Fig. 15*b*). A circular perforation extends from the base into the basin. The inner walls are straight. No traces of paint remain on this vessel, but the paste is the same as for red-on-buff pottery. A few traces of a buff slip are present. Dimensions: diameter, 9.4 cm.; height, 5.3 cm.; wall thickness, 1.5 cm.

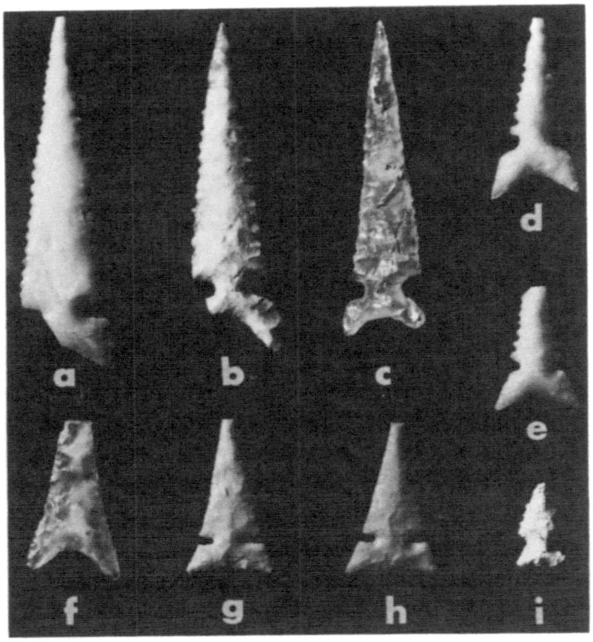

Fig. 17. Projectile points, Sedentary-period sites; a, c, e-i, *Gatlin site;* b, d, *Citrus site.* i, *1.7 cm. long.*

Sherd Discs. Seventeen sherd discs were recovered from the site. All are sherds with the edges ground into roughly circular outlines. Seven Gila Plain discs have central biconical perforations (Fig. 16 *g-h*), three have only partial perforations, and four are unperforated. The three red-on-buff discs have central biconical perforations (Fig. 16 *a-b*). Dimensions: diameter ranges from 3 to 6.4 cm.; thickness ranges from 5 to 9 cm.

Miscellaneous Ceramic Object. A small conical object of pottery is broken at the wider end. One side is slightly smoothed and the other is rough. Dimensions: length, 4.7 cm.; diameter, 2.1 cm.

Stone Artifacts

Projectile points from the Gatlin site can be divided, for descriptive purposes, into four categories. In all, 43 points were collected at the site, of which 31 were complete enough to allow them to be classified.

Twenty-one of the points are long and narrow, with concave bases, and side notches (Fig. 17, *a, c, e*). Most of these points are manufactured from translucent, white-to-grey-colored chert or chalcedony. Serrations are common. Wasley (1960b: 245) has suggested that points of this type may be ceremonial in nature. Dimensions: length ranges from 6 to 6.9 cm.; width ranges from 1.5 to 1.9 cm.

A second category has only one representative (Fig. 17*f*). The point is made from the same material as the examples described above, and also has a concave base. It differs in that it lacks side notches. Dimensions: length, 3.5 cm. (estimate); width, 1.7 cm.

The third category has two examples (Fig. 17, *g-h*). Both are triangular points, with slightly concave bases, side notches, and straight edges. Neither is serrated. Both are made from grey chert, darker in color than the materials used for the previously described types. Dimensions: both are 3 cm. long; width, 1.6 to 1.7 cm.

Seven points can be grouped together into the final category (Fig. 17*i*). Most are of obsidian. All are small and crudely made in comparison with the points described above. Bases range from convex through straight to concave. Side notches are present. Dimensions: length ranges from 1.7 to 2.3 cm.; width ranges from 9 mm. to 1.3 cm.

Knives. Three chipped-stone artifacts classifiable as knives are present in the collection. One restored example is a large blade, triangular in outline, with a convex base. It is made from a milky white chert (Wasley 1960b: 260). Dimensions: length, 14.4 cm.; width, 4.5 cm.

A second specimen was probably broken from a blade much like the one described above. Both the tip and base are missing. It is made of chert, somewhat greyer in color than the one above. Dimensions: width, 4.5 cm.

The third knife is formed from a flake removed from a water-worn pebble. One face of the knife is the original surface of the pebble, while the other is a single large flake scar. Secondary chipping is restricted to the edges. The material is dark grey andesite. Dimensions: length, 5.1 cm.; width, 2.4 cm.; thickness, 8 mm.

Crescent. The single example of this type of artifact is chipped from white chert. Similar objects found at Snaketown were divided into four groups on the basis of slightly varying forms. The example from the Gatlin site is similar to those specimens from Snaketown which had one arm flattened giving the objects a fishhook-like appearance (Gladwin and others 1937, Pl. 92*d*). It differs from the Snaketown artifacts in having a series of deep serrations around the convex edge.

Dimensions: length, 1.9 cm.; width, 8 mm.

Hoe. The only chipped stone hoe found at the site has a crescent-shaped outline. It is manufactured from a flat plate of mica schist. Secondary chipping is restricted to the edges, which are chipped all the way around the artifact. Dimensions: length, 15.7 cm.; width, 8.2 cm.; thickness, 5 mm.

Choppers. The two choppers are formed from water-worn cobbles. In one case, large flakes have been removed from both faces yielding a V-shaped cutting edge, while in the case of the second specimen flakes were removed from only one face, forming a chisel-shaped cutting edge. Use of this latter chopper has resulted in battering and rounding of the cutting edge. The hand-hold for both examples is the unmodified cobble surface. Dimensions: length, 7.6 cm. and 11.8 cm.; width, 9 cm. and 9.1 cm.; thickness, 5.3 cm. and 5.8 cm.

Scrapers. The five scrapers are manufactured from water-worn pebbles. All have been split, and as a consequence have plane surfaces formed by a few large flake scars. The opposite face is the unmodified surface of the pebble. Large flakes have been removed from the edges by the percussion technique. Dimensions: average diameter, 6 cm.

Vessels. Five stone vessels were collected at the Gatlin site. One of the vessels is an animal-effigy form. The circular vessel forms the body of the animal, with the head projecting from one side and the feet from the base. The mouth is indicated by an incised line. The walls of the basin slope slightly inward to a rounded bottom. The material is vesicular basalt. Dimensions: length, 7 cm.; height, 4.4 cm.

A second effigy vessel, also made from vesicular basalt, is fragmentary. Only a small section of the originally-circular vessel remains, and from the side of this section one leg of the figure projects. Dimensions: diameter, 13 cm. (estimate).

The third stone vessel is complete. It is a sandstone bowl, circular in outline with straight sides and a slightly convex base. The vessel is decorated with an incised cross-hatched design (Wasley 1960b: 260). Dimensions: diameter, 9.3 cm.; height, 5.3 cm.

The fourth stone vessel is represented by a fragment. Originally, the bowl was circular in outline, with outcurved sides, and a flat base. A shallow depression has been pecked into the base. A series of diagonal incised lines are present on the outcurved sides of the vessel, encircling the circumference. The vessel is made from tan sandstone. Dimensions: diameter, 6.8 cm.; thickness, 2.8 cm.

The fifth specimen is fragmentary, but was probably originally oval in outline. This vessel, of vesicular basalt, has outcurved sides and a rounded base. The basin is depressed only slightly, and it differs from the other stone vessels in having no well-marked walls. The center of the basin is more highly ground than the outside of the bowl. Dimensions: width, 13.4 cm.; thickness, 2.9 cm.

Palettes. All three of the palette fragments are of mica schist. Two have raised borders, and one of these has a running pattern of triangles and cross-hatched lines on the border. The pattern is formed of shallow lines incised into the stone. The ends and edges of all three examples are slightly rounded. Grinding striations are present on both faces. These palettes are representative of the type made during the Sacaton phase (Gladwin and others 1937, Pls. 104–105). Dimensions: width (of most complete specimen), 7.8 cm.; thickness, 5 mm. and 1 cm.

Manos. Representing some range in form were the 13 manos collected from the excavations at the Gatlin site. All are two-hand manos, and 10 are manufactured from vesicular basalt. The other three examples are of finer-grained materials, and were made from water-worn cobbles. A few examples show traces of wear on both faces, but the prevailing form has unifacial wear. The presence of end grinding on most of the specimens indicates they were used in trough metates. Dimensions: length, 20 cm. (average); width, 9 to 10.1 cm. (range); thickness, 3.5 to 5.4 cm. (range).

Metates. Fragments of four metates were found at the site. Two are vesicular basalt, and two are made from blocks of granite. Enough remains of three examples to indicate they were once trough shaped. The fourth specimen is a small section from the center of the grinding area. Dimensions: width, 36 cm. (most complete specimen).

Handstones. Two handstones were found at the Gatlin site. Both are oval water-worn cobbles with traces of pecking on the edges. The faces are ground. Both are approximately the same size.

Dimensions: length, 12.2 cm.; width, 8.5 cm.; thickness, 5.5 cm.

Pestle. The single pestle found is conical in shape. The grinding end has been broken off, but the remaining end is rounded and slightly smoothed. Traces of pecking are present over the entire surface of the pestle. Dimensions: diameter, 9.9 cm.

Rings. All six of the stone rings from the Gatlin site are manufactured from vesicular basalt. With one exception, all have large, central, biconical perforations. The exception is partially perforated and may have been broken during the manufacturing process. Two have shallow grooves encircling the outside circumference. Edges are rounded in all cases. Dimensions: diameter, 5.5 cm. to 9.6 cm. (range); thickness, 1.5 to 3.7 cm. (range).

"Medicine Stone." The single specimen in this category closely resembles similar artifacts referred to as "medicine stones" or "plummets" in the Snaketown report (Gladwin and others 1937: 112, Pl. 81). It is a small conical object with an encircling groove near the larger end. The opposite end is rounded. The material is vesicular basalt. Dimensions: length, 4 cm.; diameter, 1.9 cm. Similar artifacts have been reported from Amapa, Nayarit, in western Mexico (Meighan 1959: 4).

Ball. One ball of an unidentified stone was found. It is close to a perfect spherical shape, and the stone is quite hard and yellow-white in color. Dimensions: diameter, 2 cm.

Axe. The single axe collected is a three-quarter grooved form. It is manufactured from a water-worn cobble and is not highly finished. The wide three-quarter groove, which was pecked shallowly into the stone, is bordered by slightly raised ridges. A number of deep pits in the poll indicates a secondary use as a hammer. After the bit was broken from the axe, the broken surface continued to be used as a hammer, as is attested to by pecking and rounding of this end. Dimensions: length, 16 cm.; width, 8.5 cm.; thickness, 7.7 cm.; groove width, 4.2 cm.

Beads. Forty-one stone beads were found at the site. Of these, 38 came from the general excavation material in Trash Mound 3. They were in association with a number of small shell beads. The two groups of beads probably once formed a section of a necklace. All of the 38 beads are small discs manufactured from turquoise. Thicker examples are biconically perforated, while the thinner ones have conical perforations indicating they were drilled from one face only. Dimensions: diameter, 5 mm.; thickness, 1 to 2 mm.

Two other disc beads of stone were collected. One is of turquoise. Dimensions: diameter, 2 mm. and 5 mm.

The last bead is made from a rippled red and white stone. It is tubular in shape and biconically perforated. Dimensions: length, 9 mm.; diameter, 6 mm.

Hammerstones. Two hammerstones were collected during the excavations at the Gatlin site. One is a circular water-worn cobble with traces of pecking on the ends. Dimensions: diameter, 5.7 cm.

The other example, also a water-worn cobble, is oval in outline. A few large flakes have been removed from one end of the cobble, and the stone was then used as a hammer. This may represent a chopper reused as a hammerstone. Dimensions: length, 10.1 cm.; width, 7.1 cm.; thickness, 4.4 cm.

Miscellaneous Ground Stone Fragments. Included in this category are three small fragments of stone with traces of grinding. Two are of sandstone and one is of vesicular basalt. The ground surface of the basalt example is impregnated with red ochre.

Stone and Mineral Specimens. One of this group is a small irregular piece of fossil bone, and a second is a highly vitrified molten mass, the original nature of which is undeterminable. Also included are a pyramidal-shaped obsidian nodule and three water-worn pebbles with traces of some form of staining. The largest of these shows indications of having been used as a hammerstone or anvil. Finally, there is a spherical lump of red ochre which retains the fingerprints of the individual who molded it. The material is light red in color and readily dissolves when wet.

Shell Artifacts

A collection of unworked shell from the site, gathered for the purpose of species identification, includes the following types:

Glycymeris maculatus
Cardium elatum
Olivella dama

Vermetus centiquadrus
Pecten vogdesi
Pecten circularis
Pecten cf. *P. circularis* (possibly the variety *aequisulcatus*)
Pecten subnodosus
Cerithidea albodonosa
Cerithium stercusmuscarum
Columbella major
Turritella leucostoma
?Pinctada
? Fasciolaria
Pteria sterna
? Anomia
Spondylus cf. *S. princeps*

Plain Glycymeris Bracelets. The 203 fragmentary plain *Glycymeris* bracelets found at the Gatlin site are quite similar to those from Snaketown (Gladwin and others 1937: 142–44) and consequently the terminology devised for that site is applied here.

Thirty-one of the plain *Glycymeris* bracelets have bands which measure less than 5 mm. in width, and are therefore of the thin-band type. Of the 15 specimens which retain the umbo, five are perforated.

One hundred and sixty-eight of the plain bracelets are of the medium-width band type, as they all have bands which measure between 5 and 10 mm. Twenty of the bracelets in this group have perforated umbos.

The remaining group of 30 plain bracelets has bands measuring from 1 to 3 cm., and is consequently of the heavy- or wide-band type. One of the bracelets in this category has a perforated umbo.

Carved Glycymeris Bracelets. Three bracelet fragments, all lacking umbos, are further modified by the presence of decorative elements carved into the outer surface of the bands. Two of these have a series of V-shaped notches cut into both edges of the band, and one has a series of diagonal bars separated by small, conical, drilled perforations (Fig. 25*a-b*).

Residue from Bracelet Manufacture. Nineteen of the specimens in this category are unfinished bracelet fragments. In all cases, a large central perforation was produced in the *Glycymeris* valve by grinding the valve back and forth on an abrading stone. A few examples have a trace of some other smoothing or grinding, but for the most part these specimens seem to represent bracelets broken during the production of the original perforation.

The other two specimens are unmodified *Glycymeris* valves, probably brought to the site for the manufacture of bracelets. Both are old, eroded shells with worm holes.

Rings. Included in this category are 19 small shell rings made by grinding the convex surface from one valve of a bivalve shell. After removal of a central core, the rings were further smoothed by grinding and polishing. Several of the rings are manufactured from juvenile *Glycymeris* valves. Dimensions: band width ranges from 3 to 8 mm.

Residue from Ring Manufacture. Three juvenile *Glycymeris* valves with central perforations produced by rubbing the convex side of the valve back and forth on an abrading stone were found at the site. The bands of the rings are not finished or smoothed.

Whole Shell Pendants. Two of the whole shell pendants are valves of *Pecten circularis* (Fig. 26*n*). The only modification of the valves is at the umbo, where they have been ground to the point that a perforation is worked through the shell.

A third pendant is fragmentary. This is the flat valve of *Pecten vogdesi.* In this case a perforation is drilled through the shell near the umbo.

The fourth example is made from a *Glycymeris* valve (Fig. 26*j*). In this case, a perforation is drilled through the umbo, and the valve is ground smooth.

Cut Shell Pendants. Shell species was not identifiable for any of the cut shell pendants. Two of the cut shell pendants have circular outlines (Fig. 26*d-e*). One of these has a biconical perforation through the edge, and the other a conical perforation. In addition, both have large central perforations. One of the pendants has a series of V-shaped notches encircling the outer edge. Dimensions: diameter, 2.3 and 2.8 cm.; thickness, 2 and 3 mm.

A third pendant is oval in outline. This specimen, which is fragmentary, has three large biconical perforations in the remaining section. The example is broken across two of the perforations. Dimensions: width, 2.2 cm.; thickness, 2 mm.

Another cut shell pendant is in the form of a conventionalized bird (Fig. 26*c*). This bird is one commonly seen on pottery designs of the

Santa Cruz and Sacaton phases, but which had earlier beginnings (Gladwin and others 1937: Fig. 112). Dimensions: length, 2.2 cm.; width, 8 mm.; thickness, 4 mm.

A second carved pendant in the form of a bird is slightly more naturalistic than the one described above, but still conventional (Fig. 26*b*). The bird is shown in profile. A major part of the pendant is the body and head of the bird. A wing extends at right angles from the body. Feathers are represented by incised lines on the wing. A conical perforation forms the eye. Dimensions: length, 2.5 cm.; width, 1.6 cm.; thickness, 1 mm.

Six fragments of carved shell pendants were probably originally diamond-shaped in outline. All are biconically perforated. Perforations are near the points of the diamonds. Dimensions: length, 1 to 3 cm. (range).

Whole Shell Beads. Twelve whole shell beads were collected at the site. Eight of the specimens are *Olivella* shells (Fig. 26*f-g*), and 3 are of *Nassa* shell. The shell species could not be identified for the twelfth bead. Perforations for stringing were formed by grinding or breaking the spires from the shells.

Tubular Beads. One of the tubular beads is formed from a *Vermetus* casing. The original rough casing has been cut to length, and somewhat smoothed by grinding. Dimensions: length, 3.2 cm.; diameter, 6 mm.

The other two tubular beads have been ground to the point where species identification is no longer possible. The beads have been cut to length and ground smooth. Central biconical perforations are present. Dimensions: length, 1 and 1.9 cm.

Disc Beads. Ten small shell discs with central biconical perforations were found. All are ground to the point where identification of shell species is no longer possible. Seven of these beads were associated with the group of turquoise beads (described above) in the general excavation material from Trash Mound 3. Dimensions: diameter, 3 to 7 mm.; thickness, 2 to 4 mm.

Painted Shell. Included in this category is a single irregular fragment of a *Cardium* shell with traces of red paint on the exterior surface of the valve. One edge of the fragment is ground.

Miscellaneous Worked Shell. Eighteen assorted pieces of shell, mainly *Cardium* and *Glycymeris,* which have been slightly modified by cutting, grinding, and drilling were collected. Most of these specimens are probably unfinished ornaments, perhaps broken during the process of manufacture. Two examples, both *Cardium,* are shell sections from which pieces have been cut for ornaments. One interesting specimen in this group is a piece of abalone shell cut into a roughly square shape. Fine serrations about 1 mm. apart are present along its edges. Another small fragment of incised shell may have been used in mosaic work.

Bone Artifacts

Awls. Four awls, manufactured from splinters of bone, are present in the collection. All are fragmentary, but the remaining sections indicate that the awls once tapered from wide butts to sharp tips. Dimensions: width, 7 mm. to 1.4 cm. (range).

Miscellaneous Worked Bone Specimens. Sixteen fragments of bone bear traces of modification by man. Four pieces show evidence of having been sawed or cut, and eight fragments have polished surfaces. One fragment may have been used as a gouge.

Metal Artifacts

Copper Bells. Wasley's (1960: 259–60) description of the three copper bells found at the Gatlin site is repeated here:

> These were of the small, globular or spheroidal shape characteristic of copper bells found in other areas of the Southwest at this same time horizon (Gladwin and others 1937: 164, Pl. 113*a*). The Gatlin site specimens average 1.5 cm. in length and 1.2 cm. in width. Each has a slit in the bottom of the resonator and a copper pellet clapper. Eyelets at the top of the bells are at right angles to the slits in the resonators. Two of the eyelets are broken. It is now generally agreed that copper bells were manufactured in Mexico and reached the Southwest by prehistoric trade (Hawley 1953: 101-3; Rinaldo 1959: 275-6).

Wood Artifacts

Wooden Paddle. Wasley's (1960: 260) description of a wooden paddle found in the core material of the fifth stage of the platform mound construction is also repeated here:

> It is 21 cm. in length and 6.2 cm. in maximum width. The handle is 11.5 cm. long, and the maximum thickness, which is found in the handle, is 1.3 cm. Thickness of the paddle blade is 9 mm. The object is only slightly charred. The broad end, in particular, and the lateral edges of the paddle blade, to a lesser extent,

have not been well preserved. It is therefore impossible to tell if the broad end had been beveled, and it does not appear that the lateral edges were beveled, although they may have been slightly rounded. The blade of the paddle seems to have one slightly concave surface, but this may be a result of weathering and deterioration rather than of original manufacture. Similar paddle-shaped objects have been found in Hohokam sites of this and later horizons (Haury 1945a: 162-3, 170, 178, 182-3, Pl. 74). While some paddles of this general type may have been used in the manufacture of Hohokam pottery, Haury (1945a: 162-3) points out that modern pottery paddles used by the Pima have a slightly different shape, and he suggests that the archaeological specimens may have served as hand digging tools.

Faunal Remains

Faunal remains from the Gatlin site were submitted to the Southwest Archeological Center of the National Park Service, in Globe, Arizona, for identification and study. The mammalian material has not yet been studied. Lyndon L. Hargrave, Collaborator in Ornithology and Archeology at the Center, has kindly furnished the following identifications of the bird bones in the collection.

Bird bones. Gambel's Quail (*Lophortyx gambelii*), a left tibiotarsus from the platform mound, east side, in the fill between construction stages III and IV (Wasley 1960b: 249).

Chicken (*Gallus gallus*), a part of a sternum (breast meat) of a juvenile (fryer) from the platform mound, north side, in the fill between construction stages III and IV, at a depth of 1 to 1.5 m.

Chicken (*gallus gallus*), left tibiotarsus (drumstick) and furcula (wishbone) from Trash Mound 3, general excavation (Fig. 10). These two bones could be from the same individual.

Chicken (*Gallus gallus*), half of right tibiotarsus, but apparently not the mate of the one above, from Trash Mound 3, general excavation.

Macaw (*Ara,* sp. ?), 40 part or complete bones from a single individual, from the platform mound excavation, in a preliminary trench at the west side. Poor condition.

Discussion. Hargrave comments on the chicken bones as follows, "These are definitely chicken bones and I consider them to represent a minimum of 3 individuals." The chicken was native to southeast Asia (Gilmore 1950: 393; Zeuner 1963: 443) and presumably was not present in the New World in pre-Columbian times, with the possible exception of the still unresolved situation in South America (Nordenskiöld 1922: 1–12; Latcham 1922: 176–79; Gilmore 1950: 394; Sauer 1952: 57–60). Be this as it may, it is reasonably certain that the chicken was not present in the southwestern United States in prehistoric times. The occurrence of chicken bones in Trash Mound 3 and in the platform mound at the Gatlin site may be attributed to picnicking pot hunters within the last 30 or 40 years. The evident disturbance of the platform mound, prior to excavation, was noted previously (Wasley 1960b: 244). It was at or near the bottom of one of these larger and deeper areas of disturbance that the chicken bone from the platform mound was encountered. Similar pot hunting activity was noted in the trash mounds prior to excavation (p. 43), and it is not unreasonable to invoke the same explanation for the presence of chicken bones in Trash Mound 3.

In support of this explanation for the occurrence of chicken bones at the Gatlin site, it should be mentioned here that the metal base of a shotgun shell was encountered at a depth of nearly two meters in the southeast corner of the platform mound.

The macaw, represented by faunal remains from burials or as trophies or offerings accompanying human burials, has been found throughout the Southwest generally, in prehistoric contexts, even though it may have been imported from northwestern Mexico. Gambel's quail, on the other hand, was probably then, as it is now, at home in southern Arizona.

THE CITRUS SITE

The Citrus site (Ariz. T:13:2), the other Sacaton-phase village excavated during the second field season, is situated approximately 15 miles down the Gila River to the west of the Gatlin site (Figs. 1, 18). The village occupies a large area of nearly flat ground at the base of a gravel terrace. The southern edge of the site is marked by a large wash below the gravel terrace. The northern section of the site has been completely obliterated by agriculture, and the exact northern limit can no longer be determined. To the east and west there are no well-marked boundaries, as the cultural debris on the surface simply thins out. The origi-

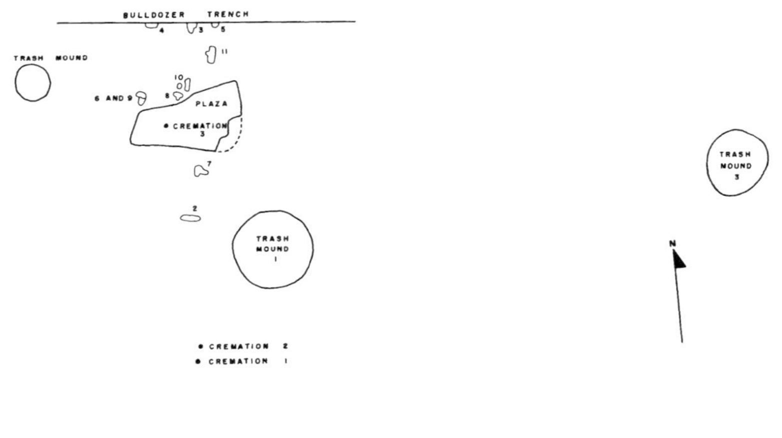

Fig. 18. The Citrus site (Arizona T:13:2). Numbers refer to houses.

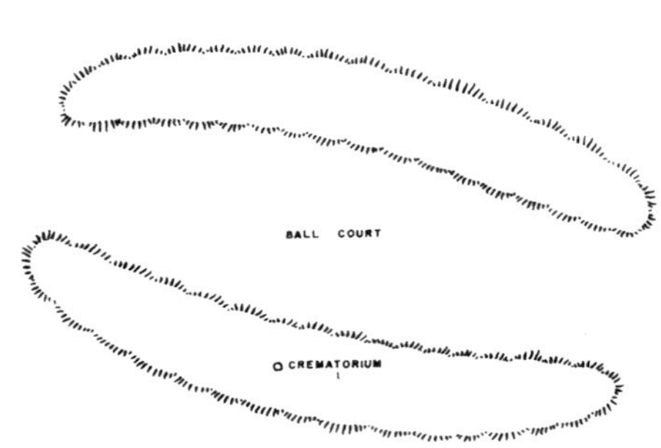

nal dimensions were probably somewhat on the order of three-fourths of a mile in length (north-south) by one-half of a mile in width (east-west).

Before excavation, the remaining section of the site was covered by a dense growth of saltbush and mesquite. The obvious archaeological features were a ball court and seven trash mounds, some of which were high enough to extend above the vegetation cover. Sherds were thinly scattered over the entire surface of the site. In connection with recent agricultural work in the area, some disturbance of the remaining section has taken place. A farm road extends through the site in a north-south direction, and this is bordered by a fence and a power line. Two old, but historic, irrigation ditches run east and west across the site, and bulldozing in connection with their construction has caused some disturbance. A small corral is also present.

The section of the site which has been leveled for agriculture is lost forever for archaeological work. This entire northern section of the site has been completely leveled with large earth-moving machinery to the point where there is no longer any possibility of salvaging any of the archaeological information which the section once contained. Norton Allen was present at the time the leveling took place, several years ago. He reports that formerly there were a number of trash mounds, cremations, and a Casa Grande-type ball court in this section. Undoubtedly there were also many houses. Allen's sketchmap of the site at that time is reproduced as Figure 67.

Trash Mounds

Seven trash mounds ranging in diameter from 12 to 25 meters are present in the remaining section of the site (Fig. 18). Six of these are relatively undisturbed, but the seventh has been nearly destroyed by the farm road which cuts through the site. All are rounded mounds of earth containing varying amounts of cultural residue. The surface of each mound is covered with quantities of sherds, stone fragments, shell residue, and some broken animal bone.

Excavations were made in Mounds 1, 2, and 3. The procedure followed in this excavation was the same as outlined for the Gatlin site, with the exception that no power equipment was used. All of the trash-mound excavations were done by hand. Only one of the mounds, number 1, was excavated in arbitrary levels. In this case, one 2 m. block was removed in this manner. Although 1.2 m. of cultural residue were present in the mound, no great time difference is indicated. The entire mound accumulated during the Sacaton phase. The Sacaton-phase occupation of this site is supported by excavations in the other mounds and features, none of which produced any locally-painted pottery other than Sacaton Red-on-buff.

Excavations in the three trash mounds at the Citrus site indicate a parallel with the Gatlin site mounds. It was noted at the latter site that only two of the mounds had trashy fills, the fill of the other mounds being relatively clean, often including lenses of unmixed sand and earth. At the Citrus site, Trash Mound 3 definitely had a trashy fill. The fill was dark and contained quantities of ash and charcoal. Mounds 1 and 2 both had relatively clean fills, quite comparable to a majority of the mounds at the Gatlin site.

As was the case at the Gatlin site, excavations in the mounds failed to disclose any evidence of associated structures. While excavating Mound 1 at the Citrus site, fragments of caliche were observed eroding from the side. Consequently, a long trench was cut most of the way through the mound in an attempt to discover the nature of the occurrence of this material. The trench disclosed the presence of several irregular layers of caliche in the fill, but all seemed to represent material which was cleaned up around the houses to the north, and not floors or platform surfacings.

Plaza

One of the most interesting features discovered at the Citrus site was a plaza (Figs. 18, 19). This consisted of a caliche-floored area some 35 m. in length (east-west) by 20 m. in width (north-south). It was probably roughly rectangular in outline, although the edges were rather indistinct. There is no evidence that the plaza was ever roofed, even in part, as no post holes were found on the floor or around the edges. The single feature on the floor of the plaza was a basin-shaped pit filled with charcoal. The pit measured 30 cm.

Fig. 19. East end of plaza, Citrus site. Piles of dirt in background from house excavations.

in diameter and was 15 cm. deep. Although it was filled with charcoal, there were no traces of burning at the edges.

The floor of the plaza was covered by only about 20 cm. of material deposited since its use ended. It rested on a layer some 30 or 35 cm. in thickness made up of trash and large masses of caliche mixed with small quantities of trash. Probably the site was occupied for some time, during which the trash and caliche accumulated, before the plaza floor was constructed over this mass of material.

Structures

Eleven houses or parts of houses were discovered and excavated at the Citrus site (Fig. 18). Ten of these were scattered about the edges of the plaza. Two trash mounds were close to the houses. It would appear from this that one form of Hohokam settlement pattern is a plaza with an irregular grouping of houses about its edges, and beyond the houses a few areas for the deposition of trash. This is interesting to note, as little is known of Hohokam settlement patterns, an important aspect of the information which can be derived from archaeology.

The eleventh house at the Citrus site adds further information about Hohokam settlement patterns. This house, Structure 1, was situated some distance north of the ball court, and was apparently an isolated example. No other houses were present in the vicinity, nor was there a trash mound close by, although a little sheet trash was present to the southeast of the house.

Houses were discovered by the use of hand-dug trenches and a soil auger. The initial step in the excavation was to dig a narrow trench through the house following the floor and thereby defining two edges. A second trench was then dug at right angles to the first, locating the other edges, and finally the four remaining quadrants were cleared. No attempt was made to separate fill and floor material as the houses were all quite shallow, the maximum depth being 50 cm. In addition, our previous excavations had been in the trash mounds, which indicated that the site was occupied during only one period, the Sacaton phase. Consequently, the problem of distinguishing houses of different phases did not arise.

Structure 1

As noted above, Structure 1 was situated to the north of the ball court, and did not form a part of the house group around the plaza. The house consisted of a poorly-preserved caliche floor which was roughly rectangular in outline. It was oriented with the long dimension north-south. Structure 1 measured 3.5 m. in length by 2.4 m. in width. A low, straight-sided, wall of caliche on the south side extended around to the west side of the structure. Another patch of this wall was preserved on the east side. Four post holes were present near the corners of the house, one in an irregularly shaped pit some 50 cm. in length by 30 cm. in width. Neither fireplace nor entrance was located.

Structure 2

This house and the ones following are all part of the plaza-house-trash mound complex mentioned above. Structure 2 was partially destroyed by a historic irrigation canal, which runs east-west across the site just south of the plaza. The canal cut through approximately the center of the house and removed the northern one-half. The remaining section of caliche floor indicates that the house was oval in outline. The southern edge of the floor slopes up abruptly to what was probably the ground surface at the time the site was occupied. Three post holes were present, two near the western end of the remaining section of the structure, and one in the center. Structure 2 was oriented east-west, with the entrance probably opening to the north, since no traces of an entrance were found along the south side. The house was 6.5 m. in length.

Structures 3, 4, and 5

These three houses were partially destroyed by a bulldozer-cut along the north edge of the unfarmed section of the site. Caliche was observed eroding from the face of the bulldozer trench, and thus it was felt that it would be worthwhile to straighten and clean this face thereby yielding a profile of one long section of the site. After the cleaning was completed, three caliche floors were observed in cross section. The overburden was stripped from these and the remaining sections of Structures 3, 4, and 5 exposed.

Structure 3 was represented by a ragged patch of caliche floor which could not represent more than one-fourth of a house. The only remaining edge of the house was along the east side. There was no evidence that the edge sloped upward; it was marked only by a smooth even end to the patch of caliche floor. No posts, hearth, or entrance were located.

Only the south edge of Structure 4 remained, the rest having been removed by the bulldozer trench. This patch of floor indicated a rectangular house with rounded corners. The edges did not slope up, nor were any posts found along the edges. Structure 4 was probably oriented east-west. The entrance may have opened to the north as no trace of an entrance was found along the south side.

Structure 5, as indicated in the trench profile, had been remodeled twice. The first remodeling consisted of a layer of caliche placed directly on the original floor. Apparently, during this period of use the house burned, since a layer of charcoal some 5 cm. in thickness was found to overlie the remodeled floor. A third floor was constructed on the layer of charcoal. In excavating the house, an attempt was made to clear each floor and record the features of each. This proved to be impossible due to the poor definition of the floors, so that only the original construction is available for description. The remaining section of this original floor indicates that Structure 5 was probably oriented with the long dimension north-south. No traces of an entrance or hearth were found. The edges did not slope upward. Two post holes were found at the south end of the partial floor. Structure 5 had a maximum width of 2.6 m.

Structures 6 and 9

Structure 6 consisted of an irregularly-shaped patch of caliche floor measuring some 5 cm. in thickness. Superimposed on the north end of this patch was a second incomplete house, Structure 9. The two were separated by about 5 cm. of sterile sand. The only feature associated with either of these floors was a circular firepit in the floor of Structure 9. The firepit was 30 cm. in diameter, and 15 cm. deep. It was lined with a layer of caliche which extended above the level of the floor in a raised rim. The edges were missing from both of the houses, and no post holes were found. The edges were found to be missing from many of the houses at the Citrus site, suggesting that perhaps the floors were broken up and the caliche reused after the houses were abandoned. The fact that caliche had to be brought

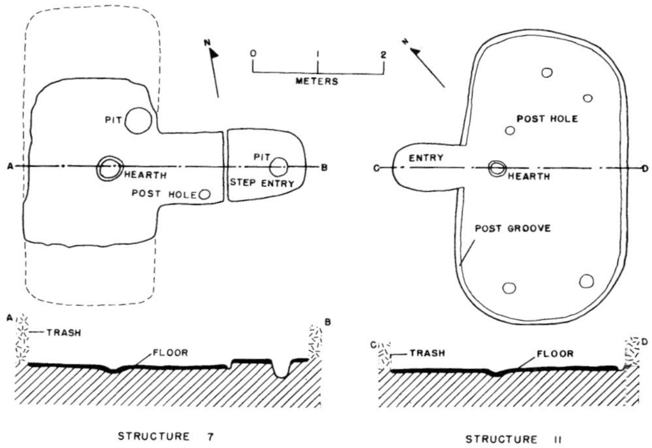

Fig. 20. Plans and sections, Structures 7 and 11, Citrus site.

Fig. 21. Step entrance (foreground), Structure 7, Citrus site. Entrance corridor and house floor behind. Caliche-lined hearth in center.

to the site from outcrops about one-half mile to the southeast somewhat supports this inference.

Structure 7

Structure 7 was discovered in a test trench on the south side of the plaza (Figs. 20, 21). Again in this case, the edges of the house were missing, except for a short section along the west side. Not enough remained of the structure to determine the shape of the original outline. The house was probably oriented with the long dimension northeast-southwest. The entrance which opened to the southeast was made in two parts separated by a narrow trench. One of the sections was a step 1.1 m. long and 1.05 m. wide. The southeastern end of this step was rounded, and a pit measuring 25 cm. in diameter was present near the center. The step section of the entrance ended at the trench, where it opened into a short corridor which gave access to the house. The corridor was 1 m. in length by 1.1 in width. A single post hole was present on the south side of the corridor.

Immediately in front of the entrance, inside the house, was a basin-shaped firepit. This consisted of a hole, some 30 cm. in diameter and 10 cm. in depth, lined with caliche. A raised rim was not present. The only other feature in the house was a basin-shaped pit in the northeast corner of the remaining section of floor. This pit was 20 cm. in diameter.

Quantities of ash and charcoal in the fill above the floor of Structure 7 indicate that the house was destroyed by fire. Further support for this interpretation comes from the fact that the caliche floor was burned to an orange color in several places. Also present in the fill of the house were numerous lumps of caliche, perhaps indicating that this material was used to some extent in the walls and roof of the house. Most of the excavated structures at the Citrus site had caliche spread for some distance around the edges, suggesting that this material may have been used in the construction of other parts of the house beside the floor.

Structure 8

Structure 8 was an incomplete house consisting of a small patch of floor, and a rectangular entrance which opened to the southwest. It was situated on the north side of the plaza. The edges of the house were completely gone, and no features were found in the remaining section of floor. The rectangular entrance passage is 1 m. in length, by 75 cm. in width. That the house had burned was indicated by the fact that the caliche was extremely hard and grey in color.

Structure 10

Structure 10 was represented by two irregular patches of caliche floor, found on the north side of the plaza, just northeast of Structure 8. House edges were missing from both sections. No features such as hearths or post holes were found in either patch of floor. The house was not burned.

Structure 11

Structure 11 was the only complete house floor found at the Citrus site (Fig. 20). It was situated on the north side of the plaza, northeast of Structures 8 and 10, but south of Structures 3, 4, and 5. The oval caliche floor of this house was oriented northeast-southwest. A bulbous entrance passage opened to the northwest. The caliche used for the floor of this house had been liberally mixed with quantities of small pebbles, many of which projected through the caliche forming a rough surface. Pebbles were not mixed with the caliche used for the entrance passage.

Floor features included a hearth lined with caliche situated directly in front of the entrance passage, and six post holes scattered over the floor. The hearth had a slightly raised rim. With the exception of the entrance passage, the entire floor was encircled by a shallow trench measuring 10 cm. in width and depth. Excavation of this trench disclosed two rows of small post holes. The walls of Structure 11 were apparently constructed of a double row of posts set in the trench. That the house was destroyed by fire is attested to by quantities of charcoal in the fill, and by the fact that the floor was burned a grey color. Structure 11 measured 4.7 m. in length by 2.6 m. in width. The entrance passage was 1 m. long and 75 cm. wide.

Ball Courts

Until a few years ago two ball courts were present at the Citrus site. One of these was a Casa Grande-type court situated in the northern section of the site which was leveled for agriculture. The leveling process completely obliterated the court, thereby removing any chance of obtaining information on its construction. The second court, a Snaketown type (Figs. 18, 22), was situated just north of the wash forming the southern border of the site and in the undisturbed section. This court was partially excavated.

The Snaketown-type ball court was marked by a large oval depression bordered on the north and south sides by rounded semicircular ridges of earth. It was oriented with the long dimension east-west, actually 20 degrees 30 minutes south of east. From the crest of the north ridge to the crest of the south, it measured 28 m. in width. The length was 60 m.

Trenches were dug at each end of the court, and in the center. At the west end, a north-south trench was dug between the earth ridges to the floor of the court. When the floor was reached, a right-angle extension of the trench was made, which followed the floor into the end unit. The end of the trench was expanded over the end unit to expose most of this feature. At the east end of

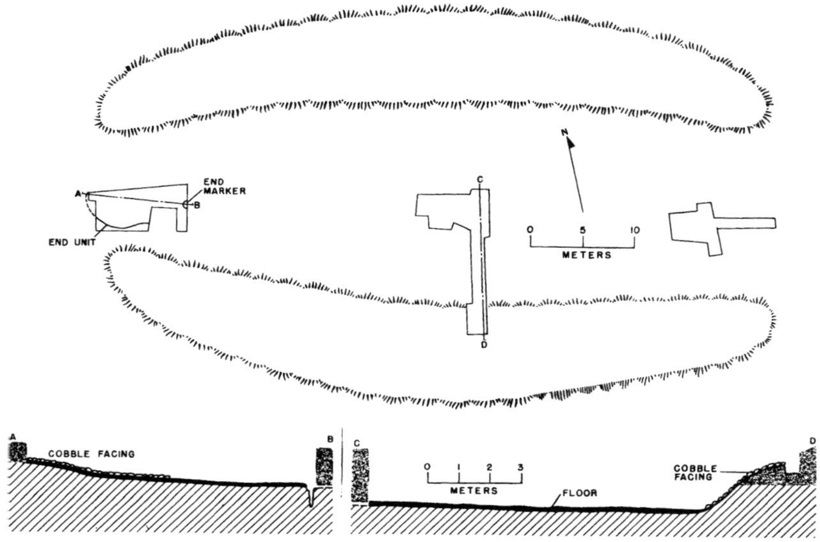

Fig. 22. Plan and sections, ball court, Citrus site.

the court a similar north-south exploratory trench was excavated, but in this case the floor was poorly preserved, and it was not possible to follow the floor into the end unit or to define this latter feature (Fig. 22).

The initial trench in the center of the court was oriented north-south. This trench was placed slightly off center to the east, and an attempt was made to follow the floor into the center and find the center marker. The floor again was poorly preserved and the center marker could not be located. An extension of the initial north-south trench was dug to the south through the earth ridge on that side of the court.

The floor of the ball court where it was preserved consisted of a single layer of caliche averaging about 5 cm. in thickness. Apparently this layer was applied over the entire prehistoric excavation. The excavation sloped up at the edges, and the slope was covered with caliche. The ridges along the north and south sides, which were formed by heaping up the earth from the excavation, were not caliche covered. The inside surfaces of the ridges were, however, paved with a layer of cobbles set directly into the ridges with no mortar. The cobbles were probably gathered from the gravel terraces to the south of the site. Most of them measured from 10 to 15 cm. in diameter.

The single end unit which could be defined, the one at the west end of the court, was constructed of caliche. It consisted of a large circular area some 5 m. in diameter, connected to the end of the court by a short neck of caliche. The end unit had a concave profile along the north-south axis. It sloped upward on a flat plane along the east-west axis, from the end of the court. The circular section of the end unit was covered with cobbles, in the same manner as the ridges around the sides of the court.

The end marker at the west end of the ball court consisted of a circular hearth measuring 50 cm. in diameter and 20 cm. in depth. The bottom of the hearth was filled with a layer of ash, which was overlain by a deposit of charcoal. The edges of the hearth were burned. A post hole measuring 20 cm. in diameter and 65 cm. in depth was present in the bottom of the hearth.

Since the floor in the center of the court and at the east end was poorly preserved, the features usually found in these sections could not be defined. Neither the center marker, nor the east end marker and end unit could be worked out. It is difficult to explain the difference in preservation found in this single feature, but perhaps more care was devoted to placing the floor in the west end of the court than over the remainder, and it therefore lasted somewhat longer.

Crematorium

Crematorium 1 was marked by the presence of calcined human bone on the surface of the ground, around rodent burrows, on the south ridge of the ball court (Fig. 18). A trench was dug

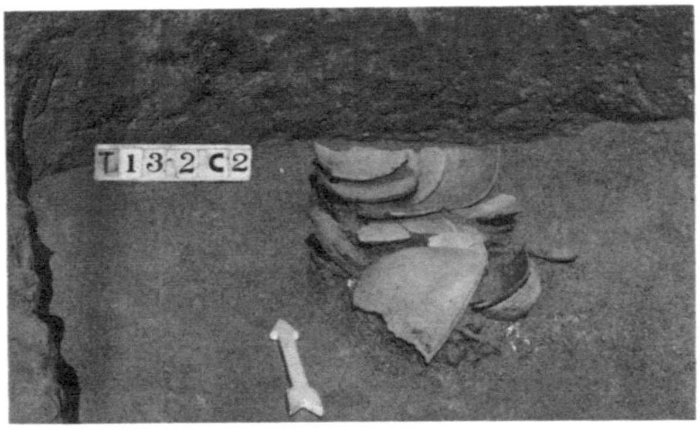

Fig. 23. Cremation 2, Citrus site.

through the heaviest concentration of this bone in a northwest-southeast direction. This disclosed the presence of a crematorium with a roughly circular outline measuring 1.6 m. in diameter. It had a basin-shaped cross section, and was 15 cm. in depth. The sides and bottom of the pit, which were unlined, were burned hard and red. The bottom of the pit was covered with a layer of poorly-reduced human bone, 10 cm. in depth. Crematorium 1 was 1.25 m. below the present surface of the ridge of the ball court. It was apparently a pre-ball-court feature, as the depth indicates it was probably let down from the level of the surface of the ground before the construction of the court. Furthermore, no pit could be discerned cutting through the ball court ridges.

Cremations

Three cremations were located at the Citrus site during the course of the field work (Fig. 18). Cremations 1 and 2 were situated in an area southwest of the plaza. They had been placed on a north-south line some 3 m. apart, and at a depth below the present ground surface of 1.1 m. Cremation 3 was discovered below the plaza floor.

Cremation 1

Cremation 1 (Fig. 18) consisted of a quantity of fragments of human bone which had been finely reduced by fire. They were concentrated under the pieces of an inverted Sacaton shouldered jar, a Gila Plain bowl, and several sherds from a large Gila Plain jar. All of the pottery vessels were fragmentary, but with the exception of the large Gila Plain jar, most of the sherds were present and they could be restored. Another offering with the cremation was a stone chopper. Perhaps this chopper was used to break the pottery vessels, a form of ceremonial killing, and then placed in the pit as an offering itself. Twelve shell beads were found mixed in with the calcined bone. All of the beads were burnt, indicating they had gone through the crematory fire. The outline of the pit, which was dug to place the cremation in the ground, could not be discerned, but the fact that the sherds were closely grouped over the burned bones in a roughly oval pattern, indicates the pit was probably this shape. The sherds overlying Cremation 1 covered an area 65 cm. in length by 40 cm. in width.

Cremation 2

Cremation 2 (Fig. 23) was quite similar to Cremation 1. The major difference was that the calcined bones were not grouped under the sherds from a single vessel, but were grouped together under one end of a pile of sherds from several vessels. All of the sherds were found to be restorable into two Gila Plain bowls, and part of a Tusayan Black-on-red bowl. A handstone was present as an offering with Cremation 2, and perhaps this was the instrument used to break the pottery vessels. One other offering was an unmodified *Cardium* shell, found under the pile of sherds. The pit of Cremation 2 could not be defined, but the sherds were grouped in a roughly oval area measuring 65 cm. in length by 50 cm. in width.

Cremation 3

Cremation 3 was discovered in a trench cut through the plaza floor to determine the nature of the underlying trash and fill. It consisted of a Gila Plain jar, lying slightly on its side, which contained a small quantity of calcined human bone and a few unburned fragments of coiled basketry. A very heavily burned *Cardium* shell was found at the mouth of the jar. A Gila Plain bowl which had been broken into many pieces was discovered over the jar as a cover. The cremation pit was roughly circular in outline and basin-shaped in cross section. It was impossible to determine the point from which the pit was dug, due to the trashy nature of the fill above.

Tests

In addition to the excavations of the features described above, the site was tested by means of 13 trenches averaging 75 cm. in width, and varying in length from 2 m. to 10 m. These trenches were placed in locations where surface material indicated the possibility of features below the surface. For the most part they were unproductive. Numerous tests with a soil auger were used to explore further the subsurface conditions at the site.

Pottery

Excavations at the Citrus site yielded a total of 6,765 sherds, one complete jar, one restorable jar, and five restorable bowls. All of the jars and bowls came from the three cremations. The sherds were collected from the various excavation units. Of the 6,765 sherds, 6,687 or 98.6 per cent were locally made, while 78 or 1.4 per cent were traded into the site from other areas. As was true for the pottery from the Gatlin site, the various types from the Citrus site are practically indistinguishable from those of Snaketown (Gladwin and others 1937: 168–228). Since the pottery from the Citrus site closely parallels that of the Gatlin site, the following comments will be in the form of comparisons with the ceramics of the latter site.

The only locally-made painted pottery type which is found at the Citrus site is Sacaton Red-on-buff. This indicates a single-phase occupation, as opposed to the Gatlin-site situation where the occupation lasted through at least one entire phase, and part of an earlier one. Evidence was presented in a discussion of the Gatlin-site pottery that the occupation of that site lasted to the end of the Sacaton phase. This is also the case for the Citrus site, where the presence of rectilinear design elements on Sacaton Red-on-buff sherds and a minor quantity of Sacaton Red sherds indicates the site was populated until the end of the Sacaton phase.

Sacaton Red-on-buff accounts for only about 10 per cent of the total number of locally-made sherds. A parallel situation was found at the Gatlin site, and an explanation is offered in the discussion of Sacaton Red-on-buff from that site. Gila Plain was slightly more common at the Citrus site than at the Gatlin site, constituting 80.4 per cent of the total of locally made pottery types.

Lower Colorado Buff is the most commonly occurring intrusive ware, as was the situation at the Gatlin site. Close trade relations with the manufacturers of this ware are indicated. Northern trade pieces include Black Mesa Black-on-white, about 900–1100 (Colton 1946: 251), Tusayan Black-on-red, about 1050-1150 (Colton 1946: 252), Snowflake Black-on-white, about 1000–1150 (Colton 1941: 62–63), and Reserve Black-on-white, about 1000–1150 (Martin and Rinaldo 1950: 502–503; Martin and others 1952: 61–63).

The dates for these types found as intrusives at the Citrus site are quite close to those assigned to northern intrusives at the Gatlin site. Again, there is a suggestion that the Sacaton-phase occupation may have lasted until 1150. A minor amount of contact is indicated with Papagueria, as a few sherds of Valshni Red were collected. Mogollon contact was minor, and is represented at the site by the presence of a single sherd of Encinas Red-on-brown (Sayles 1945: 43).

Artifacts

Ceramic Artifacts

Thick-Walled Vessels. Both of the Sacaton Red-on-buff thick-walled vessels from the Citrus site are circular in outline. One is a flat dish with straight sides, and a flat rim and base (Fig. 15*c*). The inner walls slope into a concave bottom. Traces of burning are present on the vessel, since it came from Structure 8 which was destroyed by fire. Dimensions: diameter, 9.2 cm.; height, 1.9 cm.; wall thickness, 1.8 cm.

The second thick-walled vessel has a greater height, and concave sides (Fig. 15*a*). The rim and base are flat, the sides of the basin are straight, and the bottom concave. The vessel also shows traces of burning, as it was found in Structure 7. Dimensions: diameter, 11.5 cm.; height, 5.3 cm.; wall thickness, 1.5 cm.

Sherd Discs. The six discs in this category are made from sherds, which have their edges ground to a circular outline. The edge grinding is the only modification of the sherds. One is a biconically perforated specimen made from a Gila Plain sherd (Fig. 16*f*), four are unperforated Gila Plain discs (Fig. 16*d-e*), and one is an unperforated Sacaton Red-on-buff disc (Fig. 16*c*). Dimensions: diameter, 2.9 to 5.4 cm. (range); thickness, 4 to 8 mm. (range).

Stone Artifacts

Projectile Points. Five projectile points were collected from the site. Two of the complete points have deep basal notches, side notches, and serrations (Fig. 17*b*). Both have straight edges, and both are manufactured from white chert. Dimensions: length, 3.8 and 6.3 cm.; width, 1.6 cm. (both); thickness, 4 and 6 mm.

The other complete point is made from the same material, a white chert, but differs somewhat in form. This specimen has a straight base, with side notches, and convex edges. It lacks serrations (Fig. 17*d*). Dimensions: length, 2.4 cm.; width, 1 cm.; thickness, 3 mm.

The two fragmentary points lack both bases and tips. Neither is serrated.

Knife. The single knife found at the site is represented by a small section broken from the edge of a bifacially-chipped blade. It is made of pink chert. Both faces bear large primary flaking scars, while secondary chipping is restricted to the edges.

Choppers. The three choppers are manufactured from water-worn cobbles. The only modification of the original cobble is the removal of several large flakes to produce a cutting edge. In two cases these flakes have been removed from only one side, producing chisel-shaped cutting edges. In the other example, flakes have been taken from both sides producing a V-shaped cutting edge. The hand-hold is the unmodified surface of the pebble in all cases. One of the choppers has additional modification in the form of pitting and rounding along one edge as a result of use as a hammerstone. Dimensions: length, 10.7 to 13.3 cm. (range); width, 8.1 to 10 cm. (range); thickness, 4.9 to 6.9 cm. (range).

Vessels. One of the stone vessels recovered from the Citrus site is an effigy in the form of a mountain sheep, also called bighorn sheep (Fig. 24). The vessel is oval in outline, and forms the body of the effigy. The head projects from one end of the vessel, and the tail from the other. Four legs extend down from the base of the vessel. One horn was broken off prehistorically, and the area where the horn had been was ground smooth. Eyes and nostrils are indicated by small conical holes, and the mouth by an incised line. The basin of the vessel has sloping walls and a flat bottom. Dimensions: length, 14.4 cm.; width, 7 cm.; height, 7.4 cm.

The other stone vessel is circular in outline, with outcurved sides, a flat base, and a rounded rim. It is manufactured from vesicular basalt. The basin is shallow with slightly sloping walls and a concave bottom. A phallic representation protrudes from one side of the vessel. Dimensions: diameter, 12.9 cm.; height, 10.1 cm.

Fig. 24. Stone bowl carved in form of mountain sheep, Citrus site. Length, 14.4 cm.

Palettes. Palettes are represented in the collection from the Citrus site by two small irregular plates of mica schist. Both have grinding striations on one face, but neither fragment exhibits carved or incised decoration.

Manos. The four mano fragments are from two-hand forms made of vesicular basalt. Three were used on only one face and as a consequence have plano-convex cross sections. The fourth mano shows evidence of bifacial use, and has a rectangular cross section. The ends of all the manos are ground, indicating they were used in trough metates.

Metate. The only metate found at the Citrus site is represented by a small section broken from a trough metate of vesicular basalt. The base is rounded, and the grinding surface is quite smooth. Dimensions: thickness, 4.3 cm.

Handstone. The single handstone collected is made from a water-worn cobble. Some modification of the original cobble has taken place, as is attested to by the presence of pecking marks on the edges and ends. The single grinding surface is slightly convex, and has grinding striations at right angles to the long axis. Dimensions: length, 13.3 cm.; width, 9.3 cm.; thickness, 6.7 cm.

Pestle. Pestles are represented in the collection by a single fragment of vesicular basalt. The grinding surface is broken off, so that it is not possible to determine whether the pestle was used in a wooden mortar or in one of stone. Dimensions: diameter, 6.5 cm.

Pendant. The only stone pendant from the site is manufactured from turquoise. The pendant is rectangular in outline and has a conical perforation slightly off-center near one end. Although faint grinding striations are visible on the faces, the specimen gives the impression of being well made and finished. Dimensions: length, 1.3 cm.; width, 1.1 cm.; thickness, 1 mm.

Hammerstone. The single hammerstone collected at the Citrus site is an elongate water-worn cobble with battered ends. Dimensions: length, 13.6 cm.; width, 3.6 cm.; thickness, 2.5 cm.

Paint. Red paint is represented in the collection by a piece of ferruginous shale which may have served as a source, and by a specimen of red ochre. A single piece of badly decomposed malachite may have served as a source of green paint.

Shell Artifacts

A collection of shells made for the purpose of identifying species present at the site included the following:

Cardium elatum	*Turitella leucostoma*
Glycymeris maculatus	*Olivella dama*
Columbella major	*Pecten vogdesi*

Plain Glycymeris Bracelets. Only two of the *Glycymeris* bracelets from the Citrus site are of the thin-band type. Both of these have perforated umbos. The other bracelets have medium-width bands (Fig. 26*e-d*). Of these ten, only two of which are complete, six have perforated umbos. Dimensions: diameter of complete bracelets, 4.8 and 6.5 cm.

Residue from Bracelet Manufacture. Grouped together under this heading are two unfinished *Glycymeris* bracelets, and two unmodified *Glycymeris* valves. The unfinished bracelets all have large central perforations produced by rubbing the concave side of the valve back and forth on an abrading stone. No finish work has been done on the edges of either. The two unmodified *Glycymeris* shells are old eroded valves with worm holes. They were probably traded or brought into the site for the manufacture of bracelets.

Ring. One small ring made from a juvenile *Glycymeris* valve is in the collection. A large central perforation was made, probably by grinding the convex part of the valve on an abrading stone. The band is well finished. Dimensions: band width, 6 mm.

Residue from Ring Manufacture. This category includes two small *Glycymeris* shells with large central perforations produced by grinding. The valves are unmodified, with the exception of the perforation. Both were evidently broken during the process of manufacture.

Whole Shell Pendants. Two small pendants made from juvenile *Glycymeris* valves were found at the site (Fig. 26*k-l*). In both cases, the umbo has been ground to the point where a perforation is worked through into the interior of the shell. This is the only modification of the original valve.

Cut Shell Pendants. The single cut shell pendant is rectangular in outline, and is ground to the point where identification of the type of shell is no longer possible. A conical perforation is present near one end. The edges are chipped and rough. Dimensions: length, 1.7 cm.; width, 1.3 cm.; thickness, 1 mm.

Whole Shell Beads. One of the whole shell beads is an *Olivella* shell from which the spire has been removed by breaking. The other is a *Columbella* with a hole broken through the lip.

Disc Beads. A group of 12 small, disc-shaped beads of shell were collected at the site. All have been ground to the point where identification of the type of shell is no longer possible. The two thinnest beads both have conical perforations, while the thicker examples are biconically perforated. These beads came from Cremation 1, and all show traces of having gone through the crematory fire. Dimensions: diameter, 5 to 6 mm.; thickness, 1 to 4 mm.

Etched Shell. One of the two etched shell specimens from the site is a *Cardium* fragment (Fig. 25*e*). The design consists of rough circles with central dots formed by etching the shell away from the edges of the circles and the dots. One complete and one partial circle remain on the fragment. Dimensions: circle diameter, 9 mm.

The second piece of etched shell is a fragment of a *Glycymeris* bracelet (Fig. 25*d*). The etching has produced small depressed rectangles with raised central dots, on the exterior of the band. These rectangles are grouped in two parallel lines which encircle the bracelet. The design is nearly worn off, probably as a result of long use. The bracelet was made from an old shell full of worm holes. Dimensions: band width, 9 mm.; rectangles are 3 mm. in length and 2 mm. in width.

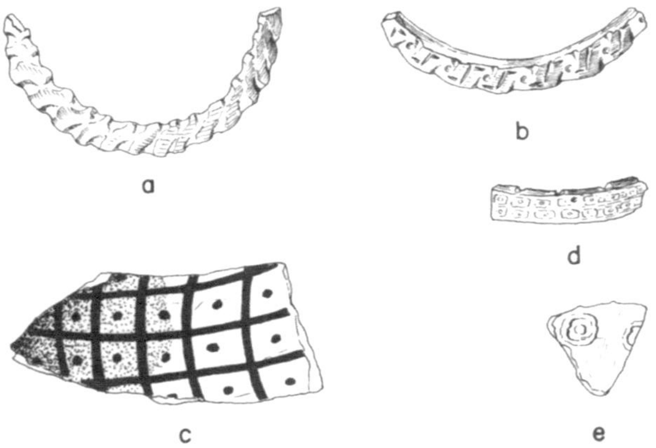

Fig. 25. Designs on carved, etched, and painted shell from Sedentary-period sites; a, b, *carved* Glycymeris *bracelet fragments, Gatlin site;* c-e, *Citrus site;* c, *painted* Cardium *fragment;* d, *etched* Glycymeris *bracelet fragment;* e, *etched* Cardium *fragment. Length of* c, *6.8 cm.*

Specimens of marine shell bearing etched designs are known from the Southwest, but they are far from common objects. Pomeroy (1959: 12–21) was able to catalog only 15 examples, although a few more have apparently been found. Probably the total is not over 20. One of the 15 previously-known specimens, an etched *Cardium* shell, was found in a cremation pit at the Gatlin site. The shell was associated with a Sacaton Red-on-buff jar. The present distribution of specimens of etched shell is restricted to the Hohokam area of southern Arizona. While all of the details of the manufacturing technique are not known, the general process has been worked out, and experiments have duplicated the prehistoric examples with the use of materials known to have been then available (Ezell 1937: 11–12; Gladwin and others 1937: 150–51).

Both of the specimens from the Citrus site are similar in design to examples previously described. One of the Citrus-site specimens is an etched *Cardium* shell, the only type of shell which was previously known to have been etched. The etched *Glycymeris* bracelet is apparently the first example of this type to be discovered.

Painted Shell. An irregularly-shaped *Cardium*

Fig. 26. Shell ornaments from various sites: a, *Arizona T:14:15;* b-g, j, n, *Gatlin site;* h, *Arizona T:14:11;* i, o, *Arizona Z:1:11;* k-m, *Citrus site;* a-c, *carved-shell pendants (bird representations);* d, e, *circular carved-shell pendants;* f-h, Olivella *shell bead;* i, Conus *bead;* j-l, Glycymeris *whole-shell pendants;* m, n, Pecten *whole-shell pendants;* o, *carved-shell frog. Length of* o, *3.5 cm.*

fragment with faint traces of a red-painted design on the concave surface of the valve was recovered from the site (Fig. 25*c*). Although the design is faint, and it is difficult to be sure, there are probably a series of connected squares, each with a dot in the center. One edge of the fragment is slightly ground. Dimensions: length, 6.8 cm.; width, 3 cm.; thickness, 5 mm.

Miscellaneous Shell Specimens. Four of the specimens in this group are irregular pieces of shell with traces of grinding on one or more edges. Of these four, three are *Cardium* and one is *Glycymeris.*

One complete and unmodified *Cardium* shell was found as an offering with Cremation 2. The shell was not burned. A slightly burned and fragmentary *Cardium* shell was present as an offering with Cremation 3.

Bone Artifacts

Awls. The only bone artifacts recovered from the Citrus site are two awl fragments. Both are manufactured from split long bones. One has a rounded tip and the other a somewhat more pointed tip. The edges of both specimens have been rounded by grinding. Dimensions: diameter, 7 mm. and 1.4 cm.

Basketry

Several small fragments of a coiled basket were found in a plainware jar with Cremation 3. These fragments are unburned, and were probably preserved by their inclusion in the jar. All are in rather poor shape. The foundation is either of the three-rod or two-rod-and-bundle type. A positive identification is impossible due to the fragmentary nature of the specimens. The stitching is not interlocked.

ARIZONA T:14:14

Ariz. T:14:14 is situated on the east side of the Gila River five and one-half miles northeast of Gila Bend (Fig. 1). The site, which was occupied during the Sacaton phase, has been badly disturbed by agricultural leveling and clearing, by relic collecting, and by a nineteenth-century irrigation canal which extends through the length of the site. Further disturbance is a result of the construction of a farm road across the west edge.

In addition to several trash mounds, the most prominent feature is a north-south-oriented ball court, marked by semicircular ridges of earth surrounding an oval depression (Fig. 27). A second court at the site has been largely obliterated by the farm road. Excavations at Ariz. T:14:14 were restricted to the complete ball court. The court was tested by means of the technique devised during the course of work at the Gatlin and Citrus sites (see above).

Ball Court

Recent agricultural activity at Ariz. T:14:14 consisted of clearing the site of brush by means of power equipment. This resulted in a certain amount of disturbance to the ball court as a number of large mesquite trees had grown in the depression, taking advantage of water which collected as a result of the high earth ridges at the sides of the court. In the removal of the trees, a bulldozer was apparently used to push them over. As a result, large holes were torn in the court, some of which extended to the floor. Patches of floor could be located in the court, but the floor could not be traced over the entire area.

The floor (Fig. 27) consisted of a layer of caliche averaging 5 cm. in thickness which sloped gradually upward from the center to a point about 1 m. from the edges. At the edges the slope was much more abrupt, the change in angle being from 5 to 15 degrees. Due to the disturbance caused by the removal of the mesquite trees, the sharply-sloping edges of the court could only be defined at the south end.

An end unit or entrance was not found at the north end of the court. The one at the south end consisted of a sloping ramp of caliche which extended to the south, beyond the edge of the floor. The center marker consisted of a small water-worn pebble set in the caliche floor. End markers were not found. A trench dug through the east bank of the court indicated a fill of fine sand and silt, undoubtedly material from the original excavation for the court which was deposited along the sides. At the north end of this bank a caliche surface was found on top of the earth ridge. This could be traced for only a short distance. Perhaps it represents an attempt to halt erosion of the banks. The most striking feature of this ball court is its great depth, 1.90 m. from the top of the earth ridges to the floor. The court is oriented 2 degrees 30 minutes west of north, and its dimensions are 24 m. in length by 16 m. in width. It was dug 1.1 m. below the present surface.

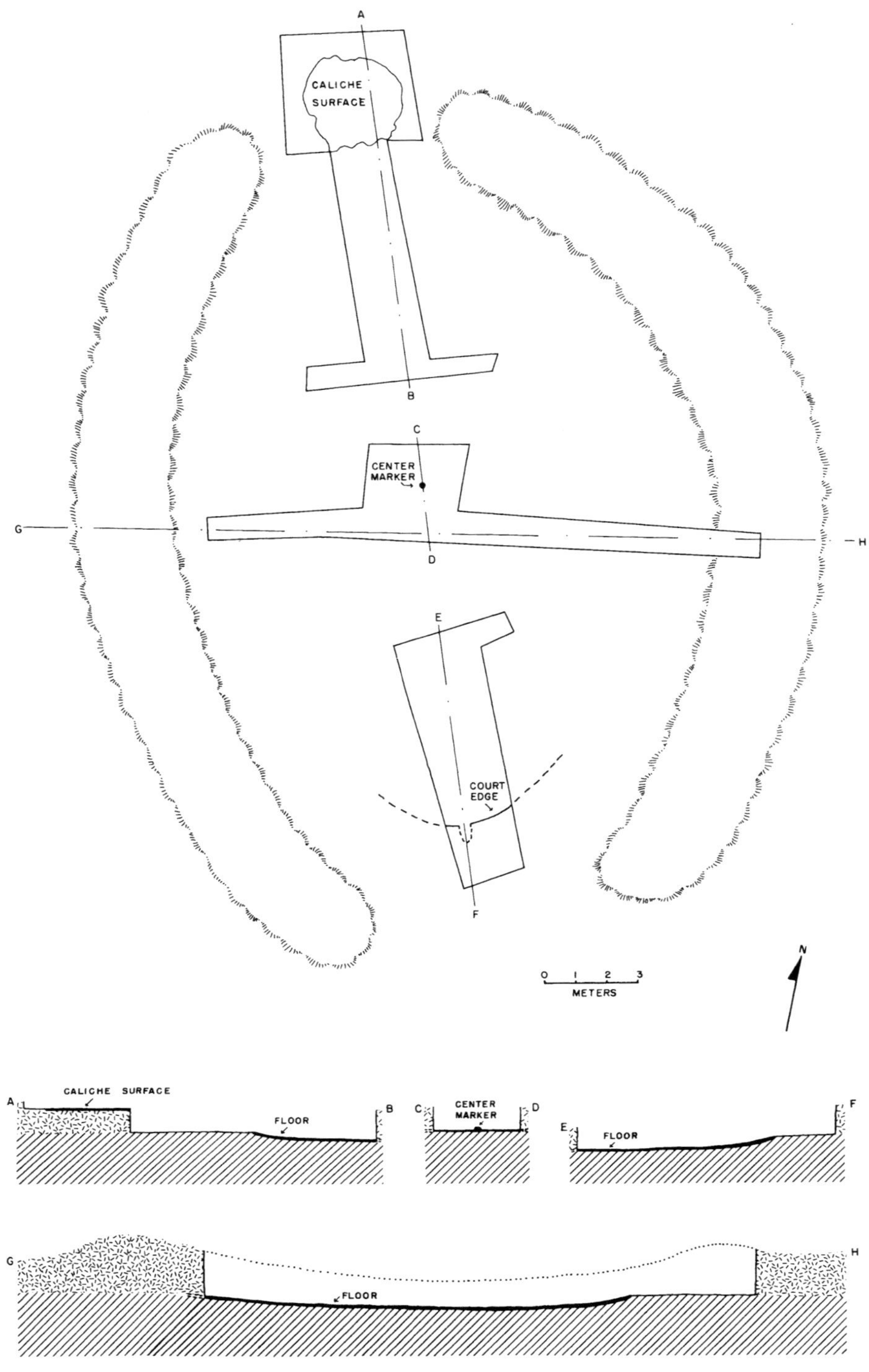

Fig. 27. Plan and sections of ball courts, Arizona T:14:14.

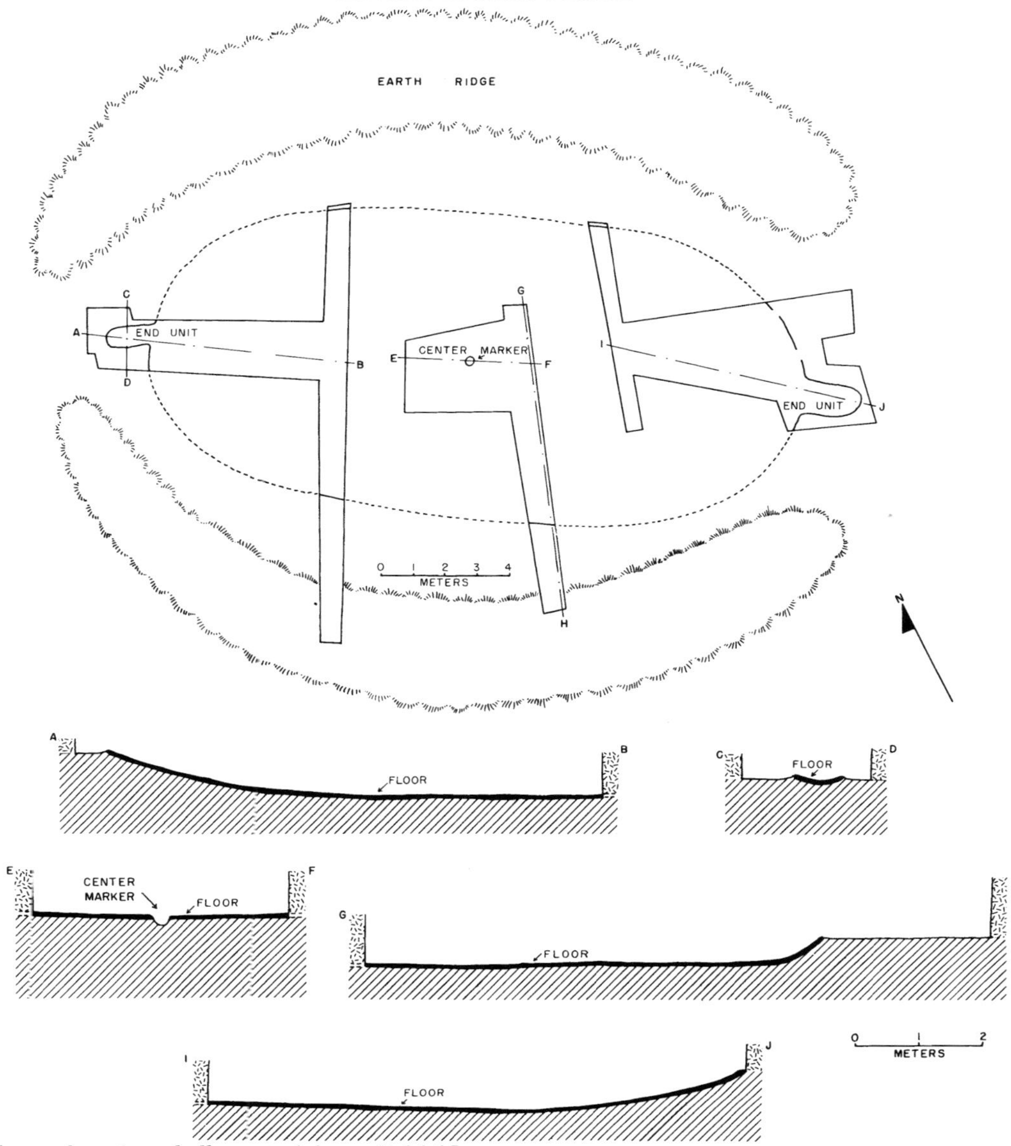

Fig. 28. Plan and sections, ball court, Arizona T:14:15.

Pottery

A total of 320 sherds was obtained from the test excavations in the court. The only locally-made painted pottery included in this sample is Sacaton Red-on-buff, sherds of which were found both in the fill and on the floor. Intrusive sherds include Lower Colorado buffware and Mimbres Black-on-white. The latter type has been assigned dates of 1000 to 1200. It seems apparent that the ball court can be assigned to the Sacaton phase.

ARIZONA T:14:15

Another ball court which was excavated in the Gila Bend area is situated one-half mile west of the court at Ariz. T:14:14 (Fig. 1). Surface sherds from the site in which the court was found range from Gila Butte through Sacaton. The east-west oriented court (Fig. 28) was tested by means of the same technique used for other courts in the Gila Bend area.

Ball Court

Trenches disclosed a well-preserved caliche floor, 5 cm. in thickness, which sloped upward from the center to the edges. At a point 50 cm. from the edges, the angle of the slope of the floor

Fig. 29. East end of ball court, T:14:15. Caliche floor, sloping edge with notches, end unit (entrance).

increased from 5 to 35 degrees. The sharply-sloping edges of the court could be traced to a height of 40 cm., and they were probably never much higher than this.

End units or entrances were present at each end of the court. The one at the east end measured 1.90 m. in length and 1 m. in width (Fig. 29). The opposite end unit was 1.40 m. in length, and 80 cm. in width. Both were sloping ramps of caliche attached to the ends of the court. End markers were not present, but a center marker was found which consisted of a hole in the caliche floor 20 cm. in diameter and 15 cm. in depth. Two other features associated with the floor were found near the east end unit. These were U-shaped notches in the sloping edge of the court (Fig. 29). The function of these notches is unknown, but they are new features for ball courts and should be looked for when future excavations are made.

The ball court at Ariz. T:14:15 was oriented 21 degrees 30 minutes south of east. It measured 23.7 m. in length by 9.5 m. in width, and it was dug to a depth of 1.4 m. below the old ground surface.

Pottery

Both Gila Butte and Santa Cruz Red-on-buff sherds were obtained from excavations in the court, but the largest number of red-on-buff sherds can be classified as Sacaton Red-on-buff. In addition, the only Hohokam painted sherds found on the floor of the court were Sacaton Red-on-buff. On this basis, the court can be assigned to the Sacaton phase.

The earlier sherds from the fill are probably fortuitous occurrences, and can be attributed to a pre-ball-court occupation of the site. Two of the Gila Butte sherds shed some light on this problem, as both were found in a trench cut into the earth bank on the south side of the court. The earth banks were formed of material from the prehistoric excavation for the court, an excavation which apparently cut through already-present deposits of trash, thereby incorporating early sherds in the banks. Additional early sherds found in the court fill can perhaps be attributed to this same source, and were washed from the banks into the court as it was filled after abandonment. Other sherds from the court are typical of several Hohokam phases, and as a consequence are of little value for close temporal placement. A single intrusive sherd found in the fill is too badly weathered for type identification. It appears to be a black-on-red sherd from the Flagstaff area.

Artifacts

Three artifacts were collected from the test excavations in the ball court. One is of clay and the other two are manufactured from marine shells. The clay artifact is an unperforated disc made from a Gila Plain, Gila Bend Variety sherd by grinding the edges to a roughly circular outline.

One of the artifacts of shell is a *Glycymeris* valve, from which the central core has been removed by grinding. The specimen probably represents the beginning of a shell bracelet, which was not completed because the valve was broken during the removal of the central core. The other shell artifact is a cut shell pendant in the form of a fairly realistic bird (Fig. 26*a*). A perforation for stringing the pendant was made through the body. The eye is represented by a shallow conical depression, which probably once held an inlay.

ARIZONA T:14:19

In an attempt to gain comparative data, some survey work was carried on following the termination of the excavation program of the third season. As a result of this reconnaissance, four sites, strung out along the west side of the Gila River for a distance of about two miles, were located. The sites are from 12 to 14 miles north of Gila Bend, and near Cotton Center (Fig. 1). They range from the Colonial through the Classic periods of the Hohokam sequence. All are out of the reservoir area.

At one of the sites, Ariz. T:14:19, a large mound was located and tentatively identified as a platform mound, similar to the mound at the Gatlin site which was excavated during the first season (Wasley 1960b). Other features at this site include two north-south-oriented Casa Grande-type ball courts, a large rectangular walled enclosure, a smaller circular walled enclosure, and a number of trash mounds (Fig. 30). Houses are probably present, although there are no surface indications of these features.

In an attempt to determine whether or not the large mound was actually comparable to the Gatlin platform mound, two test trenches were dug, one on the south side of the mound and the other on the east. At the Gatlin site, it was found that the easiest way to determine if a mound was used for the deposition of trash, or if it was an artificial platform, was to carefully strip layers of soil from the sides. If during this process prepared surfaces are encountered, the presence of a platform mound is suggested. If not, the feature under consideration is probably a trash mound. The latter situation was found to hold at Ariz. T:14:19, and consequently the tests were abandoned.

Included in the sherd sample from the trash mound are 12 Sacaton Red-on-buff sherds, 15 buff-slipped sherds not bearing paint, 7 Gila Plain sherds, 69 Gila Plain, Gila Bend Variety sherds, and 4 redware sherds. The presence of Sacaton Red-on-buff indicates that the site was occupied during the Sacaton phase. The redware sherds are most similar to the redware from Classic-period sites such as Ariz. T:14:10, Ariz. T:14:11, and Ariz. T:14:12. This is an indication that the site was also occupied during the Classic period. Whether this represents a continuous occupation from the Sacaton phase, or a reoccupation, is unknown.

DISCUSSION

During three seasons in the Painted Rocks Reservoir area, excavations were made in five sites with components which can be assigned to the Sacaton phase of the Hohokam Sedentary period. As a result of these excavations and of the surface examination of a number of other Sacaton sites, it is felt that the most elaborate development of Hohokam culture in the Gila Bend area, and probably the greatest population density, occurred during the Sedentary period.

The excavations contributed a variety of new data to the fund of Hohokam archaeology that otherwise has not been expanded substantially since the 1930's. The more significant contributions include the platform mound, the village plan of houses randomly grouped around a caliche plaza, and the information gained from excavations in five ball courts. In addition, the work at the Gatlin site suggested the possibility that the Hohokam settlement pattern may have included centers that were primarily ceremonial, perhaps in a manner analogous to the patterns of Mesoamerica (Bullard 1960).

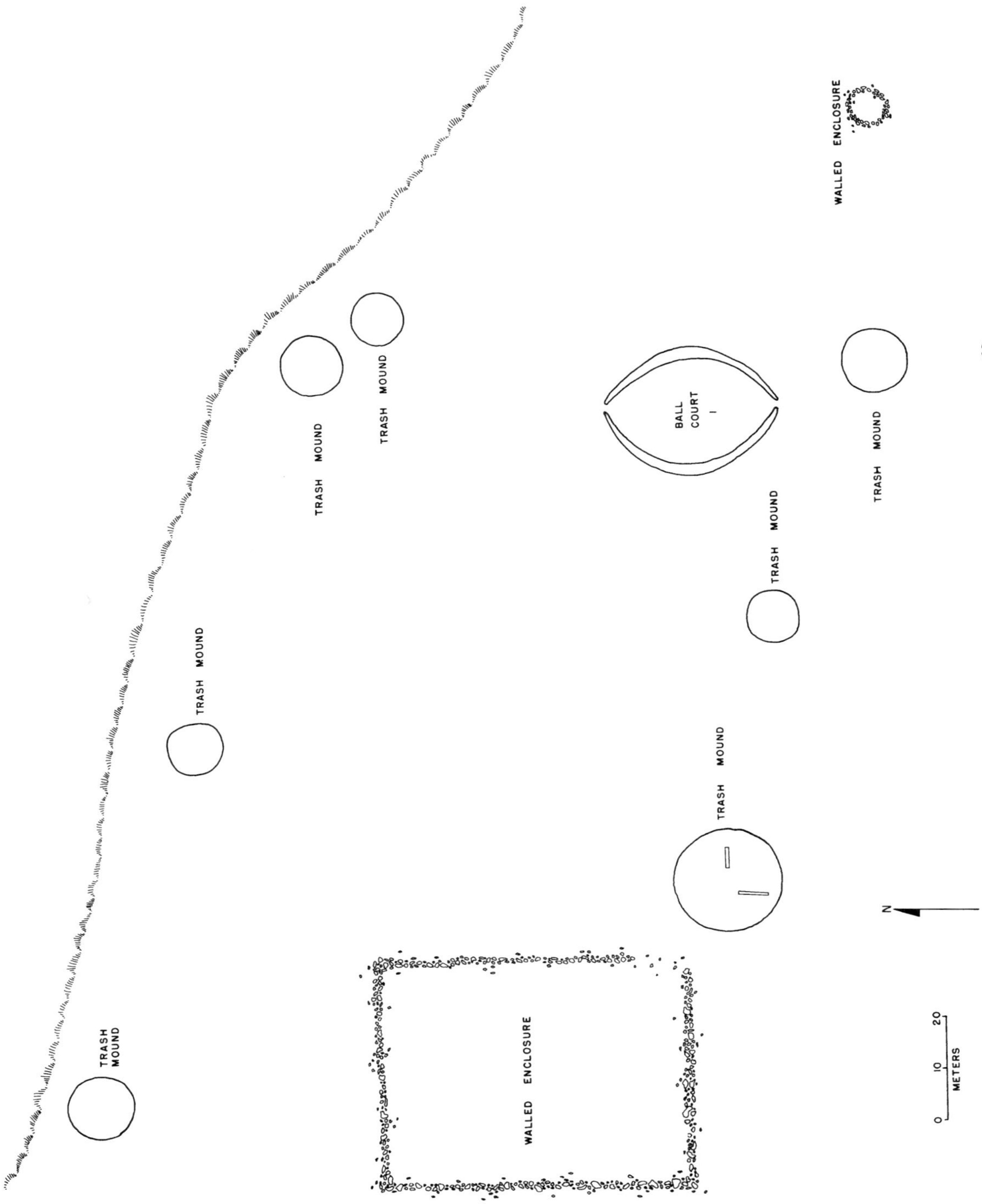

Fig. 30. Arizona T:14:19.

THE CLASSIC PERIOD

Based on the presence of pottery types such as Casa Grande Red-on-buff, Tanque Verde Red-on-brown, Gila Red, and Gila Smudged, a number of sites in the Gila Bend area have been assigned to the Classic period of the Hohokam culture. Difficulties were encountered, however, in attempting to assign these sites to the sequent Soho or Civano phases of the Classic period. Architecture has not been useful in determining phase assignments, partly because architectural data were collected from only one excavated site, partly because there was no Salado occupation of the area, and partly because so little is known of the non-Salado Civano-phase architecture in the rest of the Hohokam area. Neither has pottery been of sufficient help in making Classic-period phase assignments.

In the Gila Basin to the north and east of Gila Bend, in the Salt River Valley, and in the Tucson area, Gila Polychrome and related pottery types have been useful diagnostics for distinguishing the Soho from the Civano phase. In these areas Gila Polychrome is consistently present in Civano-phase sites, absent in Soho-phase sites (Gladwin and others 1937: 264–67). The Soho phase is characterized by Gila Red and Gila Smudged, the Civano phase by Salt Red and Salt Smudged (Haury 1945a: 81). Casa Grande Red-on-buff is relatively abundant in Soho-phase contexts and scarce in Civano-phase contexts (Hayden 1957: 191).

However, the Gila Bend area is similar to the Papagueria (Haury 1950: 6–9) in the infrequent occurrence of Gila Polychrome in Classic-period sites of the region, to the extent that its absence in a particular site is not necessarily indicative that the site belongs to the Soho phase. Casa Grande Red-on-buff is not abundant enough in the area to permit phase assignment on the basis of its frequency of occurrence. Redware appears to have been produced locally in the Gila Bend area, but while it is quite similar to the Gila Red and Gila Smudged of the Gila-Salt area, it seems to persist without the development of a Salt Red and Salt Smudged horizon.

Because neither the ceramic nor the architectural traits seem to be diagnostic, the Classic-period sites of the Gila Bend area have not been assigned to phases. One excavated site in the region, Ariz. Z:1:11, has Gila Polychrome as a constituent of the ceramic inventory, but it is represented by so few sherds that a phase assignment on this evidence could only be tentative.

Following the Sacaton phase in the Gila Bend area, there was a change in the location of Hohokam villages. Most of the sites which can be assigned to the Classic period are situated on the floodplain or on the first terrace of the Gila River, while most of the earlier Hohokam villages were on the second terrace at a greater distance from the river. As a consequence, many of the Classic-period sites have been more heavily eroded by river flooding, making it difficult to obtain much information on the Classic period occupation.

ARIZONA T:14:10

Ariz. T:14:10 (Fig. 1), located on the north side of the Gila River about four miles north of Gila Bend, may be part of the Bartley site (Arizona T:14:11) which is described next. However, Ariz. T:14:10 is separated from the Bartley site by a large wash, and for this reason it was assigned a separate site number when these sites were recorded.

Ten test trenches were dug in areas where concentrations of cultural material occurred on the surface. Only one of the trenches located any features, probably because of the great amount of erosion to which the site has been subjected.

Primary Cremation

The term primary cremation (Johnson and Thompson 1963: 470, 477–78) refers to an unusual method of burial for the Hohokam, which has been found at this site and also at Ariz. Z:1:11. The procedure involved erecting a scaffold or platform directly over a long pit dug into the

Fig. 31. Primary cremation, Arizona T:14:10.

ground. The person to be cremated was placed on the platform in an extended position, accompanied by grave offerings. As the body, platform, and offerings were consumed by fire, the remains were allowed to fall into the pit. Sometimes some of the larger pieces of cremated bone were then collected at one end of the pit, in, around, or near a ceramic vessel. The pit was then filled with earth to become a grave.

Primary Cremation 1 (Fig. 31) consisted of an east-west-oriented, oval pit measuring 1.9 m. in length, 90 cm. in width, and 45 cm. in depth. The bottom of the pit was covered to a depth of 20 cm. with a heavy layer of mesquite charcoal mixed with calcined human bones. Most of the bones, however, were concentrated on top of the charcoal layer. Many of the larger fragments were found piled together near the east end of the pit. A Gila Plain, Gila Bend Variety scoop rested upright on the pile (Figs. 31, 32*h*). In addition to the scoop, other offerings were present. These included a whole shell pendant, a shell bead, a Gila Red jar, and a large sherd from a Gila Plain, Gila Bend Variety jar. All of the offerings were burned, probably a result of having gone through the crematory fire. Four sandal fragments were also found in the crematory pit, and these are described in Appendix C.

The sequence of events for Primary Cremation 1 was apparently the following. First, an oval pit, large enough to accommodate the body to be cremated, was dug. The bottom of the pit was covered with a quantity of mesquite wood, and the body placed on the pyre. A jar, a large sherd, and several beads were included as offerings. The discovery of the sandal fragments indicates the possibility that the body was fully clothed. The entire assemblage was burned, and after the fire had died down, the obvious, larger bone fragments were gathered together and piled at the north end of the pit. The scoop was placed upright on the pile. The body had been oriented over the pit with the head to the east, as is indicated by the presence of a number of skull fragments at the east end, and bones of the feet at the opposite end.

Pottery

A total of 436 sherds was obtained from the test trenches at the site. A majority (350) was Gila Plain, Gila Bend Variety. Other Hohokam pottery types included in the collection are Tanque Verde Red-on-brown (1), Gila Red (12), and Gila Smudged (7) – types which indicate the site was occupied during the Classic period. The only intrusive sherds recovered were Lower Colorado buffware (64). The ceramic inventory of the site is similar to that at Ariz. T:14:11.

Artifacts

Other than the offerings in the cremation grave, the only artifact found at the site is a fragmentary

Fig. 32. Plain and redware vessels, Classic-period sites: a-c, e-g, *Bartley site (Arizona T:14:11);* d, *Arizona Z:1:11;* h, *Arizona T:14:10;* a, e, h, *Gila Plain, Gila Bend Variety;* b-d, g, *Gila Smudged;* f, *Gila Red. Length* h, *32 cm.*

Fig. 33. Tanque Verde Red-on-brown sherds, Bartley site (Arizona T:14:11).

mano. The specimen, which came from one of the test trenches, is a two-hand, uniface example manufactured from a water-worn cobble by pecking the edges until an oval outline was attained. Dimensions: length, 15.5 cm.; width, 10.9 cm.; thickness, 3.9 cm.

BARTLEY SITE

The Bartley site (Ariz. T:14:11) is situated on the north side of the Gila River across a wash from Ariz. T:14:10 (Fig. 1). The most conspicuous feature of the site was a large trash mound on the edge of the first terrace above the river. The mound extended to a height of about 1 m. above the surrounding terrain. The trash mound and the terrace edge marked the south boundary of the site. It extended for approximately 50 m. to the north, as was indicated by surface finds of sherds and stone artifacts.

On initial examination of the site, it was obvious that extensive relic collecting had taken place, and that the collector had removed a number of cremations from the trash mound. Information from Norton Allen indicates that this activity took place about 15 years ago, and was done by an individual from Oregon named Bartley for whom the site has been named. The cremations he excavated were apparently primary cremations in long oval trenches in which the body had been cremated and the bone fragments and offerings left in place.

The offerings which accompanied one of the primary cremations were obtained from the relic collector by Allen, who subsequently donated them to the Arizona State Museum. This material, which is listed below, is reportedly from this single primary cremation which contained painted pottery. The 26 Hohokam painted sherds are Tanque Verde Red-on-brown (Fig. 33). These came from at least one bowl and three jars. Also present are 11 sherds of Gila Red from at least one bowl and two jars, and 9 sherds of Gila Plain, Gila Bend Variety from four jars and one scoop. The 4 remaining sherds are from a small black-on-white jar, probably Puerco Black-on-white, a type made during late Pueblo II and early Pueblo III times in northern Arizona (Olson and Wasley 1956: 258). Its occurrence in a Classic-period context at Ariz. T:14:11 supports the post-1100 date for the Classic period. The only other specimen from the primary cremation is a *Glycymeris* shell pendant, formed by grinding the umbo until a hole was worked through into the center of the valve, by which the ornament could be strung.

Despite the disturbance by the collector, it was thought to be worthwhile to make excavations in the trash mound, and in the relatively undisturbed remainder of the site in hopes of obtaining information not destroyed by the unauthorized excavation. Consequently, three broadside-type excavations were made in the trash mound and five test trenches were dug in other parts of the site.

The three broadsides were dug from the terrace edge, at the south side of the site, through the trash mound. All were about 5 m. in width and 10 m. in length when completed. It was difficult to determine the exact bottom of the trash deposit in the mound, because the soil was an extremely loose, fine sand. Rodent activity and disturbance by the pot hunter further complicated matters. One meter is probably a close estimate of the maximum depth of trash in the mound. Vertical controls were not maintained, since in the large number of sherds brought to the surface by the pot hunter, no significant differences could be discerned, and since the extent of disturbance would have made such controls useless.

The five test trenches which were dug to test other parts of the site were placed in areas where surface indications gave promise of finding subsurface features. None were discovered, and the maximum depth of deposit in the area north of the trash mound was found to be only 25 cm. A probable reason for this situation is that the loose, fine, sandy soil of the site is easily eroded. Sheet erosion seemingly has removed a majority of the original surface of the site. The concentrations of sherds and artifacts on the present surface represent material which was let down from its original position. Structures, which might once have been present, are completely gone.

Burials

Unfortunately, no cremations were found during the excavations, and all indications point to the fact that the collector was quite thorough. However, he missed three inhumations.

Burial 1

Burial 1 was found in Broadside 1 at the east end of the trash mound. It was in a relatively clean sand layer, below the overlying trash-mixed sand, at a depth of 1 m. below the surface of the ground. No evidence of a pit was present. The burial was probably fully extended, but it was impossible to be sure, due to disturbance from rodent activity and earth pressure. It was oriented northwest-southeast, with the head to the southeast. Facing direction could not be determined, for the skull was completely crushed.

Offerings included a Gila Red jar, two Gila Smudged bowls, and one Gila Plain, Gila Bend Variety jar (Fig. 32,*a,c,f,g*). The Gila Red jar and the Gila Smudged bowls were arranged around the skull. The other jar was at the feet. In addition to the pottery offerings, two *Glycymeris* bracelets were found on the right arm. Both of the bracelets had umbos carved into triangular shapes.

Burial 2

Burial 2 was found in Broadside 3 at the west end of the trash mound. It was in the trash deposit at a depth of 70 cm. below the surface of the ground. A pit outline could not be discerned. The bones, those of a human fetus, were covered by an inverted Gila Plain, Gila Bend Variety bowl. A few of the bones were scattered about the bowl, probably as a result of rodent activity. An unmodified *Cardium elatum* valve was found immediately northwest of the bowl, undoubtedly an offering.

Burial 3

As was the case for Burial 1, Burial 3 was situated in the relatively clean sand layer below the trash deposit in Broadside 1. It is unknown if the burial was intruded through the trash deposit into the underlying sand, or if the trash mound grew over the burial, which then would have predated the deposition of the trash. The burial was badly disturbed, but it was probably originally fully extended. The orientation was northeast-southwest, and the head was to the northeast. The skull was crushed, so that the direction that it faced could not be determined.

The burial was accompanied by a Gila Smudged bowl (Fig. 32*b*), a large sherd of a Gila Plain, Gila Bend Variety bowl, and an unmodified *Cardium elatum* shell. All were found along the left side of the body. The large plainware sherd had been perforated by a steel probe-rod, undoubtedly the instrument used by the relic collector to locate the cremations.

Pottery

The excavation of three broadsides and a number of test trenches at Ariz. T:14:11 resulted in the recovery of 10,054 sherds, two complete jars, and four complete bowls. All of the complete specimens accompanied burials as offerings. Approximately 95 per cent of the sherds were locally made. The remaining 5 per cent consist of pottery intrusive in the Hohokam area. The basic ceramic data have been published (Johnson and Wasley 1961: 43–45). The following comments are of a summary nature and are offered as explanations to accompany the table.

Casa Grande Red-on-Buff

Casa Grande is the only Hohokam red-on-buff type which was manufactured during the Classic period. It was derived from the earlier Sacaton Red-on-buff, and was manufactured by the Hohokam in the Gila Basin. Its presence at Arizona T:14:11 indicates a Classic-period date for the site.

Tanque Verde Red-on-Brown

A more common Hohokam painted type which

occurred at Ariz. T:14:11 was Tanque Verde Red-on-brown (Fig. 33). In the Papagueria, Tanque Verde Red-on-brown is roughly the temporal equivalent of Casa Grande Red-on-buff (Scantling 1940: 27–30). This is also true for the Tucson area during the Tanque Verde phase. A slightly later variant of Tanque Verde Red-on-brown, Pantano Red-on-brown, is the Tucson (Civano) phase temporal equivalent of Casa Grande Red-on-buff in the Tucson area (Hayden 1957: 220–26). In terms of geographic proximity, however, the Papagueria can be suggested as the area from which Tanque Verde Red-on-brown found its way into the Gila Bend region. Contact with the Papagueria is known to have taken place earlier in the Gila Bend area, since several sherds of Valshni Red were found at the Gatlin and Citrus sites in Sacaton phase contexts.

Sacaton Red-on-Buff

A single sherd of this pre-Classic type was recovered from Broadside 1. Its occurrence at the site is probably fortuitous, as the remaining large quantity of sherds can be assigned to the Classic period.

Unclassified Red-on-Buff

Under this heading are grouped the Hohokam red-on-buff sherds which, due to a lack of distinctive features, cannot be assigned to type. Most are probably Casa Grande Red-on-buff.

Hohokam Buff

This category includes a few sherds with Hohokam buff paste, but without red paint. Most are probably sherds broken from unpainted areas of Casa Grande Red-on-buff vessels.

Gila Plain, Gila Bend Variety

Approximately 80 per cent of the sherds from Ariz. T:14:11 were plainware made with local sources of clay and temper. About the same proportion of the pottery was plainware during the earlier Sacaton phase.

Gila Plain

Eighty sherds collected from the site can be classified under the description of Gila Plain as it is known from Snaketown (Gladwin and others 1937: 205–11). This pottery is not believed to represent trade from Hohokam communities farther east, however, since it grades imperceptibly into the local variety of Gila Plain. Rather, it would seem that the Gila Bend potters used materials which were similar to those used at Snaketown, and thereby produced a similar product. Apparently these local materials were not as abundant, or were not used by the local potters to the extent to which they used the material which resulted in the local variety of Gila Plain.

Smudged Plainware

A large collection of plainware sherds, of the Gila Bend variety, could be distinguished from the other plain sherds at the site, since they were all bowls with smudged interiors. Polishing of the bowls was well done, but the smudging was rather poorly controlled. This category of pottery may be derived from the earlier smudged ware, Sacaton Smudged, found as a new trait, but a minor one, in the Hohokam sequence during the Sacaton phase (see Sacaton Smudged description for the Gatlin site).

Gila Red and Gila Smudged

These two types first occur in the Hohokam sequence at the beginning of the Classic period, although a forewarning of their appearance was present at the end of the Sacaton phase with the appearance of Sacaton Red (Gladwin and others 1937: 202–204). Both types are local varieties of Gila Red and Gila Smudged, differing from the described types (Haury 1945a: 80–100) in their poorer red slip, poorer control of smudging, less evidence of polishing marks, and the smaller quantity of mica in the paste. In addition, the shape inventory was apparently not as great as was the case at Los Muertos (Haury 1945a: 86–100).

Intrusive Sherds

The largest number of intrusive sherds found at the site are classifiable as Lower Colorado buffware.

Minor contact with the north is indicated by the presence of a sherd of Roosevelt Black-on-white, and one of Flagstaff Black-on-white. The latter has been assigned dates of 1125 to 1200 (Colton and Hargrave 1937: 225). Roosevelt Black-on-white is quite similar to Tularosa Black-on-white (Gladwin and Gladwin 1931: 47–49), and apparently dates about the same time, 1100–1250 (Rinaldo and Bluhm 1956: 184), or somewhat later, 1200–1350 (Pomeroy 1962: 61).

Discussion

On the basis of the presence of Casa Grande Red-on-buff, Tanque Verde Red-on-brown, Gila Red, and Gila Smudged, Ariz. T:14:11 can be

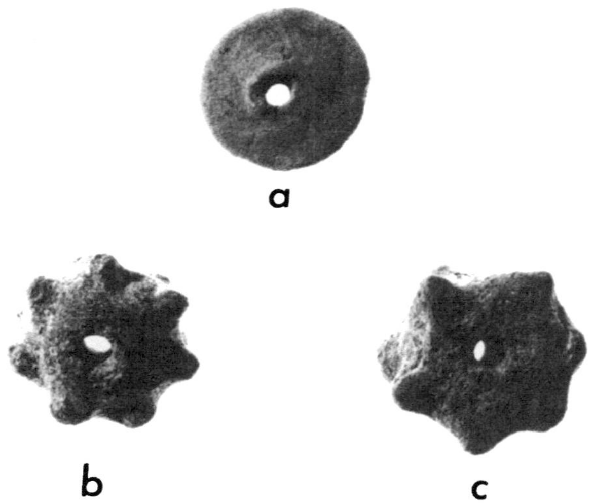

Fig. 34. Ceramic artifacts, Classic-period sites; a, *modeled spindle whorl from Arizona Z:1:11;* b, c, *modeled spindle whorls from Arizona T:14:11. Diameter of* c, *3 cm.*

assigned to the Classic period of the Hohokam sequence. The two intrusive sherds from the north, Flagstaff and Roosevelt Black-on-white which both date after 1100, further indicate a Classic-period occupation of the Bartley site.

Artifacts

Other than the large quantity of sherds obtained from the broadsides and the test trenches, artifacts were not common at the Bartley site. All of those obtained are typical of the Hohokam area, and, with the exception of two modeled spindle whorls described below, all occur in a number of the earlier Hohokam phases. Artifact proveniences have been published (Johnson and Wasley 1961: 46–48).

Ceramic Artifacts

Sherd Disc. The single sherd disc obtained from the site is manufactured from a Gila Plain, Gila Bend Variety sherd. The edges have been ground to a roughly circular shape, and a central biconical perforation is present. Dimensions: diameter, 5 cm.; thickness, 6 mm.; perforation diameter, 7 mm.

Modeled Spindle Whorls. Both of the modeled spindle whorls (Fig. 34) have a number of projections pinched up from the body of the whorl. The projections encircle the circumference in two rows. Dimensions: diameter, 2.8 and 3 cm.; thickness, 1.9 and 2.4 cm.

Modeled spindle whorls have their beginning in the Hohokam area late in the Sedentary period, perhaps through an introduction from Mexico. They gained their greatest popularity during the Classic period. Whorls with projections are apparently less common than other forms; none were in the large collection obtained at Los Muertos, for instance. A generally similar whorl was obtained by Moorehead in the Salt River Valley. This one had five points pinched out from the main body along the line of greatest circumference (Haury 1945d: 115–21).

Miniature Vessel. The single Gila Plain, Gila Bend Variety miniature vessel is cylindrical in shape. The specimen is fragmentary, and rather crudely manufactured. Dimensions: diameter, 3 cm.; height, 3.5 cm.

Stone Artifacts

Flake Knife. The single cutting tool obtained from Ariz. T:14:11 is an irregular flake of chert with sharpened edges as a result of pressure chipping. Dimensions: length, 4.4 cm.; width, 3.4 cm.; thickness, 8 mm.

Manos. Three of the four manos in the collection are two-hand, biface types. Two are manufactured from vesicular basalt, and the third from fine-grained granite. Dimensions: length, 13.4 to 20.8 cm.; width, 7.8 to 9.6 cm.; thickness, 3.1 to 4.9 cm. The fourth mano is also a two-hand form, but it exhibits traces of wear on only one face. The material is vesicular basalt. Dimensions: length, 15 cm.; width, 8.1 cm.; thickness, 5.9 cm.

Handstone. The handstone is an oval waterworn cobble with no obvious traces of intentional form modification. One face is covered with red ochre, and the stone was probably used in the preparation of paint. Dimensions: length, 10.8 cm.; width, 9.4 cm.; thickness, 5 cm.

Pestle. A conical pestle of grey granite was obtained from the site. Traces of use are present on the wider end in the form of battering and grinding. Dimensions: length, 10.2 cm.; diameter, 4.7 cm.

Hammerstones. The three hammerstones are oval, water-worn cobbles with battered ends. There is no evidence of any intentional shaping, and the only modification of the original cobble is a result of use. Dimensions: length, 7.4 to 10.1 cm.; width, 6.5 to 9.4 cm.; thickness, 5.1 to 5.4 cm.

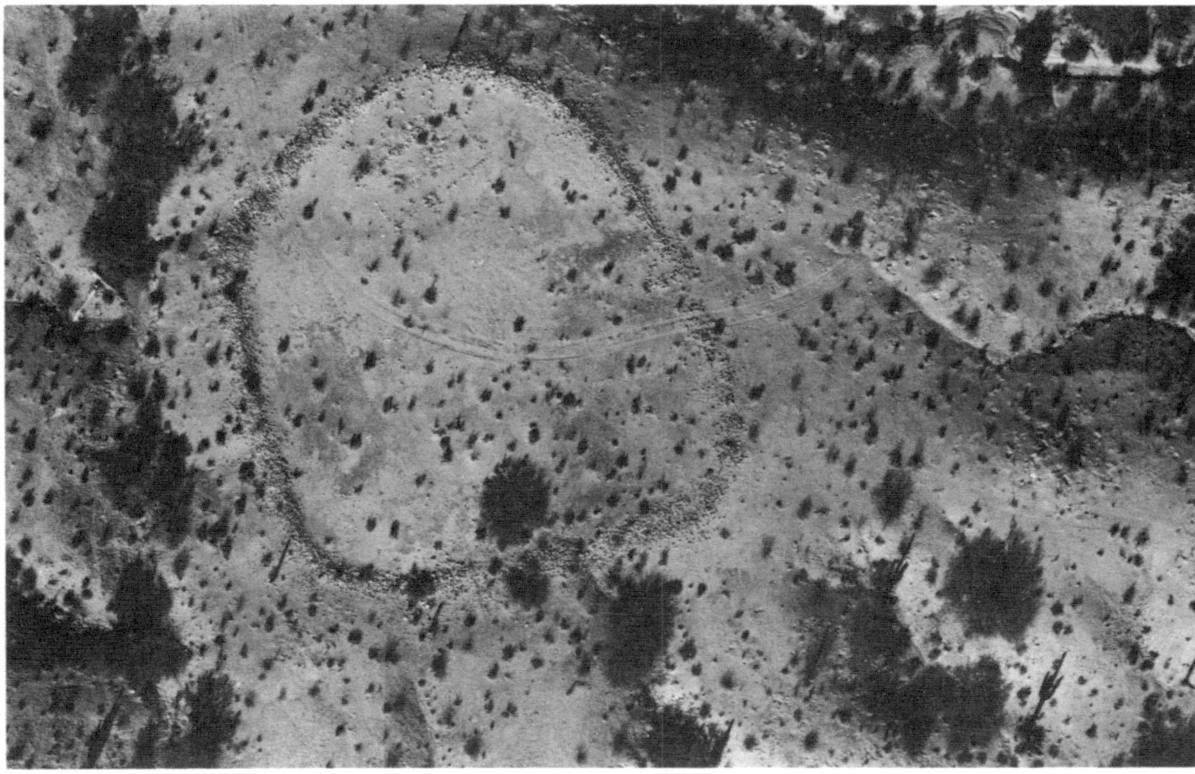

Fig. 35. Aerial view, Arizona T:14:12 prior to excavation. (Photo by D. D. Cassidy, Blanton and Cole, Tucson.)

Shell Artifacts

Plain Glycymeris Bracelets. Nine fragmentary bracelets, manufactured from *Glycymeris* valves, are undecorated. None retain the umbo. Three of the bracelets are of the thin-band variety (band width 2–5 mm.), five have medium bands (5–10 mm.), and one example has a wide band (10–30 mm.).

Carved Glycymeris Bracelet. The single carved bracelet, which is of the wide-band variety, lacks the umbo. Two diagonal lines have been incised into the band.

Residue from Bracelet Manufacture. This category includes 14 fragmentary unfinished bracelets, and two *Glycymeris* valves with ground convex surfaces. The unfinished bracelets were probably broken during the process of manufacture. The traces of grinding on the two valves indicate that central cores were to be removed, the initial step in the production of shell bracelets.

Ring. The shell ring in the collection is an unfinished example formed from an immature *Glycymeris* valve. The central core was ground out.

Whole Shell Pendants. Three of the whole shell pendants are manufactured from *Glycymeris* shells, and the fourth from a *Pecten* valve. The umbos of all the shells have been ground to the point where a perforation is worked through to the interior. This is the only modification of the valves.

Whole Shell Beads. Seven *Olivella* (Fig. 26*h*) and two *Conus* beads are present in the collection. In six cases, including the *Conus* examples, the spire has been ground off, thereby forming perforations through which the beads could be strung. The other three were strung by means of holes broken through the sides of the shells.

Miscellaneous Worked Shell. Included in this grouping is a *Glycymeris* valve which has had the sides ground and broken away, perhaps with the intent to form a shell frog, and two ground fragments, one of *Pecten* and one of *Glycymeris.*

Bone Artifacts

Bone Awls. One complete and one fragmentary bone awl were obtained from the site. The complete specimen is formed from a split bone,

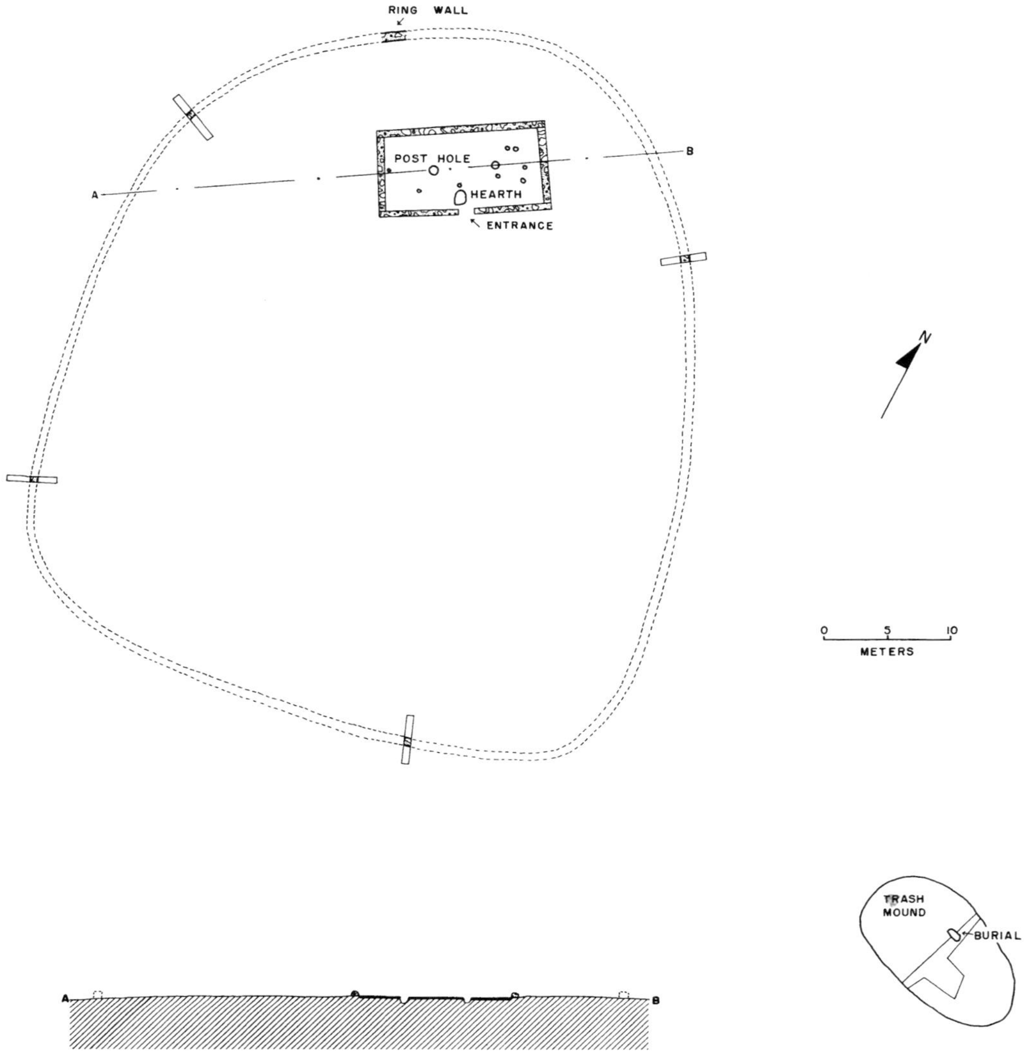

Fig. 36. Plan and section, Arizona T:14:12.

and it retains the articular end. The awl, which has been burnt, tapers from the articular end to a sharp tip. Dimensions: length, 6.5 cm.; width, 1.1 cm.; thickness, 6 mm. The broken specimen consists of the tip of a split long bone awl. This example is also burnt.

Dog Skeleton. One further discovery at the site, in Broadside 1, was a nearly complete dog skeleton. The contorted arrangement of the bones suggests that this was not an intentional burial, but rather a dog which was dumped into the trash deposit, probably to rid the village of the body.

ARIZONA T:14:12

Ariz. T:14:12 is situated on the north side of the Gila River five airline miles northwest of Gila Bend (Fig. 1). The site is on a gravel terrace immediately above the Gila River bottoms. Surface indications included a large, roughly circular ring of stones, a rectangular outline of stones within the ring, and a trash mound to the southeast of the ring (Fig. 35, 36).

Three days were devoted to the excavation of the site. During this period, the ring wall was cross-sectioned in five places, one structure was excavated, and the trash mound was tested. In addition, one burial was removed, and other sections of the site were tested by means of 13 trenches.

Ring Wall

Prior to excavation, the ring wall was marked by quantities of rocks arranged in a roughly circular pattern 50 m. in diameter. One section of the wall measuring 1.9 m. in length was excavated to determine the method of construction. This indicated that the stones forming the ring had originally been cemented together with caliche to form a wall averaging 40 cm. in width. The stone wall was faced, both on the interior and exterior, with caliche plaster measuring 10 cm. in thickness (Fig. 37).

Fig. 37. View of ring wall, Arizona T:14:12, showing caliche facing on rubble core.

The ring wall was further tested by means of four trenches which cross-sectioned the wall on all sides. The sections disclosed that the same type of construction was used for the entire wall. An entrance was not obvious from the surface remains of the wall, and time was not available to trench around the circumference and search for an opening. It is difficult to determine the original height of the wall because only about 25 cm. remained in an uneroded condition. Judging from the quantity of stones, the wall probably never reached a height of more than 1 m.

Structure

Structure 1 was marked on the surface by a rectangular outline of rock situated near the north side of the ring. Excavation disclosed a wall, of the same construction as the ring wall, measuring 50 cm. in width. The wall delimited a floor 12.2 m. in length by 6.1 m. in width. An entrance, which opened towards the middle of the ring, was present in the center of the south wall of the structure (Fig. 36).

The fill of Structure 1, measuring 40 cm. in depth, was removed in two levels. The upper level was 30 cm. in thickness and consisted of wind- and water-deposited material. The floor level included artifacts in contact with the floor, and those in the remaining 10 cm. of fill overlying the floor. Artifacts in this level were deemed most likely in association with the structure, and as a consequence of most value for dating.

Structure 1 did not have a specially-laid or prepared floor; instead the floor was marked by a layer of hard packed sandy soil, a result of human use. The hearth consisted of an irregularly-shaped, burned depression immediately in front of the entrance. The depression measured 1 m. in width, 1.25 m. in length, and 10 cm. in depth. Two primary support posts were present, situated on the midline of the long axis, at either side of the entrance. They were 50 cm. in diameter. Eight smaller posts were scattered at random over the floor of the structure.

The small quantity of rock on the surface makes it seem unlikely that the caliche and stone walls ever reached any great height. If this is the case, the upper portion of the walls must have been of perishable construction, perhaps wattle and daub, of which no trace remains today. Roof construction is not definitely known, but the pattern of posts indicates a flat roof, with beams resting on the walls and on the two primary posts. The randomly-scattered posts may have carried additional roof weight, or may have been later additions to support a sagging roof. A large quantity of charred material was found in the floor-fill level, indicating that the structure was destroyed by fire. Included in this mass of charcoal were quantities of small branches, which may have rested on the main roof timbers to support an earth or adobe roof.

Trash Mound

The single trash mound at the site was on a finger-like extension of the gravel terrace, some

25 m. southeast of the ring wall (Fig. 36). The mound was oval in outline with a width of 8 m., a length of 14.5 m., and a maximum height in the center of 75 cm. Initial excavation consisted of a trench 75 cm. in width through the shorter dimension of the mound. The trench was carried into native soil below the mound. Further excavation consisted of the removal of a 2 m. square block from the center of the mound on the southeast side of the trench. No attempt was made to obtain a stratigraphic sample, since it was obvious by the time the excavations were made that a single occupation was represented at the site. Instead, this block was removed to obtain a large sample of the material culture associated with the occupation.

Burial

The single burial found at the Ring site was situated under the north edge of the trash mound. The body was in an east-west-oriented pit, cut into native soil, which measured 1.4 m. in length, 40 cm. in width, and 10 cm. in depth. Although it was impossible to determine definitely, the burial was probably semi-flexed, with the lower legs drawn up to accommodate the body to the pit. The burial, which faced south, rested on the back, with the head to the east. The only offering was a large quartz crystal found under the neck. The pit was filled with trash. It was not possible to trace the pit outline in the overlying trash, so it is not definitely known whether the burial represents an intrusion through the mound, or whether the mound grew over the burial as trash was added through time.

Test Trenches

Further excavation at the site consisted of a series of test trenches excavated to locate features not obvious on the surface. Nine of the trenches were within the area delimited by the ring wall, and were dug in an attempt to locate more structures. None were found, and the only other information which these trenches added to the picture was the knowledge that the native caliche in the ring was overlain by a layer of sandy soil which included small quantities of trash. Four trenches were placed between the ring wall and the trash mound and around the trash mound to search for features in this area, but none were found.

Pottery

A total of 3,384 sherds were obtained from the excavations at Ariz. T:14:12. No complete or restorable vessels were found. A majority of the sherds came from the trash mound, with the second largest group coming from the fill and floor levels in Structure 1. Other sherds were found scattered through the sheet trash inside the ring wall, and outside the wall around the trash mound. Plainware accounts for 89.5 per cent of the sherd sample, a slightly higher percentage figure than for other Hohokam sites in the reservoir area. Only .5 per cent of the locally-made pottery was painted. Redware constitutes 7.6 per cent of the sample. Pottery from Ariz. T:14:12 is quite similar to that from the sites described above; to avoid repetition, reference is made to the above descriptions. Sherd counts and provenience data have been published (Johnson and Wasley 1961: 49).

The presence of Casa Grande Red-on-buff, Tanque Verde Red-on-brown, Gila Red, and Gila Smudged indicate that the site was occupied in the Classic period.

Artifacts

Provenience data for artifacts from Arizona T:14:12 have been published (Johnson and Wasley 1961: 50).

Ceramic Artifacts

Sherd Discs. One complete and two fragmentary sherd discs manufactured from Gila Plain, Gila Bend Variety sherds were collected at the site. The edges of all the sherds have been modified until a roughly circular shape was attained. In the case of the two broken examples, this modification is in the form of chipping or flaking away of the edges of the sherd. Probably this represents the initial step in the shaping of a sherd disc, and was followed by grinding, which is in evidence on the complete example. All have central biconical perforations. Dimensions: diameter, 3.3 to 4.7 cm.; perforation diameter, 6 mm. to 1 cm.

Ground Sherd. One Gila Plain, Gila Bend Variety sherd has two ground edges. The remaining fragment indicates that the original object was probably rectangular in outline. Dimensions: width, 3.3 cm.

Handle. A small fragment of a loop handle

Fig. 38. Aerial view, Fortified Hill site, Arizona T:13:8 showing masonry structures and fortification walls. (Photo by D. D. Cassidy, Blanton and Cole, Tucson.)

from a Gila Red vessel is in the collection. Dimensions: diameter, 1.3 cm.

Stone Artifacts

Choppers. The three choppers from Ariz. T:14:12 are all manufactured from water-worn cobbles. Percussion flaking has been done from one face, yielding chisel-shaped cutting edges. In all cases, the hand-hold is the unmodified surface of the cobble. Dimensions: length, 9.7 to 10.2 cm.; width, 3.6 to 8.6 cm.; thickness, 2.3 to 5.3 cm.

Handstones. The two handstones from the site are fashioned from water-worn cobbles. In one case the only modification of the original oval cobble is the presence of grinding on one face. The other cobble has been slightly shaped by pecking, and both faces are ground. Dimensions: length, 10.5 and 12.4 cm.; width, 7.7 and 8.7 cm.; thickness, 2.5 and 5.3 cm.

Shell Artifacts

Shell species included in the collection from Ariz. T:14:12 are *Glycymeris maculatus, Cardium elatum,* and *Turritella leucostoma.* The artifacts of shell were all manufactured from *Glycymeris* valves.

Plain Glycymeris Bracelets. Three unadorned *Glycymeris* bracelets were found at the site. Each is representative of a size category based on the width of the band. One has a band width less than 5 mm.; one is between 5 and 10 mm.; and the third is over 10 mm. in band width. Two retain the umbos which are perforated.

Carved Glycymeris Bracelet. A single bracelet fragment is decorated with a zig-zag design of incised lines on the outer surface of the band. It is of the thin type (band width less than 5 mm.).

Ring. The fragmentary shell ring is fashioned from an immature *Glycymeris* valve, by the removal of a central core and further finish work by grinding. The umbo is perforated.

Whole Shell Pendant. A whole shell pendant was fashioned from an immature *Glycymeris* valve. The only modification of the valve is a perforation which is the result of grinding the umbo.

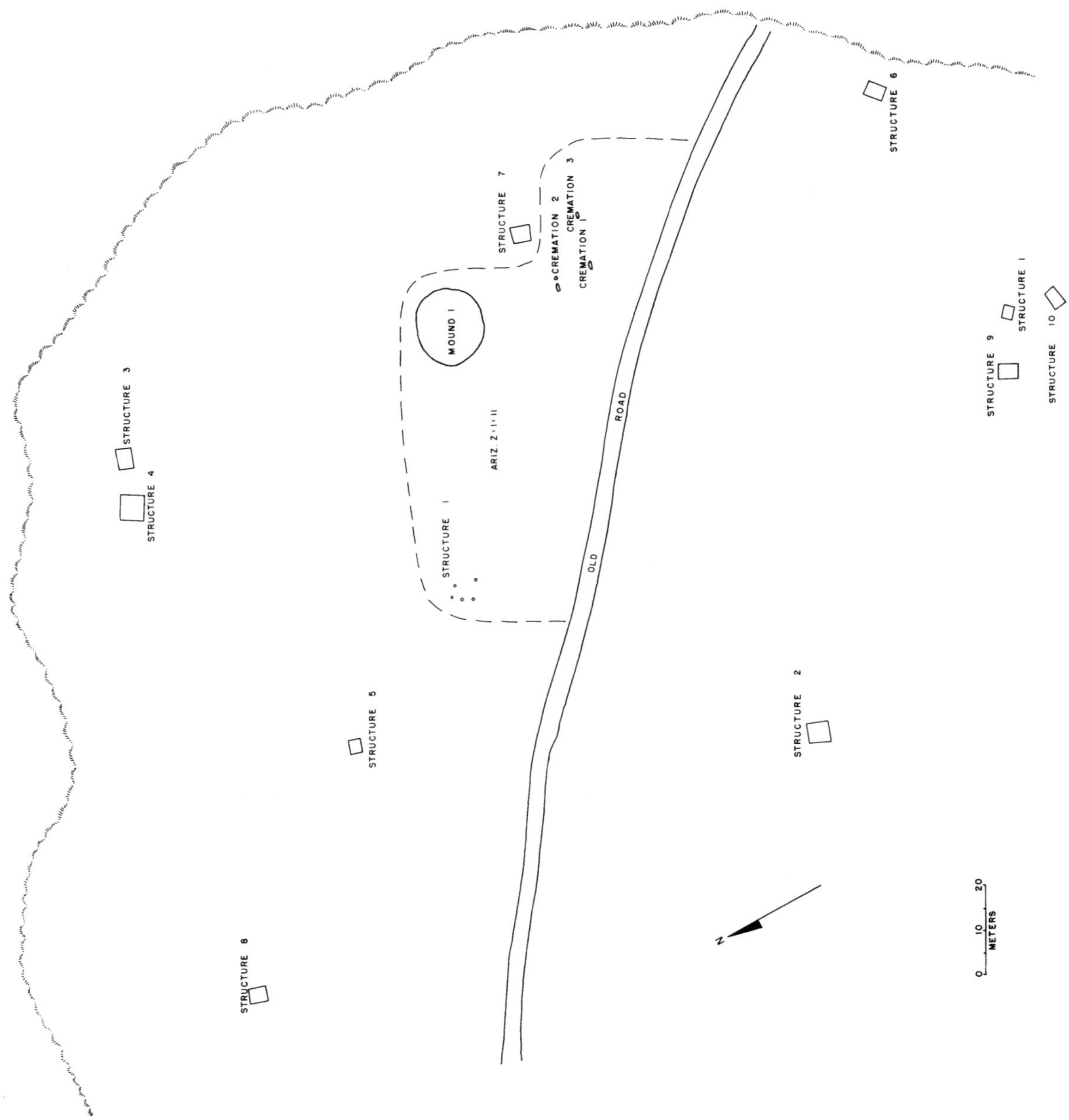

Fig. 39. Arizona Z:1:11 and Arizona Z:1:13. Excavated portion of Arizona Z:1:11 outlined by dashed line.

FORTIFIED HILL SITE

One of the most spectacular sites in the Gila Bend area (Ariz. T:13:8) is situated on a huge uplifted and tilted block (Fig. 38) four and one-half miles northwest of Gila Bend and three-fourths of a mile west of Ariz. T:14:12 (Fig. 1). The block is locally known as the "jump-off" in recognition of the sheer cliff on the north side. Access is easy only from the west, although possible on the east and south.

Lumholtz (1912: 337) visited the site early in the twentieth century, and supplied the following description.

> Crossing the wide river-bed of the Gila River, on the banks of which batamotes grew exuberantly, the village is found on top of a detached hill, which was admirably adapted for defense, being protected on the side easiest of access by a stone wall two hundred yards long, from six to eight feet high and from four to five feet wide, running east and west. The houses, like the wall, are made of stones set without masonry. One of the largest houses measured sixteen by twenty feet, and the walls were three feet thick in all of them. A dozen dwellings were found outside of the wall, and nearly thirty were counted inside, standing in irregular groups. The Papagos call the fortress *kokulisik* (*kokuli,* corral).

Schroeder (1961: 12) recorded *ko-klee-tsat* (rocks all around) as the current Papago name for the site.

The dimensions given by Lumholtz are somewhat too great, but there remains no question as to what site he was describing (Fig. 38). More recent examinations have added some detail to the description. In addition to the main defensive wall there are one and possibly two less conspicuous walls spanning the top of the hill. Today some of the walls stand to a height of four feet, having been eroded perhaps more by sightseers than by the elements since the time of the visit by Lumholtz. Built of dry-laid masonry, occasionally the walls were constructed by filling the area between two parallel boulder walls with a rubble core. The three transverse walls and the total of about 40 rooms on top of the block cover an area of about two acres. A few more houses are built in niches down the south side of the block. Petroglyphs, which cover many boulders on the south side of the block, extend to the gully below. These are described in a subsequent section.

Because the height of the block placed the site on top well out of danger from the water of the reservoir, salvage excavations were not conducted. More recently, however, the ruin has been partially dug, stabilized, and reconstructed by means of a National Science Foundation grant to the Arizona State Museum. Sherds collected from the site include Tanque Verde Red-on-brown, Gila Red, and Gila Plain, Gila Bend Variety, indicating that it is roughly contemporaneous with the Classic-period sites described herein.

ARIZONA Z:1:11

This prehistoric site underlay all of the area covered by Ariz. Z:1:13 (a historic Papago site), and in addition extended beyond to the south and east (Figs. 1, 39). Excavations were made only in the area covered by Ariz. Z:1:13, and were incidental to the work at that site. Test trenches, dug to locate features at Ariz. Z:1:13, consistently turned up prehistoric material which was, for the most part, thoroughly mixed with the historic specimens. Consequently, attempts were made to isolate features which could be attributed to the prehistoric occupation. Features located which pertain wholly or in part to this earlier occupation include a trash mound, four primary cremations, and a structure.

Trash Mound

The trash mound, which was 15 m. in diameter, extended only 50 cm. above the surface of the surrounding terrain. Initial excavation consisted of a trench through the center of the mound, which was carried into native soil, found at a depth of 1.25 m. Further excavations consisted of the removal of two 2-m. square columns, one from each side of the initial trench. Each of the columns was excavated in 25 cm. arbitrary levels in hopes of being able to separate the two occupations in a stratigraphically controlled situation.

An analysis of the artifacts from the mound indicates that its primary period of use was during the prehistoric occupation of the site. By far a majority of the sherds and non-ceramic artifacts are prehistoric. A few objects attributable to the Papago occupation are present throughout the mound, but they are concentrated in the upper 25 cm., and the ones from greater depths can be

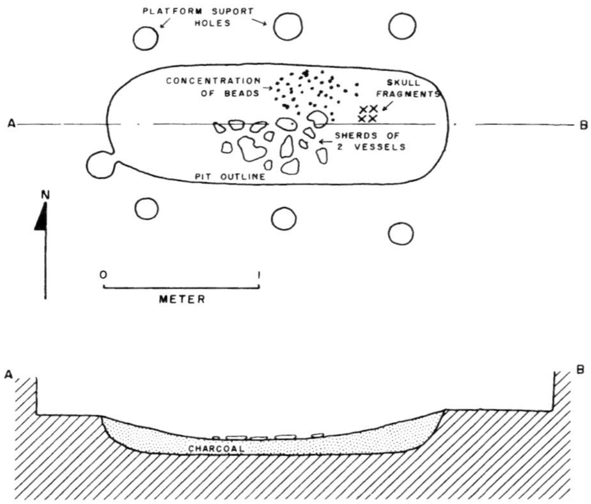

Fig. 40. Plan and section, Primary Cremation 1, Arizona Z:1:11.

explained as a result of mixture by rodents and other causes.

Primary Cremations

Three primary cremation burials, similar to those described for Ariz. T:14:10 were excavated at Ariz. Z:1:11.

Primary Cremation 1

Primary Cremation 1 (Figs. 40–42) consisted of an oval pit 2.2 m. in length and 80 cm. in width. The pit was oriented with the long axis east-west. In the pit, a layer of mesquite charcoal 10 to 20 cm. in thickness was found to cover the bottom, sides, and ends. Most of the bone fragments were found on top of the layer of charcoal. Skull fragments were near the east end of the pit, indicating that the body had been placed with the head to the east.

Six post holes, three on each side of the pit, arranged in rows along the long axis were present (Figs. 40–41). These probably supported a framework which held the body above the fire in the pit (Fig. 42). Further support for this inference comes from the discovery of bone fragments arranged along the midline of the pit, as if the framework had burned through in the middle allowing the body to slide into the center of the pit. A seventh "post" hole, with an unknown function, was connected to the southwest corner of the pit.

All of the offerings which accompanied the burial had gone through the cremation fire. Hundreds of tiny stone and shell disc beads, which apparently once formed a necklace, were concentrated around the skull fragments at the east end of the pit. The stone beads average 3 mm. in diameter, and the shell beads 4 mm. A fragment of a stone vessel made from vesicular basalt was found. The vessel was probably circular in outline. Pottery offerings included a small Gila Plain, Gila Bend Variety jar, a Gila Red seed jar, and a Gila Smudged bowl. Other offerings were several badly-burned fragments of a *Cardium elatum* valve and several kernels of charred corn. The latter may represent food offerings.

Primary Cremation 2

Primary Cremation 2 consisted of an oval pit 1.7 m. in length and 25 cm. in depth. The sides and bottom of the pit were burned, but there was no heavy layer of charcoal, only scattered chunks of mesquite charcoal in the fill. The quantity of calcined bones was small, and offerings were represented only by sherds. The sherds were Gila Red and Gila Bend Variety. Shapes represented by the sherds were two jars and one bowl.

One meter east of the east end of Primary Cremation 2 and on the same level, an inverted Gila Smudged bowl was found (Fig. 32*d*). A quantity of large fragments of burned human bone was present under the bowl. Probably these were a portion of the bones from Primary Cremation 2 which were gathered up and buried separately.

Fig. 41. Primary Cremation 1, Arizona Z:1:11.

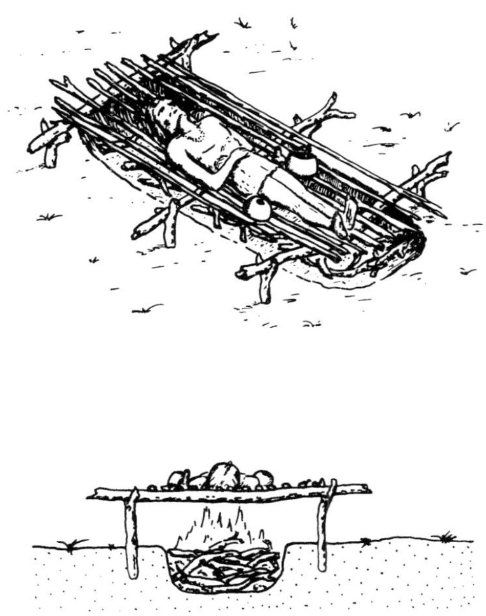

Fig. 42. Artist's reconstruction, Primary Cremation 1, Arizona Z:1:11.

Primary Cremation 3

Primary Cremation 3 was another oval pit. Its dimensions were 2 m. in length, 80 cm. in width, and 30 cm. in depth. The walls of the pit sloped gradually inward to the bottom. The bottom and sides of the pit were covered with from 10 to 15 cm. of mesquite charcoal, which represented the remains of the crematory fire. After the body was burned, the larger fragments of bone were piled together near the center of the pit, and on top of the charcoal layer. The bones were then covered with an inverted Gila Plain, Gila Bend Variety bowl, which showed traces of having gone through the crematory fire. Also found in the pit were several burned sherds from a small Gila Plain, Gila Bend Variety jar. These were probably offerings. No post holes were found around the edges of the pit, and the body may have rested directly on the mesquite fire rather than on a framework above.

Structure

The only structure found in association with Ariz. Z:1:11 was marked by an irregular post-hole pattern, a hearth, and a hard-packed floor level. The hearth was a basin-shaped pit, near the west edge of the structure, measuring 25 cm. in diameter and 10 cm. in depth. The structure was poorly defined, and perhaps represents some sort of a temporary ramada, rather than a formal house. Historic artifacts were common in the fill of the structure, but only prehistoric specimens came from the floor. On this basis, the structure is assigned to the prehistoric component of the site.

Tests

In an attempt to locate more features attributable to the occupation of Ariz. Z:1:11, several tests were made in areas of the site which were least mixed with historic materials. Most of the tests took the form of trenches, averaging 75 cm. in width, and varying in length according to the conditions. In addition, two broadside excavations were made. On completion these were about 10 m. in width, and from 5 to 10 m. in length. One was placed in the area where Primary Cremation 1 was discovered, and this broadside succeeded in locating Primary Cremation 3. The other broadside was near Structure 1, and was an unsuccessful attempt to locate more structures.

Pottery

Sherd counts and provenience data on the sherds collected at the site have been presented previously (Johnson and Wasley 1961: 51–53). Most of the types found at Ariz. Z:1:11 have been described above, and to avoid repetition, the following comments will refer only to types so far unmentioned and to unusual occurrences.

Gila Butte and Sacaton Red-on-Buff

Three sherds of these pre-Classic-period Hohokam red-on-buff types were found during the excavation of Ariz. Z:1:11. All came from the test excavations. The small number of these sherds and the fact that they were not found associated with any definite archaeological features indicates that their presence at the site was probably fortuitous. It is possible, however, that they found their way into Ariz. Z:1:11 from an early section of the site, which was not located. The remaining large quantity of sherds from the site all indicate a Classic-period date.

Intrusive Sherds

As was true for a number of other Hohokam sites in the Gila Bend area, Lower Colorado buffware was the most common intrusive type found at Ariz. Z:1:11. The presence of Lower Colorado buffware in quantity in Hohokam sites indicates a considerable amount of trade and contact with the people to the south and west.

Ariz. Z:1:11 is the only site which was excavated in the Painted Rocks Reservoir where Gila Polychrome was found, and only four sherds were recovered. As mentioned above, the Gila Bend area parallels the Papagueria (Haury 1950: 6–9) in this lack of Gila Polychrome during the Classic period. The origin of Gila Polychrome has been attributed to the Salado culture (Haury 1945a: 63). Although an earlier beginning date of 1250 has been suggested (Smiley 1952: 62–65), the type is usually assigned dates of 1300 to 1400 (Hayden 1957: 122) in southern Arizona.

A single sherd of Roosevelt Black-on-white was found at the site. This type may be a regional variety of Tularosa Black-on-white (Colton and Hargrave 1937: 240–41), with dates of about 1200 to 1350 (Pomeroy 1962: 61).

Papago Pottery

Several sherds which can be attributed to the historic Papago occupation of the site were found mixed in areas which were mainly prehistoric.

Discussion

The pottery complex from the site, including Gila Red and Gila Smudged, indicates a Classic-period assignment. The presence of a few sherds of Gila Polychrome, a diagnostic of the Civano phase in Hohokam areas farther east (Gladwin and others 1937: 267), suggests the site may belong in this phase. Based only on the four sherds of Gila Polychrome, however, such a phase assignment must be considered tentative. No architectural features characteristic of the Civano phase were found.

Artifacts

Provenience data for the artifacts from Ariz. Z:1:11 have been published (Johnson and Wasley 1961: 54–56).

Ceramic Artifacts

Modeled Spindle Whorl. One modeled spindle whorl is circular in outline, and has a deep groove encircling the circumference (Fig. 34*c*). The plainware whorl was apparently modeled around a stick. Dimensions: diameter, 2.5 cm.; thickness, 1.4 cm.

Sherd Discs. Two complete and five fragmentary sherd discs were discovered. One is made from a sherd of Hohokam buffware and four are from Gila Plain, Gila Bend Variety sherds. The other two discs are made from Gila Red and Gila Smudged sherds. Four of the sherds are biconically perforated, and one other is only partially drilled. Two are unperforated. The edges of all are ground. Dimensions: diameters range from 4.2 to 5.9 cm.

Stone Artifacts

Mano. The single mano recovered is a two-hand, bifacial form manufactured from vesicular basalt. Dimensions: length, 22 cm.; width, 9.7 cm.; thickness, 6.6 cm.

Handstone. One handstone made from an oval water-worn cobble was collected. It is unmodified except for traces of grinding on both faces. Dimensions: length, 10.1 cm.; width, 8.7 cm.; thickness, 4.4 cm.

Axe. A fragment of a three-quarter grooved axe was found. It is broken across the groove and the poll is missing. Raised ridges around the groove are not present.

Flake Knife. The only cutting tool from the site is an irregular flake of stone which has one edge sharpened by pressure flaking.

Hammerstone. The hammerstone is a water-worn cobble modified by use. Both ends are battered. Dimensions: length, 10.1 cm.; width, 5.5 cm.; thickness, 5.1 cm.

Shell Artifacts

Shell species included in the collection from Ariz. Z:1:11 are *Glycymeris maculatus, Cardium elatum, Conus* sp., and *Olivella dama*. Specimens of *Glycymeris* were most common.

Plain Glycymeris Bracelets. Three fragmentary bracelets made from *Glycymeris* valves were found at the site. One has a thin band (less than 5 mm. in width), and two have medium-width bands (5 mm. to 10 mm.).

Residue from Bracelet Manufacture. Represented in this group are six unfinished *Glycymeris* bracelets, apparently broken during the process of manufacture. Two have perforated umbos. The remaining specimen is a *Glycymeris* valve from which the central core has been removed by grinding.

Rings. Both of the shell rings were made from immature *Glycymeris* shells. One is a section of the band of a finished ring, and the other is a fragment of an unfinished ring.

Cut Shell Pendant. One pendant, made from a *Glycymeris* valve, is cut and ground into a representation of a frog (Fig. 26*o*). The pendant was strung through a hole in the umbo.

Whole Shell Beads. Three of the whole shell beads from Ariz. Z:1:11 are made from *Conus* shells (Fig. 26*i*) and the fourth is from an *Olivella* shell. In all cases, the only modification of the shells has been the removal of the spire by grinding, so that the beads could be strung.

Miscellaneous Objects of Shell. This category includes a small *Cardium* fragment with traces of grinding and a *Conus* shell which has been cut. Both are perhaps sections broken from shell ornaments.

Faunal Remains

Faunal remains from Ariz. Z:1:11 were submitted for identification and study to the National Park Service Southwest Archeological Center at Globe, Arizona. Identification of bird bones was made by Lyndon L. Hargrave, Collaborator in Ornithology and Archeology at the center.

Bird Bones. Golden Eagle *(Aquila chrysaetos)*, 77 part or complete bones from a single individual, encountered in one of the exploratory trenches (p. 65).

This is not a unique occurrence of the Golden Eagle in prehistoric sites of southern Arizona. It was reported as present at Snaketown (Gladwin and others 1937: 156), although it was not recorded in the faunal remains from Ventana Cave (Haury 1950: 152, 160).

ARIZONA Z:1:12

Ariz. Z:1:12 is situated at the west edge of Ariz. Z:1:11 and Ariz. Z:1:13. The site was marked by a blowout in the terrace sand, in which were concentrated many sherds and stone fragments. As a result of the initial survey, it was believed that the sherds were primarily Lower Colorado buff, and therefore that the site should be aligned with this complex in the Gila Bend area. Test trenches, 11 in all, were dug in the blowout and in the surrounding area, but no archaeological features were found.

A larger sample of sherds was obtained from the test trenches, and these indicate that rather than a Lower Colorado buffware site, Ariz. Z:1:12 is a Hohokam site. Included in the sherd sample are 1 Gila Plain sherd, 133 Gila Plain, Gila Bend Variety sherds, 13 Gila Red sherds, 8 Gila Smudged sherds, and 7 Lower Colorado buffware sherds. The evidence obtained from the trenches indicates that the site is another section of Ariz. Z:1:11, the Classic-period Hohokam site underlying Ariz. Z:1:13, the historic Papago site. No artifacts other than sherds were found at the site.

DISCUSSION

During the course of the salvage operations in the Painted Rocks Reservoir, five sites were excavated which can be assigned to the Classic period of the Hohokam sequence. In addition, survey data were collected on a number of other sites of this period, one of which, the Fortified Hill site, has been described herein. The criteria established farther east for distinguishing the phases of the Classic period were found to be unusable in the Gila Bend area, and as a consequence it has not been possible to assign the sites to phases.

It is unfortunate that more information on architecture and village plan was not obtained for Classic-period sites in the Gila Bend area. The two sites which produced the most data on these subjects — Ariz. T:14:12 which was excavated and the Fortified Hill site which was not excavated — do not appear to represent typical habitation sites, on the one hand, and on the other hand their geographical locations and the fact that both employed rubble-core wall construction further differentiates them from the rest of the Classic period sites in the area. While the Fortified Hill site was quite obviously built for defensive purposes, this function need not necessarily be imputed to Arizona T:14:12.

The burial practices revealed by excavation in Classic-period sites of the Gila Bend area include both inhumation and cremation. Inhumation in the Hohokam area, usually attributed to Salado influence, became fairly common during the Classic period, while cremation represents an old Hohokam tradition. However, the primary-cremation burial practice in the Gila Bend area represents a variation of cremation burial not previously associated with the Hohokam. Primary cremations have been recorded for the Sacaton phase (Gladwin and others 1937: 93), but these apparently were not of the trench-platform type.

LOWER COLORADO BUFFWARE SITES

Up to this point the prehistoric sites which have been described in the Gila Bend area have been attributed to the Hohokam culture. During the latter part of the Hohokam occupation of the Gila Bend region, particularly during the Classic period, another cultural group, the bearers of Lower Colorado buffware, appears to have filtered into the area from the south or west. Eventually, more-or-less permanent camps were established on the first terrace above the river channel, often on low dunes, and it is likely that these new people practiced flood-water farming in the adjacent areas. This intrusion of a foreign group into territory previously occupied exclusively by the Hohokam appears to have taken place peacefully. At least there is no archaeological evidence to the contrary.

The culture pattern to which the Lower Colorado buffware sites in the Gila Bend area belong has variously been referred to as Yuman (Gladwin and Gladwin 1930; Rogers 1945), Patayan (Colton 1938, 1939, 1945; Hargrave 1938; Harner 1958), and Hakataya (Schroeder 1957, 1960, 1961: 3–5). Whatever this cultural pattern may be called, the Lower Colorado buffware sites of the Gila Bend area would belong to some subdivision of this pattern as it was defined under the term Yuman.

Lower Colorado buffware has been described by Schroeder (1952a) for the Lower Colorado River area, where it seems to center, and for the Gila Bend area. In the latter region the ware is intrusive in Hohokam sites, and in addition it forms the major component of the ceramic inventory of a number of other sites, two of which were excavated.

ARIZONA T:13:7

Ariz. T:13:7 is situated on the first terrace above the Gila River channel about one and one-half miles west of Ariz. T:13:9 (Fig. 1). The terrace is composed of fine sand and silt deposited by the river. In places this material has blown into dunes. Over most of the site, sheet erosion has removed the surface on which the aboriginal occupation took place. Consequently, most of the artifacts on the surface of the site today may have been redeposited and are not *in situ*. Despite the erosion, it was felt worthwhile to test the site in hopes of locating features and materials that had not been disturbed.

Three days were devoted to testing the site, and during this period 30 trenches were excavated. Only three of these succeeded in locating archaeological features. In the other trenches, sherds and artifacts were found to a depth of about 25 cm., but none of the objects were found in areas where there could be any assurance that they were in their original positions.

Hearths

Two of the excavated features were observed on the surface as roughly circular areas of fire-cracked rock. Trenches were cut through the centers of each to obtain cross-sections. Both of the features were shallow basins filled with fire-cracked rock. One was 1.8 m. in diameter and 25 cm. in depth, and the other was 1.4 m. in diameter and 25 cm. in depth. Although the pits did not appear to have been burned, the presence of quantities of fire-cracked rock in each indicates that they may have been hearths or ovens. The rocks may have been warmed elsewhere and then deposited in the pits, and it is possible that the basin-shaped pits represent only the bottoms of deeper pit ovens, the upper sections of which had been eroded away.

Living Area

Trenches in a stabilized sand dune near the south edge of the site disclosed an irregularly-shaped pit, about 2 m. in diameter, cut into the native brown sand. The pit was filled with a small amount of trash, some charcoal, and gray sand. The level from which the pit was cut into native soil was 40 cm. below the present surface of the ground. This level may represent an old living surface. The aboriginal excavation of the pit was another 30 to 40 cm. After this pit had been refilled, a basin-shaped hearth, marked by an area of intensely-burned sand and a concentration of mesquite charcoal on the bottom, was intruded into the fill of the pit. The hearth was about 1 m. in diameter and 25 cm. deep. Other than occasional sherds, no other evidence of occupation was found in the area.

Pottery

A total of 322 sherds was collected during the test excavation of Ariz. T:13:7. A majority of the sherds (83.9 per cent) was Lower Colorado buffware. The remaining portion of the ceramic inventory (16.1 per cent) consisted of Hohokam pottery, represented by Sacaton Red-on-buff, Gila Plain, and Gila Plain, Gila Bend Variety. The Hohokam sherds, which are considered to be intrusive in this Lower Colorado buffware site, suggest a date between A.D. 900 and 1150.

Artifacts

A small number of artifacts was obtained from the test trenches and from the surface of the site.

Ceramic Artifacts

Modeled Spindle Whorl. A single modeled spindle whorl with a biconvex cross-section was recovered from one of the test trenches. The central perforation was made either by modeling the whorl around a small stick or by perforating the whorl while the clay was still in a plastic state. Dimensions: diameter, 3 cm.; thickness, 1.1 cm.

Stone Artifacts

Projectile Point. The only projectile point, which was found on the surface of the site, is a fragment manufactured from obsidian. It is triangular in outline with a convex base and concave sides. Dimensions: length, 2.9 cm.; width, 1 cm.; thickness, 4 mm.

Three-quarter Grooved Axe. One fragmentary three-quarter grooved axe was collected from the surface of the site. The bit had been broken from the specimen. Raised ridges around the groove suggest the possibility of Hohokam influence or manufacture.

Ring. Also found on the surface of the site was a stone "ring" made of vesicular basalt. It is roughly cylindrical with a biconical perforation and a faint, shallow groove encircling the outer circumference. Dimensions: height, 4.5 cm.; diameter, 7.6 cm.; diameter of perforation, 1.2 cm.; thickness of walls at rim, 2.9 cm.

ARIZONA T:13:13

This site is about 14 miles northwest of Gila Bend and one mile southeast of Arizona T:13:9 (Fig. 1). It is on the first terrace above the Gila River and occupies most of a large stabilized dune made up of fine sand and silt. The site was tested with 11 trenches. Probably because the site had been farmed a number of years ago, no archaeological features were encountered.

Pottery

A majority of the sherds (86.9 per cent) from the test trenches at this site were Lower Colorado buffware. Most of the remaining sherds (12.1 per cent) were Hohokam intrusives, including Sacaton Red-on-buff, Gila Red, Gila Plain, and Gila Plain, Gila Bend Variety. The Sacaton Red-on-buff sherds indicate that contact with the Hohokam first took place during the Sacaton phase, while the Gila Red sherds suggest that this contact lasted into the Classic period.

Artifacts

The two artifacts collected from the site both came from test trenches.

Stone Artifact

Mano. The single mano is a two-hand, uniface type manufactured from vesicular basalt. Dimensions: length, 18.4 cm.; width, 10.1 cm.; thickness, 5.3 cm.

Shell Artifact

Whole Shell Pendant. A pendant made from a *Pecten excavatus* shell came from one of the test trenches (Fig. 26*m*). The only modification of the shell is a biconical perforation through the umbo.

DISCUSSION

The relatively meager amount of information derived from excavation in two sites in which Lower Colorado buffware was the predominant pottery does not provide a sufficiently detailed basis on which to define the nature of this second cultural occupation of the Gila Bend area in prehistoric times. However, Yuman-speaking groups of people are known to have been in the Gila Bend area at the time of the earliest historic contact by the Spanish (Ezell 1963*a*). It is possible that the Lower Colorado buffware sites represent former camps of Yuman-speaking groups, and if this is the case, they were in the Gila Bend area as early as the Sacaton phase of the Hohokam culture, but apparently no earlier. This latter conclusion is based on the occurrence of Lower Colorado buffware intrusives in Hohokam sites and on the presence of Hohokam intrusives in Lower Colorado buffware sites.

Fig. 43. Petroglyph designs, Painted Rocks (Arizona S:16:1.)

Fig. 44. Petroglyph designs, Fortified Hill site (Arizona T:13:8.)

PETROGLYPHS

In addition to data collected from village sites in the vicinity of Gila Bend, information of another type was gathered on the aboriginal occupation of the area. Many of the cliff faces and boulder-strewn sections of the region have been utilized for the execution of petroglyphs. The technique used throughout the area was to peck the design through the desert varnish or patina which covers the surface of the rock. As a result the design appears as a light area surrounded by the darker weathered surface of the stone. Anthropomorphic, zoomorphic, and geometric designs were produced in this manner.

Three of the petroglyph sites in the Gila Bend area have been selected for description. Most of the typical designs of the region are exhibited in the petroglyphs at these sites. Since the area was inhabited over a long period of time by several cultural groups, it is not possible to assign the petroglyphs definitely to any single time period or cultural group. It is probable that a majority of the designs can be attributed to the Hohokam for the following reasons: (1) the major occupation of the area was by the Hohokam; (2) many of the petroglyph designs are the same as those used on Hohokam pottery; (3) petroglyph sites are often near Hohokam villages. In no case have any definite associations been found, however, and for this reason the Hohokam origin of the petroglyphs can only be offered as a probability.

PAINTED ROCKS

The Painted Rocks site (Arizona S:16:1), about four airline miles southwest of the Painted Rocks Dam (Fig. 1), constitutes the most elaborate and best preserved of the petroglyph sites in the region. It consists of an isolated boulder outcrop on the desert floor, and formed a conspicuous local landmark along the earlier Indian trail and later stagecoach route, both of which passed close to the outcrop. The present dam and the Painted Rocks Mountains just to the east both derive their names from this petroglyph site. Zoomorphic, anthropomorphic, and geometric figures are represented (Fig. 43).

This particular group of petroglyphs has been known historically at least since 1749 when the German Jesuit missionary, Jacobo Sedelmayr, saw them and mentioned them in his report the following year (Dunne 1955: 56–57). Coues (1900: 117, note 24) apparently thought that Sedelmayr had seen the Painted Rocks on his first trip to the area in 1744, and it seems possible that Father Kino and Captain Juan Mateo Manje (1954: 121) may have seen the petroglyphs in 1699 unless they followed too closely the banks of the river in this area.

Among the first Americans to see and report on the Painted Rocks were Emory (1848: 89–91), Johnston (1848: 604), and Eccleston (1950: 218). One of the better early descriptions, accompanied by three pages of illustrations, was made by Bartlett (1854: 206):

> After crossing a plain for about 5 miles, we reached the object of our search, which consisted of a pile of large boulders, heaped some forty or fifty feet above the plain, and standing entirely alone. Such of these rocks as present smooth sides are covered with sculptures, rudely pecked in, of animals and men, as well as of various figures, apparently without meaning. There are hundreds of them so ornamented, showing that the place has long been the resort of the Indians for this purpose; for there seems to be nothing else to attract them here. Many of the inscriptions bear the stamp of great age, others having been made over them repeatedly, rendering it impossible to trace out either the earlier or the later markings.

Painted Rocks is a literal translation of Piedras Pintadas, the name used during the Spanish period of colonization. The name implies that the designs were painted, rather than just pecked, into the rocks. Although Bartlett and the earlier American writers cited do not mention it, Sedelmayr said that the designs were painted (Dunne 1955: 56–57), and some of the later nineteenth-century writers (Browne 1950: 102; Hinton 1954: 176) make it clear that the figures were first pecked and then some of them were also painted. This is not an unusual technique, as petroglyphs made by pecking and then painting are known from other localities in southern Arizona, particularly in caves and rock shelters or overhangs where the paint stands a better chance of being preserved. There is little trace of paint now at the Painted Rocks because they are so exposed.

Unfortunately, since the time of the nineteenth-century visitors to the Painted Rocks, and particularly since World War II, a large number of the more easily-portable rocks with petroglyphs have been carted off to line driveways and private yards. Others of the petroglyphs have been defaced by the pecking of initials and dates, the earliest of which is in the 1860's and the most recent in the 1950's. About two years ago the area containing the Painted Rocks was fenced by the Bureau of Land Management, and steps are now underway to incorporate this site into the Arizona State Park system.

There are no village sites in the immediate vicinity of the Painted Rocks, and although a few plainware sherds have been found around the boulder pile, these are not distinctive enough to allow the assignment of the petroglyphs to any one time period or cultural group.

FORTIFIED HILL SITE

A second extensive set of petroglyphs is to be found on the southern slope of the large uplifted and tilted block on which the Fortified Hill site (Ariz. T:13:8) was built (Fig. 1). The petroglyphs extend down the slope of the block to the arroyos at the bottom, where the best examples are to be seen on a large isolated boulder (Fig. 44). The Fortified Hill site has been assigned to the Classic period of the Hohokam culture, and the proximity of the petroglyphs to this site suggests the possibility that they were produced by the Hohokam inhabitants of the site.

ARIZONA T:14:20

The petroglyphs at Ariz. T:14:20 (Fig. 45) have been executed on the smooth faces of boulders which cover the southern side of a small hill detached from the main mass of the Gila Bend Mountains (Fig. 1). The site is within about 200 m. of Ariz. T:14:10 and Ariz. T:14:11, which have been described herein, and it is possible that the inhabitants of these Classic-period villages may have been responsible for the petroglyphs.

Fig. 45. Petroglyph designs, Arizona T:14:20.

DISCUSSIONS

THE HOHOKAM PHASE SEQUENCE

As a result of the excavation of the site of Snaketown and the analysis of the large collection of artifacts, a Hohokam sequence of seven phases grouped into three periods, beginning with the Pioneer, was established (Gladwin and others 1937: 32, Fig. 9). In addition, data which had been collected prior to the work at Snaketown were crystallized into sequent phases for the fourth period, the Classic, following the abandonment of Snaketown. This sequence, which is believed to cover the entire time span of the Hohokam occupation of southern Arizona, is given below:

CLASSIC PERIOD (A. D. 1150–1450)	Civano phase Soho phase
SEDENTARY PERIOD (A. D. 900–1150)	Sacaton phase
COLONIAL PERIOD (A. D. 500–900	Santa Cruz phase Gila Butte phase
PIONEER PERIOD (A. D. 1–500)	Snaketown phase Sweetwater phase Estrella phase Vahki phase

Since publication of the Snaketown report several attempts have been made to revise the sequence. These attempts have been made without advantage of further excavation (Gladwin 1948), or as a result of excavation in areas peripheral to the center of Hohokam development (DiPeso 1956). Rather drastic changes have been suggested.

One of the most complete revisions of the original sequence, excluding the Classic period, was given by Gladwin (1948: 1–124). He reconsidered the Snaketown data, and concluded that "instead of a vertical succession of seven cultural phases, each defined by a distinct type of decorated or red pottery, the series is now reduced to two – Santa Cruz followed by Sacaton – with the possibility that the pure Vahki deposits at the bottom of Trench III may represent a short pre-Santa Cruz occupation." Painted pottery types which, in the original Snaketown report (Gladwin and others 1937: 189–202), were presented as diagnostics of the Estrella, Sweetwater, and Snaketown phases, were felt to overlap with one another and to be partly or wholly contemporaneous with Santa Cruz and Sacaton Red-on-buff (Gladwin 1948: 80).

> Gila Butte Red-on buff, which formerly had been compressed between Snaketown and Santa Cruz Red-on-buff, is now expanded into a blended type which was present throughout most of the life of Mound 29, having been identified in the lowest, the intermediate, and the uppermost levels of the Mound (Gladwin 1948: 80).

The presentation of this revision of the original report caused Lehmer (1950), Schroeder (1951a), and Dixon (1956) to reexamine the basic data presented in the report. Lehmer (1950), through the application of a statistical formula to test the validity of associations of earlier and later pottery types, concluded that the original sequence was correct. The same conclusion was reached by Schroeder (1951a) through a comparison of the Snaketown data with that from the Salt River Valley (Schroeder 1940). Dixon employed the Brainerd-Robinson (1951) statistical method of chronological ordering on the raw ceramic data from Mound 29 at Snaketown (Gladwin 1948: 239–63) with some success to demonstrate the accuracy of the original Snaketown sequence.

The recent work in the Painted Rocks Reservoir also suggests that the original sequence presented in the Snaketown volume (Gladwin and others 1937) is essentially correct. No new information was gained on the Pioneer period, but the presence of a Gila Butte phase, which Gladwin (1948) would remove from the sequence, is now definitely established. The principal occupation of the Rock Ball Court site (Ariz. T:13:9) was during this phase. The only Hohokam painted type other than Gila Butte Red-on-buff found at the site was Santa Cruz Red-on-buff, which accounted for 3.5 per cent of the sherds. There was nothing at the site to indicate that the sherds of Santa Cruz Red-on-buff were contemporary with the Gila Butte Red-on-buff examples, as they should have been if Gladwin's (1948) revisions were correct. Rather, it seems apparent that there was a continuous occupation from the Gila Butte phase into the early part of the Santa Cruz phase, since the earlier type graded imperceptibly into the later. No features were excavated at the site where Santa Cruz Red-on-buff was the dominant type.

Be this as it may, it is apparent from the excavations in the Painted Rocks Reservoir that there is a Gila Butte phase, as defined by the stratigraphic work at Snaketown (Gladwin and others 1937), which can be identified on the basis of single component sites. In other words, there was a period of time during which Gila Butte Red-on-buff pottery was being produced as the only locally-made painted pottery type in the Hohokam area. One of the great advantages of the excavation of small uncomplicated sites occupied for a short period of time, is that a clearer picture can often be gained of a single period of time. Sites with considerable time depth are often complicated by disturbance caused by later occupation in already-present habitation levels.

The validity of the Santa Cruz phase has not been specifically questioned, although DiPeso (1956: 239) has hinted at some doubts, as a result of the excavation of the Paloparado site. It should be noted that data collected in the Painted Rocks Reservoir support the validity of a Santa Cruz phase. In addition to the evidence for this phase collected at the Rock Ball Court site (Ariz. T:13:9), further data are available from excavations at the Gatlin site (Ariz. Z:2:1). At the latter site, the lower two levels in Trash Mound 3 contained Santa Cruz Red-on-buff as the only locally-made painted pottery type, indicating a period of time when this type was being made as the only Hohokam painted pottery. Upper levels in the mound contained both Santa Cruz and Sacaton Red-on-buff, a parallel to the Snaketown situation where one type was observed grading into the other (Gladwin and others 1937). Also, at the Gatlin site, the trash layer between the two major construction periods in Ball Court 1 contained both Santa Cruz and Sacaton Red-on-buff sherds. The trash was probably deposited during the transitional period between the two phases. Consequently, the first construction period in the court would seem to date to the Santa Cruz phase.

The Sacaton phase was well documented at Snaketown (Gladwin and others 1937), and the Gila Bend data support the validity of this phase. The major period of occupation at the Gatlin site was during the Sacaton phase, and the only occupation at the Citrus site (Ariz. T:13:2) was during this phase. Further evidence for the existence of a Sacaton phase comes from Ariz. T:14:14 and Ariz. T:14:15. Ball courts were constructed and used at both of these sites during the phase.

In the Snaketown report (Gladwin and others 1937: 264) a transitional Santan phase between the Sacaton and the Soho phases of the Classic period was introduced. Work since the excavation of Snaketown has failed to substantiate this Santan phase as more than a local manifestation (Hayden 1957: 178–79, 184), and as a consequence it has been dropped from most presentations of the Hohokam phase sequence. In the Gila Bend area no sites were located which seemed to fit the criteria of the Santan phase.

As was noted above, difficulties are encountered in the Gila Bend area in assigning Classic-period sites to the sequent Soho and Civano phases. The lack of Gila Polychrome at several of the Classic-period sites, and its minimal presence at others, makes the phase assignments tenuous. In other words, sites with Gila Polychrome can be assigned to the Civano phase, but those without could be either Soho or Civano phase or both. Gila Polychrome was not introduced in quantity in the Gila Bend area, and it may not have found its way into all of the Civano-phase sites. The lack of change in Classic-period redwares of the Painted Rocks Reservoir has been a further deterrent to distinguishing between phases. Due to these difficulties, there is only an indication that sequent Soho and Civano phase sites or components may have been represented in the area.

Summarizing the above discussion, evidence was obtained from excavations in the area about Gila Bend, Arizona, which supports the original Hohokam sequence from the Gila Butte phase through the Classic period as defined at Snaketown

(Gladwin and others 1937: 256–67). No information was obtained on the Pioneer period. As at Snaketown, in the Gila Bend area there was a sequence of phases, each related to the one preceeding and following, but distinctive enough to be isolated at one period in its development.

In addition to the attempts which have been made to revise the Hohokam phase sequence, attempts have also been made to change the calendrical dates assigned to the various phases. Because little in the way of new information was obtained on this problem, it will not be considered in detail. Suffice it to say that since the publication of the Snaketown report, several attempts have been made to push the dates up in time (Gladwin 1942; DiPeso 1956).

Intrusive sherds which have been assigned dates on the basis of tree-ring analysis were found in Sacaton-phase and Classic-period contexts in the Gila Bend area. The pottery types represented and their assigned dates are listed below. At the Gatlin site (Ariz. Z:2:1) the following dated intrusives were found:

- Black Mesa Black-on-white, about 900–1100 (Colton 1946: 251)
- Red Mesa Black-on white, about 900–1100 (Gladwin 1945: 56)
- Sosi Black-on-white, about 1050–1150 (Colton and Hargrave 1937: 211-13)
- Puerco Black-on-white, about 950–1150 (Colton 1941: 58-59)
- Tusayan Black-on-red, about 1050–1150 (Colton 1946: 252)

Additional intrusives came from the single-component Sacaton-phase, Citrus site (Ariz. T: 13:2). These included Snowflake Black-on-white, about 1000–1150 (Colton 1941: 62–63); and Reserve Black-on-white, about 1000–1150 (Martin and Rinaldo 1950: 502–503; Martin and others 1952: 61–63).

On the basis of trade sherds found at Snaketown, the Sacaton phase was assigned dates of A. D. 900–1100 (Gladwin and others 1937: Fig. 106). The dated intrusives listed above for Sacaton-phase sites in the Gila Bend area are in full accord with the Snaketown dates, and consequently it appears that the Sacaton phase in the Gila Bend area was essentially contemporaneous with the phase as it is known farther east. There is some indication from the dates listed above that the Sacaton phase may have lasted until about A.D. 1150 in the Gila Bend area.

Northern intrusives found in Classic-period sites in the Gila Bend area include Flagstaff Black-on-white, about 1120–1225 (Colton 1946: 251); and Roosevelt Black-on-white, about 1100–1200 (Pomeroy 1962: 61).

Little in the way of refinement is added to the absolute dating of the Classic period by the recovery of these few sherds. They support the post-A.D. 1100 assignment of the Classic period which has previously been given (Gladwin and others 1937, Fig. 106). The phase-by-phase occurrence in the Gila Bend area of northern intrusives of different time periods offers still further support to the validity of the original Snaketown sequence and chronology from the Colonial period through the Classic period.

While on the subject of the Hohokam phase sequence, mention should be made of the attempts at revision based on migration. To date, several authors, writing on Hohokam archaeology and related subjects, have proposed migrations to account for the Mesoamerican traits which appear in southern Arizona during the Gila Butte and later phases (Jennings 1956: 92–93). An early proposal of this type was offered by Gladwin (1948: 232). More recently, Ferdon (1955: 29–31), DiPeso (1956) and Schroeder (1960) have suggested that Mesoamerican traits in Hohokam sites appeared as a result of a migration.

In the Gila Bend area, a number of the previously-recorded Mesoamerican traits, such as copper bells, were noted, and in addition a few traits of possible Mexican derivation were added to the list. They include the Gatlin-site platform mound, the possibility that the Gatlin site represents a ceremonial center, and the plaza-house-trash-mound arrangement noted at the Citrus site. Despite these additions to the list, it is believed that the Hohokam culture represents a long local development. Mesoamerican traits in Hohokam sites are felt to be a result of trade and culture contact, not the result of migration.

One reason for this belief rests in the observation of the intimate relationship of the Gila Bend Hohokam to the local environment. The utilization of local resources, as was done by the Gila Bend Hohokam, required a long period of development and "settling-in" to use Braidwood's term (1957:

105–106). It is doubted that the archaeological remains of a newly-arrived migrant group would exhibit this intimate relationship.

To cite one example, the utilization of caliche can be mentioned. Caliche is a calcium carbonate formed in arid regions through ground-water activity. Its occurrence is quite as variable as its form (Hayden 1957: 203). The material makes an excellent plaster when mixed with water, but its potentialities are not obvious from the material itself. Often, as at the Rock Ball Court site, it occurs as a cementing agent in gravel terraces, and in these cases refining was necessary to remove the larger rocks.

It is not known when the first use was made of caliche in the Hohokam area, but by the Gila Butte phase, in the Gila Bend region, its use was an established pattern. The desirability of the material is obvious when it is noted that it was carried a distance of one-half mile to a mile at the Gatlin and Citrus sites for use on house floors, ball-court floors and features, the platform mound, and the plaza floor. The utilization of a less-than-obvious material such as caliche for building purposes indicates a long period of local development in the area, and not a migration of new peoples unacquainted with the local environment.

In summarizing a series of papers on migrations in New World culture history, Rouse (1958: 64) set forth five conditions which should be satisfied to demonstrate adequately that a migration has taken place:

> 1) identify the migrating people as an intrusive unit in the region it has penetrated; 2) trace this unit back to its homeland; 3) determine that all occurrences of the unit are contemporaneous; 4) establish the existence of favorable conditions for the migration; and 5) demonstrate that some other hypothesis, such as independent invention or diffusion of traits, does not better fit the facts of the situation.

Let us examine the proposed migration of Mesoamerican peoples into the Hohokam area in terms of these conditions. It has not been possible to identify an alien group of people in the Hohokam area on the basis of physical type, since all of the prehistoric inhabitants of the area practiced cremation burial during most of the prehistoric period. However, this first condition might still be met if it were possible to demonstrate that a) "there suddenly appears in a cultural continuum a constellation of traits readily identifiable as new, and without local prototype," and b) that "the products of the immigrant group not only reflected borrowed elements from the host group, but also, as a lingering effect, preserve unmistakable elements from their own pattern" (Haury 1958: 1). About two dozen Mesoamerican traits have been listed by Haury (1945b: 62–64) as having been introduced into the Hohokam area. To these may be added the few new ones from the Gila Bend area, and additional Mesoamerican traits have been suggested (Jennings 1956: 92–93). However, these do not appear in the Hohokam culture as a cohesive constellation or unit but as dribblets and small clusters over a period of some 1,400 years. Except for copper bells, whose probable place of origin was in the Jalisco-Nayarit section of the west coast of Mexico (Meighan 1960: 15–34; Pendergast 1962: 376–77), it has not been possible to pinpoint the homeland sources of the other Mesoamerican traits which occur in Hohokam sites. Furthermore, most of the other objects of manufacture occur in the Hohokam area as altered copies and not as direct imports. Finally, the conditions for migration were not ideal. While migration was geographically possible, if not easy, by a number of routes, it would be difficult to justify or define the incentive that would lure a group of Mesoamerican migrants to the Hohokam desert environment.

Therefore, 1) it has not been possible to identify a Mesoamerican migratory group intrusive into the Hohokam area, or 2) to trace it back to its homeland, or 3) to demonstrate that all occurrences of the unit are contemporaneous, or 4) to establish particularly favorable conditions for migrations, and so we must conclude that 5) a diffusion of traits, probably at different times and over different routes from Mesoamerica, better fits the facts of the situation. The continuum of Hohokam culture history was not broken, nor was its course measurably altered, by the Mesoamerican innovations.

This discussion has considered data collected in the Gila Bend area on the Hohokam phase sequence and chronology. Suggestions which have been presented for revisions of the sequence have been evaluated in the light of the work done in the Painted Rocks Reservoir. All of the Gila Bend data are in support of the original Hohokam sequence set forth in the Snaketown report (Gladwin and others 1937). Little new information was obtained from the Gila Bend excavations on the problem of absolute dates for the Hohokam phases, but the information which was collected on this problem supports the dates originally assigned to the Sacaton phase and to the Classic period. Attempts to revise the Hohokam sequence by introducing a Mesoamerican migration hypothesis have been discussed, with the conclusion that there is no current support for such a migration.

SETTLEMENT PATTERNS

Most of our knowledge of Hohokam archaeology was gathered before the concept of settlement patterns (Willey 1953) had gained wide acceptance as a useful tool for the study of archaeological cultures. Partly for this reason, but no less because of the relatively-expensive undertaking that comprehensive excavation in a Hohokam site represents, data pertaining to Hohokam settlement patterns have been insufficient. The little information which can be used has been summarized by Haury (1956: 7–9).

Therefore, the Painted Rocks Reservoir salvage project was welcomed as an opportunity to gain more knowledge about broad settlement patterns and specific village plans of the Hohokam culture. Yet in spite of a conscious effort to achieve this goal, the results were disappointing in several respects. A large portion of some of the sites had been destroyed by erosion or by modern agricultural expansion. A prohibitive expense would have been involved in the thorough investigation of some of the other sites. Nevertheless, some valuable data on settlement patterns were obtained.

Vogt (1956: 173) suggests that analysis of settlement patterns should include the whole range: the nature of individual domestic house types, the spatial relationships of these to one another, the relationship of domestic structures to special architectural features within a village, the over-all village or community plan, and the spatial relationships of villages over large areas. Of course, temporal relationships must also be taken into consideration. What is not clearly expressed in these comments on settlement patterns is the basic premise of the concept: the settlement pattern reflects the nature of man's adaptation to his environment (Willey 1953: 1). Too frequently archaeologists in writing about "settlement pattern" have dealt only with architectural comparisons, village layout and type, and the distribution of settlements, without reference to the possible effects and role of environment. Yet one does not have to believe in environmental determinism before he can discuss the nature of man's adaptation to his environment.

The distinction between the River Hohokam of the Gila and Salt rivers and the Desert Hohokam of the Papagueria (Haury 1950: 15, 546–48) was based partly on the different environments of the two areas (the Papagueria could boast no permanent streams or rivers), and partly on differences in cultural inventory and emphasis, not all of which can be attributed to the different environments. Certainly the hallmark of River Hohokam cultural development was the attainment of an extensive and affluent agricultural community in riverine locales. This was made possible first of all by the presence of the rivers and valleys, but particularly and more importantly by the fact that the Hohokam seized upon and developed to a high degree the concept and practice of canal irrigation to exploit this environment to the fullest. Although sharing in part this same riverine environment, the Lower Colorado buffware peoples of the lower Gila River, and sometimes neighbors of the Hohokam, did not practice canal irrigation, did not develop an agricultural subsistence economy past fairly rudimentary stages, and consequently they had to rely more heavily on other subsistence pursuits.

Let us turn now to the Gila Bend area for a more detailed consideration of data pertaining to settlement pattern. Village location is usually determined to a considerable extent by the availability of water. Without some means of diverting water away from the river channel, people tended to build habitation sites close to the river: on the river bank, on the floodplain, or perhaps even on the first terrace, depending upon the profile of the valley at any given point. This was the pattern of the Lower Colorado buffware peoples. By means of canals, however, it was possible for the Hohokam to divert water not only for irrigation but also for domestic consumption to habitation sites sometimes located a considerable distance from the river (for example, Los Muertos, in the

Salt River Valley some six miles south of the river; Haury 1945a: 40). Areas more suitable for agriculture were put under cultivation, and these usually included the floodplain and part of the first terrace.

At least by the early part of the Colonial period in the Gila Bend area, the Hohokam pattern of building villages some distance from the Gila River was apparently well established. All of the unexcavated Gila Butte-phase (A.D. 500–700) sites recorded in the surveys, and the one excavated site of this phase, Ariz. T:13:9, are situated well back on the first terrace or on the second terrace above the river. No canals have been found which can be attributed to this period, but their use at this time may be inferred from the village locations.

This pattern of locating villages at some distance from the river continued until the end of the Sedentary period about A.D. 1150. During the Sedentary period the canal passing close to the Gatlin site was certainly in use, and there was probably a canal servicing the Citrus site, although modern agriculture has apparently obliterated all traces of it. At the end of the Sedentary period a radical change seems to have occurred. Sites which had been occupied for as long as several hundred years were abandoned, and new villages were established closer to the river, on the floodplains or on the edge of the first terrace. There are some exceptions, but in a majority of cases this situation seems to hold true.

Haury (1945a: 204) has noted similar changes in the Salt River Valley, where Soho-phase trash is seldom found in conformable relationship to Sacaton-phase trash. New village locations are indicated. Also in this region Soho-phase sites apparently are found in a more restricted area, nearer the river, than was the case during the Sacaton phase. By compiling data from Gila Pueblo's surveys, Schroeder (1952b: 331) has been able to show that fewer than 8 per cent of the surveyed sites show a continuous occupation through the Sacaton-Soho transition in the Gila Basin, and that in the Verde Valley fewer than 4 per cent were occupied through this period. Obviously, as Haury (1945a: 204) has stated, "a disruptive influence was present in the area, causing a wide-spread adjustment of the population."

What this disruptive influence may have been has never been adequately explained, and unfortunately the work in the Gila Bend area does not seem to clarify the question at all. However, at least in the immediate Painted Rocks Reservoir area, a change in agricultural techniques may be inferred from this change in village location. Although the Hohokam may have utilized a number of farming methods at any given period, undoubtedly greater reliance was placed on canal irrigation after the systems were established. The abandonment of sites relying on canal water for domestic use as well as for irrigation, such as the Gatlin and Citrus sites, the absence of any evidence for the later occupation of these sites, and the lack of definite evidence for Classic-period canal systems in the Painted Rocks Reservoir, all indicate that reliance must have shifted from canal irrigation to some other types of farming and irrigation.

What cannot be invoked to explain the abandonment of canals and the consequent shift of habitation sites is a categorical statement that drought or extensive flooding or a general raising or lowering of the water table or some other climatic change made canal irrigation no longer possible. Some sites serviced by canals continued to be occupied throughout the Classic period: witness Casa Grande in the Gila River Valley and Los Muertos in the Salt River Valley, to mention only two outstanding examples. Similarly, Ariz. T:14:16 and Ariz. T:14:17 (Fig. 1), not far north of the Painted Rocks Reservoir area, may have been serviced by a canal during the Classic-period occupation of these unexcavated sites.

Hohokam villages typical of the riverine agrarian society appear through the Sedentary period to be not much more than a random clustering of houses and associated trash mounds. Ball courts, if present, tend to be at or near the outskirts of the village. Isolated farm houses are not uncommon, and some appear to have been located in areas where the tenant could tend or guard the local section of canal. Hohokam settlements in the Gila Bend area follow this same general pattern, but there were exceptions. At the Citrus site a group of houses was randomly clustered about a raised, caliche-surfaced plaza floor, suggesting that the plaza concept had been introduced to the Hohokam at least by the Sedentary period. At the Gatlin site the presence of a platform mound probably ceremonial in nature, the relative paucity of domestic structures, and the relatively numerous "trash" mounds suggest that this site may have been primarily a ceremonial center. The Classic-period Fortified Hill site introduces a new dimension to Hohokam settlement patterns in the Gila Bend area. Constructed of dry-laid stone masonry and perched in a defensible position of difficult access that was also controled by a series of defensive walls, this site is more characteristic of the Papagueria and of the Trincheras area (Johnson 1963) in northwestern Sonora than it is of the River Hohokam. The difference in building materials and construction techniques between this site and the more common Hohokam wattle-and-daub or post-reinforced adobe construction is not so startling when one realizes that expediency must have been the guiding factor. There is so little soil on this forbidding bedrock eminence on which the village was built that dirt probably had to be hauled up just to level the floors a bit, whereas the malpais (basalt) boulders were readily at hand for the walls. The need for a defensible location is the factor which is more at variance with the data of earlier Hohokam history. That this was a retreat used in times of social unrest rather than a permanent habitation site is attested to by the contemporaneous unfortified farming communities of the Classic period dotting the valley below. Who indeed were the aggressors, and for what reasons? Speculation will not answer this question in the Gila Bend area which by this time represented a usually peaceful frontier for several cultures.

BALL COURTS

Large oval depressions with surrounding ridges of earth were reported for many years in the literature on Southwestern prehistory before their recognition as ball courts during the excavations at Snaketown (Gladwin and others 1937: 36–49). In 1918 Pinkley drew together the various reports on these depressions and found that speculations on their function varied greatly. These speculations included assumed uses as reservoirs, wells, threshing floors, corrals to hold stock, dew ponds, and ceremonial chambers (Pinkley 1935a: 385). Unsatisfied with many of these theories, Pinkley made tests in the depressions at Casa Grande, the Grewe site, and the Adamsville ruins (Pinkley 1935a, 1935b) and concluded that they may have been used for "ceremony, games, or festivals" (Pinkley 1935a: 388). However, Pinkley's findings were not generally known for several years, and during the 1920's Turney (1929: 24) and others referred to the depressions as "sun temples," while still other workers continued to call them reservoirs.

The identification of these features as ball courts was effected during the visit to Snaketown in July, 1935, of a group of Mesoamerican archaeologists (Anonymous 1935: 154–55; Gladwin and others 1937: 38), although similarities between the Hohokam features and Mesoamerican ball courts had been noted during the course of excavation at Snaketown (Gladwin and others 1937: 38). No rubber balls, or balls of any kind, have been found in direct association with Hohokam courts, although two prehistoric rubber balls have been reported from the Hohokam area (Lloyd 1911; Amsden 1936; Haury 1937). While there is still a possibility that these Hohokam courts may have served some other ceremonial purpose such as dancing, there has been no evidence over the years or as a result of the recent work in the Gila Bend area to negate the ball-court theory. Therefore, it seems wisest, even nearly 30 years after Snaketown, to continue to accept the ball-court identification as the most likely explanation for the function of these features.

The classification of Hohokam ball courts into two basic types has been based primarily on five criteria: size, orientation, end units, shape, and temporal relationship. The Snaketown type has been characterized as being relatively large and oriented in a general east-west direction. It has bulbous end units large enough to accommodate at least small end fields. This type of court has a center field with nearly parallel sides but rounded ends, and it appeared in the Hohokam area during the Colonial period. The Casa Grande type of court is described as relatively small and oriented in a general north-south direction. The diminutive end units or entrances are too small to accommodate end field areas, and there is a decided oval or bulging shape to the center field. The first appearance of the Casa Grande type of court in the Hohokam area was thought to have been in the Sedentary period.

This classification was originally based on the excavation of the large east-west court at Snaketown and on the excavation or testing of the small north-south courts at Snaketown, the Casa Grande ruin, the Grewe site, Adamsville, and courts in the Flagstaff area, as well as on the visible surface indications of a number of unexcavated courts. Subsequent ball-court excavation and testing for the most part substantiated this classification, such as in the Snaketown type of court at the Hodges site and the Casa Grande type of court at Pueblo Grande. General characteristics of both types of courts were center markers and end markers in the floor along the long axis of the center field, raised banks along the sides, and caliche or clay surfacings on the playing floors and banks. The nature of center and end markers varies considerably within each type of ball court, and end markers are not always found in Casa Grande ball courts. Only three ball courts of the Snaketown type have been excavated or tested (including the one at the Citrus site in addition to the two listed above), and this would appear to be an inadequate sample on which to determine whether floor markers are consistent features in this type of court.

Two Southwestern ball courts have been suggested as transitional between the "earlier" Snaketown type of court and the "later" Casa Grande type, implying that one type developed from the other through a contraction in size, a degeneration of the end units, and a shift in orientation. These "transitional" courts consist of one in the middle Verde Valley and the court at Tres Alamos on the San Pedro River (Schroeder 1949a: 30). Both courts are large enough to fall well within the size range of the Snaketown type, but both are oriented essentially north-south. The Verde Valley court has not been excavated or tested, but Schroeder (1949a: 30) claims it does not have end fields. No end fields were defined for the Tres Alamos court, but the report does not indicate that excavation was extended to try to locate end courts (Tuthill 1947).

Since the absence of surface evidence to indicate end fields or the lack of excavation to locate them does not prove their absence, we cannot legitimately assume, on the one hand, that this feature represents a transitional "loss" in changing from the Snaketown to the Casa Grande type of court through time. On the other hand, with only three Snaketown-type ball courts excavated or tested in the Southwest, neither can we be sure that the presence of end fields was a consistent feature of this type of court. Thus, these two courts may be judged to be transitional on the basis of only two proven criteria – size and orientation: Snaketown type in size and Casa Grande type in orientation.

On the basis of excavated ball courts and ball courts recorded in the Arizona State Museum and Gila Pueblo site surveys of Arizona, it would appear that there are no Snaketown-type ball courts shorter than 50 m. (range 52 m.± to 65 m.±) and no Casa Grande-type courts longer than 35 m. (range 18 m. to 33.5 m.). There is absolutely no overlap in size known to date. On the other hand, the orientation from true north has been calculated for as many of these courts as has been possible in a survey of the literature and on the basis of firsthand knowledge of a few other courts. These results are graphically presented in Figure 46, which shows that there is a complete overlap in orientation of Snaketown- and Casa Grande-type courts, although there is a tendency for Snaketown courts to be oriented east-west and for Casa Grande courts to be oriented north-south.

Returning again to the "transitional" courts, we find that Schroeder's criterion of orientation is seriously in question and that the lone remaining criterion is size, which would indicate that these two courts are – being in excess of 50 m. long – of the Snaketown type, as McGregor (1941: 89) originally reported the large Verde Valley court to be. It should be mentioned at this point that one other large (57 m.) court was recently (1962) recorded in the Arizona State Museum site survey (Ariz. FF:7:2). This court is at the Leslie Canyon site in southeastern Arizona on the eastern side of the Chiricahua Mountains. The orientation is essentially north-south, and it may or may not have end fields: the surface indications were not conclusive, and the court has not been excavated. This, then, constitutes a third possible "transitional" type of court, although it was referred to at the time of survey as a "north-south Snaketown" type.

If these three "north-south Snaketown" ball courts are indeed transitional between an earlier and a later ball-court development in the Southwest, then they should meet two basic requirements quite aside from size and orientation. (1)

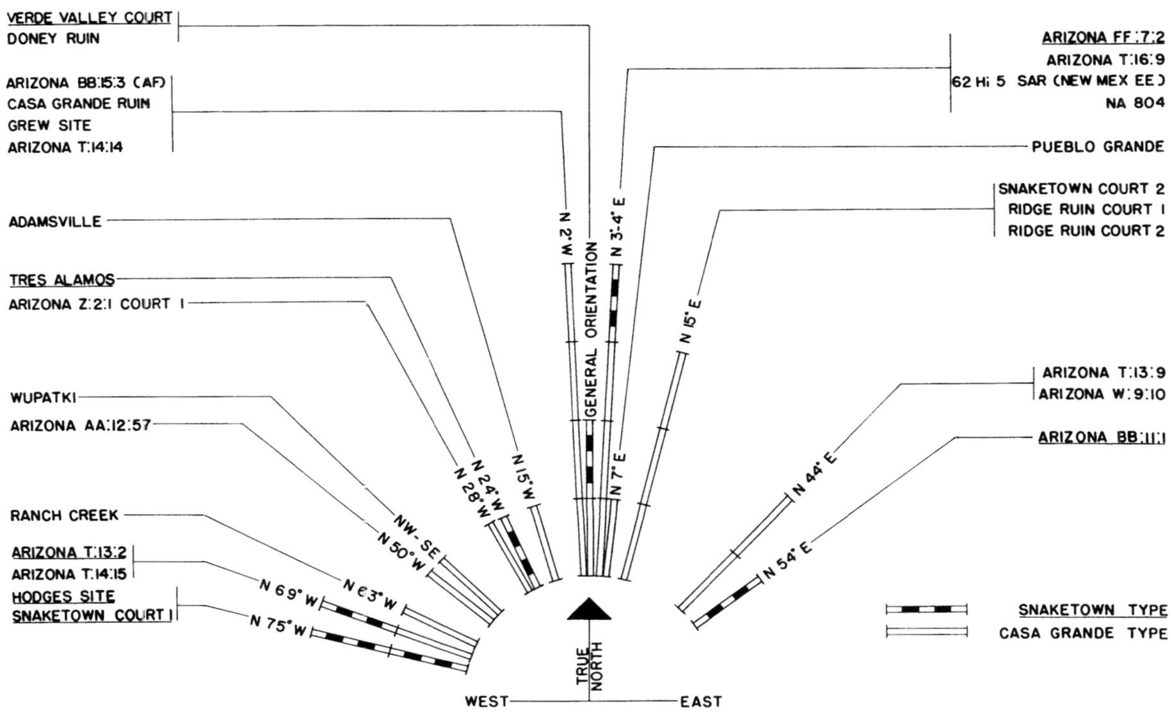

Fig. 46. Orientation of Southwestern ball courts. These have been selected (1) to encompass a wide geographical area and (2) within the area of concentration to include only those in which enough testing has been done so that orientation of the long axis could be more precisely determined.

Such a change should have taken place in the Hohokam area where the ball-court idea was first received and developed (there are as many ball courts in the limited Gila-Salt area of central Arizona as in all the rest of the state combined), and (2) it should be possible to demonstrate that the Snaketown type of court definitely appeared earlier than the Casa Grande type, regardless of any later overlap. The first of these requirements can easily be dismissed. None of the three possible "transitional" courts is located in – or particularly near – the central Hohokam area. Indeed, this fact was noted by Schroeder (1949a: 30) for the first two of these courts. Before proceeding to a consideration of the temporal sequence of ball-court types, it will be well to digress long enough to firm up, by means of redefinition based on the foregoing discussion, the significant differences between two types of ball courts.

We recognize two basic types of ball courts in the Southwest. One of these may still be called the Snaketown type, characterized as having absolutely the longer center field of the two types. At present the known range of center-field length for six courts within this type is about 13 m. There is a tendency for the Snaketown type of court to be oriented east-west, but the range of variation extends to almost due north-south. This type of court usually, if not always, has end fields, and the center field has relatively parallel sides. The second type of court, which may still be referred to as the Casa Grande type, has absolutely the shorter center field of the two types. The known range of length for 14 courts of the Casa Grande type is about 15 m., and the longest center field is 19.5 m. less than the shortest Snaketown type. There is some tendency for the Casa Grande courts to be oriented north-south, although the range of variation extends to nearly east-west. The Casa Grande type has small end units or entrances too small to accommodate end fields, and the shape of the center field is decidedly oval or bulbous. It must be expected that within these two types of ball courts there may be considerable variation in detail. If there can be general agreement on this redefinition of ball court types, based now primarily on size and only secondarily on other criteria, the temporal relationships of the

Snaketown and Casa Grande courts may be considered.

Only three – or four if one is willing to include the court at Tres Alamos – Snaketown-type ball courts have been excavated or tested in the Southwest. One of these was Court No. 1 at Snaketown which Haury was able to say was probably constructed during the Gila Butte phase of the Colonial period (Gladwin and others 1937: 40–41). The second was the ball court at the Hodges site in the Tucson area, which was not tested sufficiently to determine its age (Haury, personal communication 1963). The third was the court at the Citrus site (Ariz. T:13:2), reported herein, which was built and used entirely within the Sacaton phase of the Sedentary period. Dating of the Tres Alamos ball court was not attempted in the site report (Tuthill 1947), but it would appear to date from the time of the Santa Cruz or Sacaton phases (Tuthill 1950: 57–58). There is no question about the fact that other known, but unexcavated, Snaketown-type courts exist in sites with strong Colonial-period components. However, surface indications are not always infallible. The Painted Rocks-area ball court at Ariz. T:14:15, a small court oriented east-west, was thought on the basis of surface pottery to be Gila Butte phase in time but excavation proved that it was built during the Sacaton phase.

Prior to the Painted Rocks Reservoir project, all of the small, Casa Grande-type ball courts that have been excavated have been thought to date from the Sacaton phase of the Sedentary period, or later, or in the Flagstaff and Verde areas from late Pueblo II or later. Included in this group would be Court No. 2 at Snaketown, the three courts tested by Pinkley, the court at Pueblo Grande, the courts tested by McGregor (1941: 83–89), the Sacred Mountain ball court tested by Schroeder (1949b), the San Simon court (Sayles 1945: 31–32), the court at Ariz. BB:15:3 (Amerind Foundation survey number) excavated by DiPeso (1951: 257–60), and the ball court at the Stove Canyon site (Ariz. W:9:10) in the Point of Pines area (Johnson 1961: 565–66). In addition to these, all of the ball courts tested in the Gila Bend area and reported herein, with two exceptions, also date from the Sacaton phase. However, in the Gila Bend area, the ball court at the Rock Ball Court site (Ariz. T:13:9) appears to have been built during the Gila Butte phase, while Court No. 1 at the Gatlin site (Ariz. Z:2:1) was built during the Santa Cruz phase, and was remodeled during the Sacaton phase. On the basis of size, the primary criterion used here for the classification of ball courts, the court at the Rock Ball Court site falls well within the range of the Casa Grande type, in spite of some of the apparently unique idiosyncrasies of this court. The bulging sides of the center field of this court, as a secondary criterion, also indicate that it should be considered as one of the Casa Grande courts. Similarly, it is doubtful if anyone would challenge assignment of Court No. 1 at the Gatlin site to the Casa Grande type.

There is, then, one Snaketown-type court and one Casa Grande-type court which probably date from the Gila Butte phase of the Colonial period, with other courts of both types dating from later horizons. One other ball court that may be as early as these Gila Butte phase courts has been reported by Brandes (1957). It is the Ranch Creek Court, a Casa Grande type oriented nearly east-west (Fig. 46). This would hardly seem a strong enough basis on which to claim that one type did or did not precede the other in the Hohokam area. With reference to the "transitional" court problem, the present evidence does not indicate any order of priority, and thus the second basic requirement for defining a transitional stage in ball-court type development in the Southwest has not been met either. For the present, therefore, it seems best to consider the three "north-south Snaketown" courts as such and not as transitional in a developmental sequence that took place in the Hohokam area. Parenthetically, it might be pointed out that the time of construction of these "north-south Snaketown" courts has not been determined.

One further consideration remains. "The change from the Snaketown court to the Casa Grande type court is marked by a contraction in size, a degeneration of the end units, and a shift in orientation" (Schroeder 1949a: 30), and this degeneration is also marked by the change in shape of the center fields from those with nearly parallel sides to those with decidedly bulbous sides. All of these changes appear to be degenerate in the sense that they lead farther and farther away from the basic concept of a Mesoamerican ball court. On this stylistic basis, the Snaketown type of ball court would certainly appear to be ancestral to the Casa Grande type of court, but if this is the case, the change may already have taken place by the time both types of court reached the Southwest. If this were the case, it might mean that the two types of courts were introduced to the Hohokam area along different routes of diffusion, but at about the same time.

Regardless of the route or routes involved in the transmission of the trait, a Mesoamerican origin for Hohokam ball courts is fairly certain. The distribution of Mesoamerican court types extends from Casas Grandes, Chihuahua (Wasley 1959: 148; 1960a: 445), where the appearance is on a late time horizon, south to Honduras and El Salvador (Proskouriakoff 1956: 441; Wicke 1957: 55), but the concentrations seem to be in the Valley of Mexico and in the Maya area. In the latter area, for instance, Smith (1955, Table 1) located 40 ball courts in a survey of a restricted section of central Guatemala.

Many features characteristic of Mesoamerican courts are not recognizable in ball courts of the Southwest. Two factors may account for these differences. First of all, the ball-court idea was introduced from Mesoamerica into an area a great distance from the major centers of ball-court concentration. Changes that took place in the course of this diffusion probably account for some of the differences. Secondly, other variations may be a result of using different building materials: earth in the Southwest and dressed stone masonry in Mesoamerica.

The only example of ball-court remodeling in the Gila Bend area was observed in Ball Court 1 at the Gatlin site. This is not a unique feature, since the Snaketown type court at Snaketown was remodeled twice (Gladwin and others 1937: 41), and one of the Ridge Ruin courts was remodeled five times (McGregor 1941: 86). Ball court remodeling is also known from Mesoamerica. The court at Yagul, for instance, was reconstructed once (Wicke 1957, Fig. 31).

Upward-sloping extensions of the ball-court ends in Casa Grande-type courts have previously been labeled entrances (Gladwin and others 1937, Fig. 13). With one exception, wherever it was possible to define these features in the Gila Bend courts, they conform to this pattern. The one exception was in the southeast end of Court 1 at the Gatlin site, where an extension conforming in general outline and shape was found, but which had almost no slope at all (Fig. 11, profile F-G).

A noticeable difference between the Casa Grande-type courts of the Gila Bend area and previously excavated examples from other areas in the Southwest is the lack of end markers in the former group. Possibly they did not occur in the Gila Bend area, possibly they were not preserved, or possibly they were not recognized during excavation. However, center markers were found, and they differed in type from one court to another, exhibiting about as much variation as elsewhere in the Southwest.

Although the extent of preservation varied from court to court in the Gila Bend area, enough information was obtained to indicate that sloping sides were consistent features. In some cases these sloping sides were constructed by applying caliche plaster to the sides of the excavation made for the ball court, and sometimes to the surfaces of the earth mounds built up above the court excavations. The angle of slope averaged about 15° with no great range of variation. It was impossible to determine the original height of the caliche-plastered side walls because in many cases there was evidence that the upper portions had been removed by erosion.

The only Snaketown type of ball court tested in the Gila Bend area was at the Citrus site (Fig. 22). One of the interesting features of this court was the cobble facing over the sloping sides and end unit. An examination of the literature on ball courts in the Southwest indicates that stone facings are not unknown, but neither are they very common in the Hohokam area. The most striking use of stone in ball-court construction in the Southwest is at Wupatki, where the walls of a Casa Grande type of court were constructed entirely of this material (McGregor 1936: 55; 1941: 88). Stone also appears to have been used in the end unit of the court at N.A. 804 northwest of Wupatki (McGregor 1936, Fig. 1). Farther south, along Beaver Creek, Schroeder (1949b: 56) noted the presence of numerous river boulders on the crest of the ridges of the Sacred Mountain ball court. Near Rimrock in the Verde Valley, Schroeder (1951b: 61) recorded another Casa Grande type of court with a "surrounding low embankment composed of earth with a course or two of boulder rock being evident along the interior base of the court." Recently a Casa Grande type of court was tested during the course of a survey along the Gila River near Safford, Arizona. The test disclosed the presence of cobbles in the earth ridges, which may have formed a facing (Tuohy 1960, Fig. 5).

The use of stone in ball courts of the Verde and Flagstaff areas seems not so unusual in a region where strong influences from the Anasazi architectural tradition are bound to be felt. However, cobble facings on ball courts of the Hohokam area are not at all in the Hohokam architectural tradition in which stone was almost never used. If the cobble facing in the court at the Citrus site was an attempt to control erosion of the court sides, it is difficult to explain why this appears to be a unique occurrence and not a fairly common trait in Hohokam ball courts. River cobbles were similarly used on the basal portion of Stage VI of the platform mound at the Gatlin site (Wasley 1960b: 257).

An alternative explanation for the occasional use of cobble facings in the Hohokam area is that they represent a watered-down survival of the Mesoamerican emphasis on the use of stone. If this were the case, the trait would represent still another Mesoamerican feature in the Hohokam area.

BURIAL PRACTICES

Cremation was the typical method of disposal of the dead among the Hohokam (Haury 1945a: 43). In the Anasazi (Haury 1945: 43) and Mogollon areas (Wheat 1955: 66–71) inhumation was the common practice.

Although few examples are known, inhumation may have been the burial pattern throughout the span of the Cochise culture. Perhaps the oldest-known human remains from southern Arizona come from Sonora F:10:17, a Cochise site dating either to the Sulphur Spring or Chiricahua stage, situated some nine miles northwest of Douglas, Arizona (Sayles and Antevs 1941: 50–51). The first evidence of formal inhumation burial seems to date to the San Pedro stage of the Cochise sequence. In the Cienega Creek Basin of southeastern Arizona, Eddy (1958: 52) excavated eight inhumations which had been placed in pits in a midden deposit. Other pre-ceramic burials are known from Ventana Cave (Haury 1950: 460).

Pre-ceramic occurrences of cremations are rare in the Southwest, but are known from the Cienega site at Point of Pines (Haury 1957: 11), in the Guadalupe Mountains of New Mexico (Howard 1935: 67–69), and at the mouth of the Pecos River in Texas (Cosgrove 1947: 162–63).

The early occurrence of both of these types of disposal of the dead perhaps indicates that the two methods were known as alternatives to the people of the Cochise culture. If so, this could explain the striking difference in burial methods of the Hohokam and Mogollon, since both cultures are believed to be derived from the Cochise pattern (Haury 1943: 260–63; Martin and others 1952: 500–501). In this interpretation, the Hohokam may have selected the alternative of cremation, while the Mogollon chose inhumation as the preferred method.

Be this as it may, it is apparent that by the first phase in the Hohokam sequence, Vahki, the practice of cremation was a definite trait in the Hohokam culture (Gladwin and others 1937: 95). Although there are variations in the techniques of burying the cremations, the practice continues until the end of the Hohokam sequence (Haury 1945: 43). Late in the Hohokam sequence during the Sacaton phase (Gladwin and others 1937: 93) and in the Classic period (Haury 1945a: 209), inhumations occur in Hohokam sites. The later occurrences have been attributed to the Salado invasion (Haury 1945a: 209).

In the Mogollon area, by way of contrast, inhumation is the most prevalent method of burial through all of the periods (Wheat 1955: 66–71). Cremations appear in Mogollon sites during late horizons, but these are far from common. In the Mimbres area, 1,009 inhumations were found at the Swartz Ruin as opposed to only 6 cremations (Cosgrove and Cosgrove 1932: 23, 111). At the Point of Pines ruin (Ariz. W:10:50), cremations are only slightly outnumbered by inhumations on the Pueblo III and Pueblo IV horizons. With the exception of the early Cienega Creek finds, however, inhumation was the only method of disposal of the dead in the Point of Pines area until the Tularosa phase, the local Pueblo III equivalent (Breternitz 1959: 67–68; Wheat 1954: 74). Another Mogollon area where cremation appears on a late time horizon is the San Simon branch. In this region, inhumation is the only method of disposal of the dead until the Encinas phase which is equated with the Sacaton phase of Hohokam sequence in time. During the Encinas phase a few cremations appear, but inhumation remains the prevailing technique. Interestingly enough, it is during the Encinas phase that Hohokam influence is most strongly felt in this area (Sayles 1945: 62–68, Fig. 32).

In the Gila Bend area, data on burial methods were collected for the Gila Butte phase, the Sacaton phase, and the Classic period of the Hohokam sequence. The two Gila Butte-phase cremations, which were found at the Rock Ball Court site (Ariz. T:13:9), were simple pits cut into native caliche. Each contained a quantity of calcined bone and some mesquite charcoal. No offerings accompanied the cremations.

Three types of cremations could be assigned to the Colonial-period occupation at Snaketown. One type consisted of pits which contained burned bones, charcoal, and offerings. A second type was marked by a number of small holes placed close together and filled with bones and offerings. Pits or trenches filled with small sherds, apparently the remains of offerings, and some calcined bone account for the third type (Gladwin and others 1937: 93–95).

At Roosevelt:9:6, pit cremations were the pattern. Holes from one to three feet in depth were dug into sterile soil. Calcined human bone and the burned remains of offerings were placed in the pits. In several cases no offerings accompanied the cremations (Haury 1932: 113). In the Salt River Valley, pit cremations including a few offerings were common during the Gila Butte phase (Schroeder 1940: 140). Pit cremations were also found in Colonial-period associations at the Grewe site (Woodward 1931: 11).

From the considerable amount of information which has been gathered on Colonial-period burial practices, it is apparent that pit cremations occurred most commonly. The two cremations discovered at the Rock Ball Court site conform to this pattern established by the excavation of a number of other sites.

The practice of gathering together the larger bone fragments and offerings from the crematorium and depositing them in pits continued as the Hohokam custom through the Satcaton phase (Gladwin and others 1937: 93). Two of the cremations at the Citrus site (Ariz. T:13:2) were of this type, as were those at the Gatlin site according to information obtained from Norton Allen (Wasley 1960b: 245). The meager amount of information obtained on Sacaton-phase cremations in the Gila Bend area indicates that the pattern defined at Snaketown (Gladwin and others 1937: 93) was followed in the Gila Bend area.

In the case of one cremation from the Citrus site, the calcined bone fragments were found in a plainware jar, which was covered by an inverted bowl. This method of burying the cremated remains which becomes the common practice during the Classic period (Gladwin and others 1937: 92), apparently had earlier beginnings as is indicated by the Citrus-site discovery. In addition to the cremations, two Sacaton-phase crematoriums were excavated in the Gila Bend area. One of these, found at the Gatlin site, was a large rectangular pit, and the other, at the Citrus site, was a circular pit. Crematoriums were also found at Snaketown (Gladwin and others 1937: 95). They differed from those in the Gila Bend area in being oval pits, of sufficient size to hold an adult body. Apparently they were in use during the Colonial and Sedentary periods.

Burial practices of the Classic period in the Gila Bend area include both inhumations and cremations. Examining first the cremations, it was noted in the above descriptions that these are of a special type designated as primary cremations. Essentially these are long oval pits in which the body was cremated and the bones and offerings left in place.

On the surface, this would seem to be a marked contrast with Hohokam areas farther east where the custom during the Classic period was to gather up the calcined bone fragments and bury them in a pottery vessel (Gladwin and others 1937: 92). A closer examination of the data collected on Classic-period primary cremations in the Gila Bend area indicates, however, that there are significant parallels with Hohokam sites to the east. In the case of two of the excavated primary cremations, the larger fragments of calcined bone were concentrated in one section of the pit. In one case a pottery vessel rested upright on the pile of bones, and in the second a bowl was inverted over the bones. In addition, in the case of Primary Cremation 2 at Ariz. Z:1:11, the bones were gathered up and buried under an inverted bowl some distance from the pit. These examples would seem to indicate a closer parallel between the two areas than is apparent from an examination of the gross forms of the two types of cremation burial.

Ethnographic data collected from Yuman-speaking groups indicate that both techniques were practiced. The Yuma (Forde 1931: 208) and the Yavapai (Gifford 1936: 302–303) both had primary cremations. The Cocopa (Forde 1931: 208) cremated the dead separately from the place of actual burial.

In summary, it appears that the general Hohokam practice was to cremate the body in a pit and to gather together the larger fragments of bones for separate burial. Both this method and the other of leaving the remains in the crematorium were practiced in California, and by Yuman-speaking groups. As it is probable that Yuman-speaking groups were in the Gila Bend area during the Classic period, it is possible that the practice of primary cremation was adopted by the Hohokam from these groups. Large fragments of bone are often piled together under a pottery vessel in the primary cremations of the Gila Bend area, and this feature was a Classic-period Hohokam practice. Perhaps a fusion of the two techniques is indicated.

Classic-period inhumations were found in the Gila Bend area at Ariz. T:14:11 and Ariz. T:14:12. It has been suggested that inhumations occurring in Classic-period sites were made by the puebloan Salado invaders of southern Arizona (Haury 1945a: 43–49). While this may have been true in Salado sites of the Gila-Salt area, it is doubtful that inhumations were made by, and for, the Salado in the Gila Bend area where there is little evidence of Salado contact and no evidence of Salado occupation. The Hohokam trait of inhumation burial in the Gila Bend area may have been borrowed either from the Salado or from the desert Hohokam of the Papagueria where inhumation was apparently a common practice (Haury 1950: 6–13).

The recent statement (Ezell 1963b: 63) that the Pima burial pattern of inhumation is not in the Hohokam tradition of cremation loses its significance as an argument against a Hohokam-Pima culture continuum when two other facts are taken into consideration. First, apparently during the Classic period at least, the Hohokam as well as the Salado were practicing inhumation. Second, the Pima used to cremate their war dead (Russell 1908: 52, 194; Ezell 1961: 90–92). In the light of this information it can be suggested that there has merely been a change in preference from one method of burial to another over a period of time, and that this change began late in Hohokam prehistory and culminated not long ago in modern Pima history. The obscuring cloud over this situation has been the fact that this change, if it did take place as suggested above, happened during a period for which we have little information from archaeology and history.

POTTERY AND ARTIFACTS

On the basis of macroscopic examination, Hohokam painted pottery from the Gila Bend area is indistinguishable from that found in Hohokam sites farther east such as Snaketown (Gladwin and others 1937). It is possible that more detailed analyses would succeed in distinguishing local varieties, on the basis of differing mineral constituents in the paste. These detailed studies were not made, however, and on the basis of the more obvious characteristics such as paint, slip, and design, the types from the two areas appear to be essentially the same.

Haury (1932: 116–26) has previously called attention to the uniformity of Hohokam pottery from different sites during the Colonial period. The present study indicates that this uniformity is also present during the Sedentary period, as Sacaton Red-on-buff sherds from the Gila Bend sites are essentially the same as those from Snaketown (Gladwin and others 1937: 171–78). This ceramic similarity argues for a uniformity of Hohokam culture during the Colonial and Sedentary periods. Contacts between the various Hohokam villages during these periods must have been frequent and of a peaceful nature for the widespread dissemination of standard techniques of pottery manufacture.

By way of contrast, Classic-period painted pottery in the Gila Bend area indicates the possible breakdown of earlier contacts and the establishment of closer ties with other areas. Specifically, Tanque Verde Red-on-brown appears as a frequent occurrence in Classic-period sites, indicating closer relationships with the Tucson area or with Papagueria.

Plain or utility pottery from Hohokam sites in the Gila Bend area can be distinguished, on the basis of macroscopic examination, from plainware which has been recovered from Hohokam sites farther east. The essential difference between the Gila Bend plainware and that of Snaketown (Gladwin and others 1937: 205–11), for instance, is the lack of mica in quantity in the paste of the former and its presence in quantity in the latter. This difference can probably be attributed to the utilization of differing local sources of materials.

Artifacts recovered from the various Hohokam sites in the Gila Bend area were quite comparable to those found during the excavation of Snaketown (Gladwin and others 1937). In this respect they reinforce the postulated uniformity of Hohokam culture over wide areas mentioned above in the discussion of the pottery from the sites. One significant difference is in the quantity of artifacts found in Gila Bend sites, and at Snaketown. It is obvious from a perusal of the Snaketown report (Gladwin and others 1937) that a much larger quantity of artifacts was obtained from this site.

There are several factors which suggest explanations for this difference. First is the greater size of Snaketown, and the fact that the site was occupied over a long period of time. The combination of these two factors, in part, explains the concentration of artifacts which was found at the site. In addition, an interesting statement referring specifically to stone palettes is that "while an occasional fragment was found in rubbish, no other objects appeared so consistently with cremations" (Gladwin and others 1937: 121). Since artifact proveniences are not given in the Snaketown report, a search through the raw data recorded as a result of the Snaketown program seemed in order.

An examination of all the catalog cards pertaining to Snaketown was made to determine how many of the artifacts from the site had been found with cremations and how many came from other excavation units, such as houses, trash mounds, test trenches, etc. The artifacts from Snaketown are recorded on over 3,000 cards, and many of the cards include several artifacts of a particular kind from a specific provenience. As the actual number of specimens is not always listed, some skewing of the sample is undoubtedly present. Despite this factor, it is apparent that approximately 50 per cent of the Snaketown artifacts came from cremations. The other 50 per cent were recovered from all of the other excavation units at the site.

These percentage determinations suggest another explanation for the lack of artifacts in quantity in the Gila Bend area. Only a few cremations were found during the current work, and judging from the Snaketown situation the artifact sample would have been greatly increased had it been possible to excavate more of these features. At this point it is worth noting that the cremations which were excavated by amateurs at the Gatlin site (Ariz. Z:2:1) produced artifacts in quantity (Wasley 1960b: 244–45). A good deal of time was devoted, during the second season at the Gatlin site, to attempt to locate additional cremations. The effectiveness of earlier efforts by relic collectors became apparent when no undisturbed cremations were found.

The descriptions and illustrations of the artifacts from the Norton Allen collection from the Gila Bend area, which are included in Appendix A of this report, give a rough idea of the quality and quantity of artifacts which might have been obtained had the Arizona State Museum program been accomplished some 30 years earlier.

MESOAMERICAN INFLUENCES

One of the biases stated in the preface was a predilection on the part of the authors for the notion that Mesoamerican influence on Hohokam culture, expressed often in subtle ways, might be greater than it has generally been considered to be. To keep this discussion within bounds, mention will not be made of such obvious traits as ball courts, copper bells, or modeled spindle whorls, to list only a few which have been amply treated elsewhere (Haury 1945b). While some, or perhaps all, of the traits which are discussed in this section may have an ultimate Mesoamerican derivation, it is recognized that more direct evidence is needed in many cases to substantiate such claims.

Certainly one of the highlights of the work in the Gila Bend area was the excavation of the platform mound at the Gatlin site (Wasley 1960b). The original structure was modified and enlarged through five subsequent stages of construction. The mound consisted of earth and trash fill covered with adobe or caliche veneer. After most of these remodelings the flat-topped structure had sloping sides. No evidence of stairs or ramps was encountered, but there were hearths associated with two of the tops and the post-hole outline of a rectangular structure on top of the Stage IV mound. Ancillary mounds connected to the main mound unit by radial walls were in use during part of the history of this mound complex. This ceremonial platform mound, as well as the concept of periodic enlargement, is seen to represent a northward extension into the Hohokam area of the Mesoamerican pyramid idea.

The Gatlin site was tested thoroughly enough to make it clear that there were never many domestic structures at the site. This situation suggests that the Gatlin site may have been a ceremonial center serving a greater or lesser portion of the Gila Bend area during the Sacaton phase. The rich cremations that have come from this site lend weight to this idea. Somewhat in the sense of the minor ceremonial centers described by Bullard (1960: 367–68), the Gatlin site may have served a community of adjacent habitation sites. If this were the case, it could reflect another area of Mesoamerican influence.

At both the Gatlin site and the Citrus site it was noted that only a few of the trash mounds contained the abundance of cultural debris which characterized the mounds excavated at Snaketown. The rest of the mounds contained a considerable amount of relatively clean earth or a large amount of earth dispersed throughout the trash. This gave rise to the idea that the less trashy mounds may have been constructed as substructures for houses, another prominent Mesoamerican feature. However, careful observation in all of these mounds failed to reveal evidence of house floors or features of any sort. If the mounds had been used as house mounds, any caliche or adobe floors on top would have been vulnerable to rapid erosion; the problem still begs solution.

Wall construction at two Classic-period sites, Ariz. T:14:12 and the Fortified Hill site (Ariz. T:13:8) is similar to a type of Anasazi construction which has been called core masonry. Walls of this type have a rubble hearting over which a veneer of dressed stones was placed. The technique apparently appeared among the Anasazi during Pueblo III times (Morris 1939: 41). Walls at the Fortified Hill site have a similar rubble hearting, but the facing, on both sides, is of dry-laid, large, irregular boulders. At Ariz. T:14:12 the rubble core was cemented together with caliche, and the facings consisted of a thick caliche plaster applied directly over the core. Ferdon (1955: 3–4) points out that there appears to be no precedent for core masonry in the Anasazi area, and this also seems to be true for the Hohokam area, where the technique appears as a new trait during the Classic period, post 1100. However, the technique of core masonry was well known in Mesoamerica where it dates back to at least the Classic Maya and Teotihuacan III times. Thus, core masonry would appear to be another trait in the Southwest with possible Mesoamerican origin, although it still remains to be demonstrated conclusively that it did not have a local development.

We have considered here, as of probable or possible Mesoamerican origin, a group of traits extending the list or range of those previously cited (Haury 1945a; Ferdon 1955; Jennings 1956: 91–98). Even taking these additions into consideration, should they prove more valid than we have been able to indicate, we would postulate that Mesoamerican influence arrived in the Southwest by some means other than migration, since the conditions (pp.77–79) for establishing migration beyond a reasonable doubt cannot be met (Haury 1958: 6; Rouse 1958: 64–67).

Thus far we have not considered the possibility of another source of origin for these traits. However, there are parallels in the Mississippian complex of the southern United States. This complex was characterized by an influx of traits of Mesoamerican derivation. The most obvious of these is the pyramidal earthen mound which served as a base for the important dwellings of the community (Griffin 1952a: 361). These mounds were often rebuilt and enlarged (Jennings 1952: 265). Several mounds are grouped around a plaza, and the complex of mounds and plaza formed the heart of a ceremonial center. The earlier domed burial mounds continued in use, and they were occasionally grouped loosely about a pyramidal temple mound, as at the site of Lake George (Jennings 1952: 265). Dates for the Mississippian complex are not firmly established, but there may be contemporaneity with the introduction of some Mesoamerican traits into the Southwest (Griffin 1952b: 369). There are gross similarities between this Mississippian pattern and the situation at the Gatlin and Citrus sites, but regardless of the dating problems, it seems more logical to derive Mesoamerican influences in the Southwest from Mexico than to derive them from the Mississippian complex.

APPENDIX A

Illustrations from the Norton Allen Collection of Artifacts Recovered in the Gila Bend Area

COLONIAL PERIOD

For some 25 years the Norton Allens have been students of Hohokam archaeology in the Gila Bend area. Spending winter months each year at Gila Bend, they have gathered an invaluable collection of Hohokam material, primarily from cremations. Allen's father, Ernest G. Allen, played a major role in amassing this collection through his outstanding ability for being able to locate rich finds. This collection is particularly important to the archaeological profession because it is painstakingly documented. Beyond this, Allen possesses a unique insight into subtle changes in burial pattern within a Hohokam phase, as well as into some of the more elusive changes in burials, ceramic styles, and artifact types and frequencies from one phase to another. This latter aspect of Allen's work should be recorded in published form by Allen himself, for contained in it are the feelings and convictions that come after long reflection and study. This is the type of information, or knowledge, that is most difficult, if not impossible, to record in field notes. It can never be adequately presented, secondhand, by one who was not a part of this total experience.

It was a privilege to be allowed to photograph and to obtain documentation for the Norton Allen collection, as well as to be permitted to present these data as a part of this report. At the same time it is regrettable that the entire collection could not be photographed and that not even all that was photographed can be included here. Presentation has had to be limited to an equitable representation of the collection, permitting more illustrative space to some of the more important finds.

Hohokam materials in the Norton Allen collection were excavated for the most part in the spirit of salvage archaeology: cremations and burials that were exposed by erosion, or purposeful excavation in sites that the Allens knew were to be – or were in the process of being – leveled in the course of agricultural expansion, or in sites that were already being stripped by troops of weekend relic seekers. In quite another sense the Allens were salvage archaeologists in tracking down, sometimes only after the expenditure of considerable time and effort, individuals from Arizona and California known to have collected from the Gila Bend area, finding out what they had collected, and from where, and what had been associated with it.

To some of their sites the Allens gave names. Two of these were changed, perhaps without warrant: the Allens' Big Ball Court site is the Citrus site of this report, and the Gatlin site was the Allens' Gila Bend site. Designations for other sites, such as the Twelve Mile site, referred to the distance of the site by road from the Allens' camp on the Gatlin ranch. Some of these have been referred to in this report simply by the Arizona State Museum site-survey designation: the Allens' Three Mile site has been divided between Ariz. T:14:14 and Ariz. T:14:15. The Allens' Twelve Mile site, however, had been completely destroyed before any of the museum surveys of the area were made.

To provide some continuity and a logical sequence, the Norton Allen collection is presented in terms of the Hohokam phase sequence, beginning with the Gila Butte phase of the Colonial period and ending with the Civano phase of the Classic period. Admittedly this is an arbitrary arrangement, and it involves skipping from one site to another and then back to the first in some instances, but at least a temporal progression is maintained by which cultural change may be more readily perceived.

Two items in the collection should be mentioned at the outset. They have not been illustrated here because they have been dealt with in publications. A large ceramic bell from the Twelve Mile site was the subject of an article by Allen (1953). A report on an etched *Cardium* shell in the Norton Allen collection from the Gatlin site has been made by Pomeroy (1959: 19).

GILA BUTTE PHASE

All of the Gila Butte-phase objects illustrated came from a single site, Ariz. T:14:15. These include a bowl and two scoops from one cremation (Fig. 47), two jars and a scoop associated in another cremation (Fig. 48), and two figurines associated with grooved Gila Butte-phase sherds (Fig. 79*c,e*). The large jar in Figure 48 is the only illustrated vessel with the characteristic exterior grooving. There are about six other sites in the Gila Bend area with evidence of Gila Butte-phase components, one of which, the Rock Ball Court site, is reported here (pp. 5–15).

SANTA CRUZ PHASE

The Santa Cruz-phase material illustrated from the Norton Allen collection came from five sites

Fig. 47. Gila Butte Red-on-buff bowl and scoops from a cremation west of ball court, Arizona T:14: 15. Length of scoop, left, 14.5 cm.

Fig. 48. Gila Butte Red-on-buff vessels from a cremation southwest of ball court, Arizona T:14:15. Jar grooved and painted on exterior. Found in fragments covering calcined bone of cremation. Jar height, 24.8 cm.

Fig. 49. Offerings from Santa Cruz-phase cremation, Twelve Mile site. Santa Cruz Red-on-buff jar and miniature bowl, vesicular basalt pipe, sculptured stone palette, carved stone bowl of vesicular basalt with a rattlesnake representation encircling it. Pipe length, 6.6 cm.

Fig. 50. Carved stone bowl from Santa Cruz-phase cremation, Twelve Mile site. Diameter, 13.4 cm.

Fig. 51. Santa Cruz Red-on-buff jars from Gila Bend area; a, *a site between old Indian school and Sisson's cotton gin;* b, e, f, *Four Mile site;* c, *Citrus site;* d, *north end, Gatlin site. Height of* e, *14.3 cm.*

Fig. 52. Late Santa Cruz Red-on-buff bowl and carved stone effigy pipe from early Sacaton-phase cremation that also contained sherds from a Sacaton Red-on-buff platter. Length of pipe, about 15 cm.

Fig. 53. Late Santa Cruz Red-on-buff jar and palette from cremation, northwest end, Gatlin site. Palette length, 12 cm.

Fig. 54. Late Santa Cruz or early Sacaton Red-on-buff vessels from cremation about one-tenth mile northeast of platform mound, Gatlin site. Bowl has two small animals modeled on rim. Bowl diameter, 13.4 cm.

Fig. 55. Early Sacaton-phase palette, bowl, and jar associated in cremation southwest of platform mound, Gatlin site. Bowl diameter, 7.2 cm.

in the Gila Bend area. In addition, there are about six other sites recorded in the Gila Bend area with Santa Cruz-phase components.

The objects illustrated in Figure 49 came from a single cremation at the Twelve Mile site, a ruin which has been completely leveled during the course of agricultural expansion since the Allens worked there. Before this site was destroyed, Allen noted that there were five Casa Grande-type ball courts, three of which were quite deep and in an excellent state of preservation. The occupation of this ruin was during the Colonial and Sedentary periods.

From another cremation at the Twelve Mile site came a carved stone bowl (Fig. 50). Associated in the same cremation were a miniature palette, burnt shell beads, and sherds of a pottery bowl. The stone bowl with the rattlesnake representation was carved from a reddish vesicular basalt. The vesicles of the basalt had been filled with a matching reddish colored plaster, apparently to give a smoother finished appearance. The interior of the bowl shows a rather pronounced fire blackening. This has been noted in many of the stone and thick-walled ceramic vessels found in the Hohokam area and suggests that they may have been used as incensarios in which some pungent herbaceous material may have been burned.

Santa Cruz Red-on-buff jars from various sites in the Gila Bend area are illustrated in Figure 51. Note the burden-basket carriers represented in *a,* the mountain sheep (desert bighorn) in *b,* and the scorpion-like figures in *c.* This group of vessels illustrates the striking similarity between the Santa Cruz Red-on-buff from the Gila Bend area and that from Snaketown (Gladwin and others 1937, Pls. 154–70).

SANTA CRUZ-SACATON TRANSITION

The latter part of the Santa Cruz phase and the early part of the Sacaton phase is represented by the material in Figures 51*d* and 52-55. The transitional nature of this material is reflected by the presence of traits of both phases in most of it. It is interesting to note that with the exception of the objects shown in Figure 52, all of this transitional material came from the Gatlin site.

SEDENTARY PERIOD

SACATON PHASE

The Sacaton phase is represented in several sites in the Gila Bend area and by many artifacts in the Norton Allen collection. Sacaton Red-on-buff jars are illustrated in Figure 56. Jars *e* and *f* in this figure represent late forms, as well as the late design on *e,* that presage the development of Casa Grande Red-on-buff in the Classic period.

The jar in Figure 56*b* has been restored. It was found broken, in a cremation about one-tenth mile northeast of the platform mound at the Gatlin site. The cremation pit was about 50 cm. deep. In the bottom of the pit was a slight depression in which most of the bones were gathered. These were covered with a large sherd from the bottom of the jar. The other fragments of the jar were piled around and on top of this, along with two rocks and a one-handed mano. On the floor of the pit to the east of the bones was a thick-walled vessel one-third filled with fine fragments of charcoal. The remainder of the thick-walled vessel and of the cremation pit was filled with a light, whitish ash. This pit fill also contained fragments of burnt *Cardium* shell and scattered small pieces of bone. About two-thirds of the way up from the floor of the pit, a niche had been cut into the east side. This niche contained as additional offerings for the cremation a small scoop and a miniature Sacaton Red-on-buff jar.

The jar pictured in Figure 56*d* came from a cremation at the Gatlin site about one-fourth of a mile northwest of the platform mound, along the prehistoric canal. Associated with it were some long, white projectile points (of the type illustrated in Figure 60) and a small hemispherical Gila Plain bowl. A late Sacaton Red-on-buff jar (Fig. 56*e*) came from a cremation about 1 m. deep in a section of the Four Mile site which has since been leveled for cultivation. The jar contained coarse fragments of cremated bone – another late trait – and was covered with a hemispherical Gila Plain bowl.

Fig. 56. Sacaton Red-on-buff jars from Gila Bend area; a, *Twelve Mile site;* b-d, *Gatlin site;* e, *Four Mile site;* f, *Arizona T:14:15. Diameter of* f, *29.2 cm.*

a b

Fig. 57. Sacaton Red-on-buff platters from Gila Bend area; a, *Arizona T:14:15;* b, *Gatlin site. Diameter of* a, *30.5 cm.*

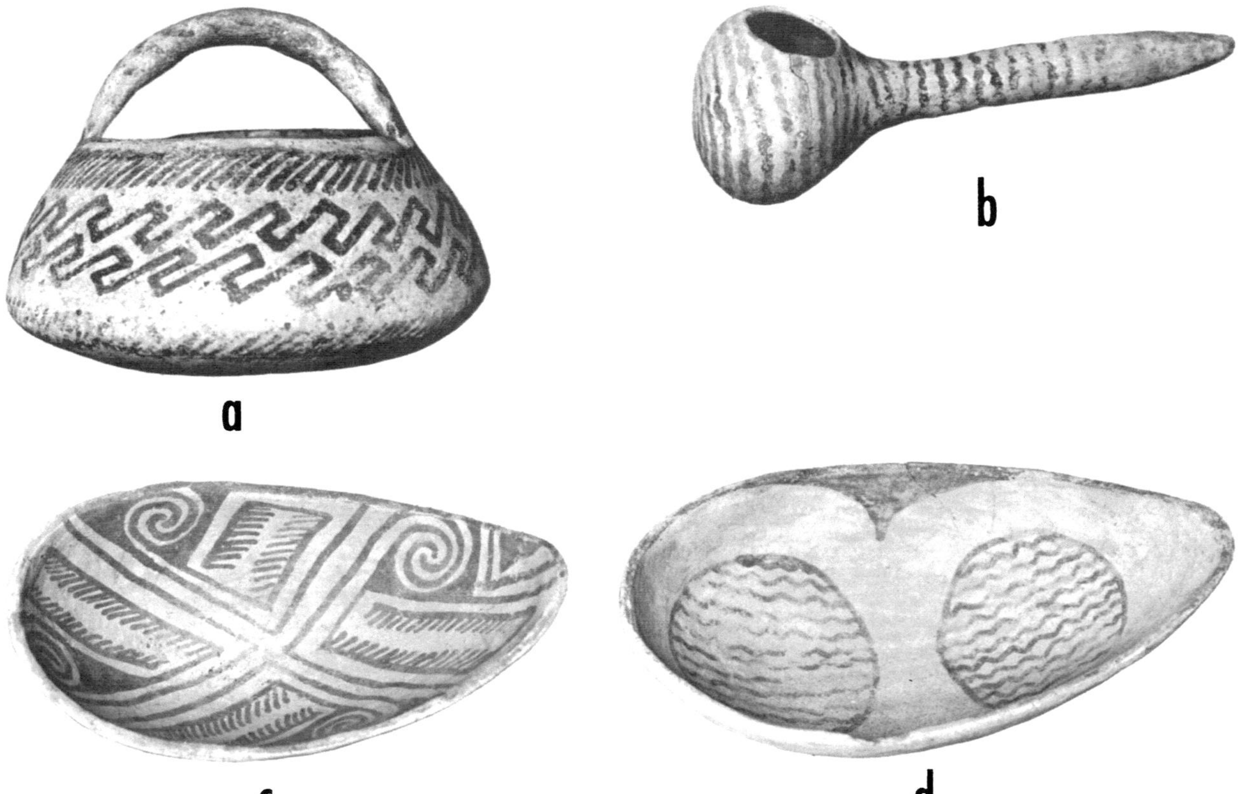

a b c d

Fig. 58. Sacaton Red-on-buff vessels from Gila Bend area; a, *Twelve Mile site;* b, d, *Arizona T:14:15;* c, *Gatlin site. Length of* d, *28 cm.*

In Figure 57 are illustrated two typical Sacaton Red-on-buff platters or large plates. Fig. 57*a* came from a cremation at Ariz. T:14:15 in association with a Sacaton Red-on-buff carinated or shouldered bowl. The platter in Figure 57*b* was found northeast of the platform mound near the prehistoric canal at the Gatlin site. It was associated with the Sacaton Red-on-buff scoop shown in Figure 58*c*.

Two rather unusual vessel forms are illustrated in Figures 58*a* and 58*b*. The former is a bowl with a strap handle of the type usually associated with baskets. The latter is a ceramic dipper or ladle, fashioned to simulate a common gourd-type of dipper. It was found in a cremation just to the east of the ball court at Ariz. T:14:15.

It has been mentioned previously (Wasley 1960b: 245) that a relatively large number of copper bells are known to have come from the Gatlin site. Only a small number of these have found their way into the Norton Allen collection, and they are illustrated in Figure 59. The bell in the bottom row, right, has a double-wire loop or ring. Still lodged within this ring is a small shell disc bead, suggesting that the bell may have been on a string of beads. This bell came from a cremation southwest of the platform mound, associated with the projectile points shown in Figure 60 and Sacaton Red-on-buff sherds.

Two thick-walled Sacaton Red-on-buff effigy vessels, representing mountain sheep (desert bighorn) came from the Gatlin site (Fig. 61). They were found north of the platform mound and north of the prehistoric canal. A third mountain sheep thick-walled effigy vessel, undecorated, came from a cremation at the Citrus site (Fig. 62). Another cremation at the Citrus site produced a small bi-lobed Sacaton Red-on-buff jar (Fig. 63) associated with a beautiful Sacaton Red-on-buff platter (Fig. 64).

Trade pottery from northern Arizona is not common in sites of the Gila Bend area, but in addition to the few sherds that have been reported there are two Black Mesa Black-on-white vessels in the Norton Allen collection. One (Fig. 65) is a canteen from a cremation at the Gatlin site, in which were associated pieces of a Sacaton Red-on-buff platter and long, white projectile points of the type illustrated in Figure 60. The Black Mesa Black-on-white pitcher shown in Figure 66 came from a cremation at the Twelve Mile site in association with a Sacaton shouldered jar containing the cremation, plainware vessels, and some of the typical long, white projectile points.

Shell Cache from the Citrus Site

Certainly one of the richest finds in the Gila Bend area has to be the cache of objects found by the Allens in a portion of the Citrus site which was already under cultivation at the time of the Arizona State Museum work in the area. The location of this cache with respect to the other features of the site is shown in Allen's sketch map (Fig. 67).

Contained in this pit cache were a stone bowl, two chunks of obsidian weighing a half pound or more each, several types of beads, although not many beads altogether, about 235 projectile points, and about 70 carved shell ornaments. There was also a suggestion that there may have been a cotton textile associated. The entire cache had been thoroughly burned, as would have been the case had it accompanied a cremation. However, not a single fragment of calcined bone was found in the pit. The exact number of objects originally placed in the cache could not be determined because of the presence of small fragments without matching parts and because of the evidence of rodent activity.

The burnt shell ornaments constitute the most interesting group of objects in the cache. Included were 11 human representations (Figs. 68–69). Two very similar examples have been reported from the Swarts Ruin (Cosgrove and Cosgrove 1932: 67 and Pl. 76). It would appear that at one time there may have been inlays of some sort for the eyes of the Citrus-site figures. Similar human forms, carved from shell, have also been noted in collections in Guadalajara, Jalisco, Mexico (Haury, personal communication). A recent visitor from Guadalajara, upon seeing the photographs of the figures from the Citrus site, commented that they appeared to be virtually identical to six shell figures recently found in the San Isidro-Cofradia area west of Guadalajara.

Some of these ornaments have a single perforation, indicating that they may have been used as a pendant, but others have two perforations which suggest that they may have been sewn to

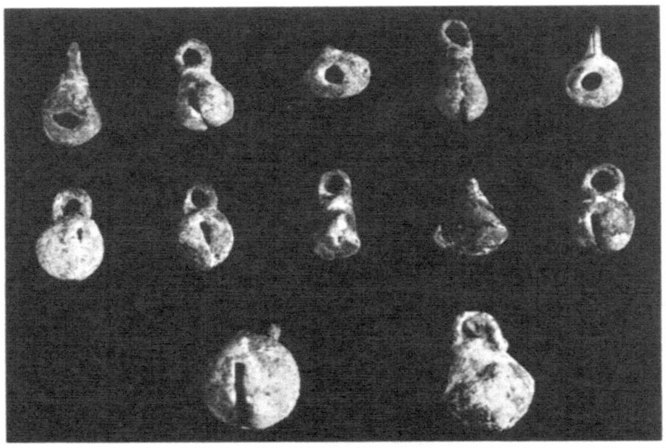

Fig. 59. Copper bells from Gatlin site. Ten small bells obtained by screening back dirt from a looted Sacaton-phase cremation. Bell in lower left from surface. Bell in lower right from cremation described in caption to Fig. 60. Bell diameter, lower left, 1.3 cm.

Fig. 60. Projectile points from Gatlin site; a few of many found in cremation southwest of platform mound. Also in this cremation were a copper bell (Fig. 59) and Sacaton Red-on-buff sherds. Point length, center bottom, 10 cm.

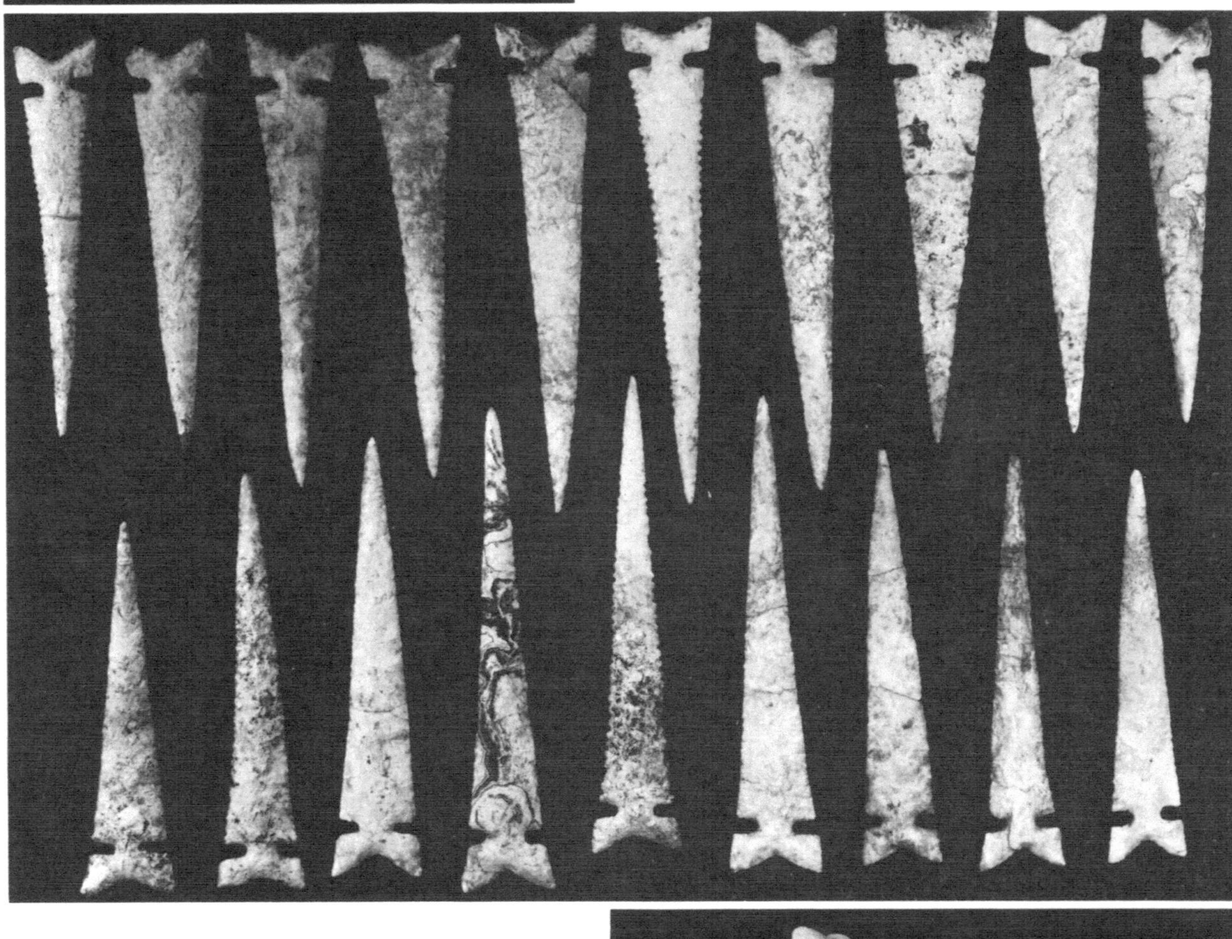

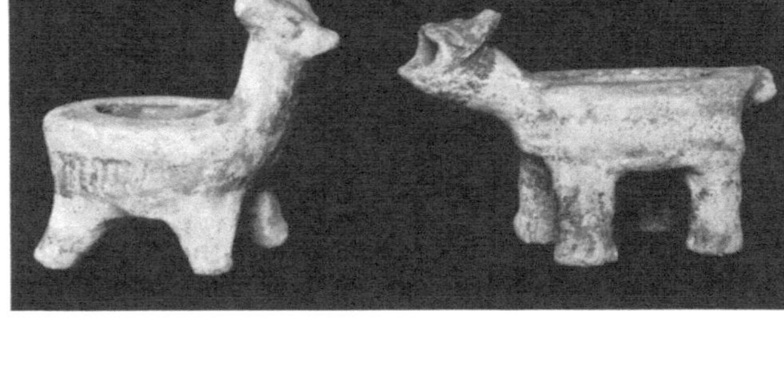

Fig. 61. Sacaton Red-on-buff thick-walled vessels from Gatlin site. Vessel length, right, 15.8 cm.

Fig. 62. Sacaton Buff thick-walled vessel from cremation, Citrus site. Height, 11.4 cm.

Fig. 64. Sacaton Red-on-buff platter, Citrus site, associated with jar Fig.63. Platter diameter, 35 cm.

Fig. 63. Sacaton Red-on-buff bi-lobed jar from cremation, Citrus site, associated with platter, Fig. 64. Jar height, 18.4 cm.

Fig. 65. Black Mesa Black-on-white canteen from cremation, Gatlin site. Height, 10.4 cm.

Fig. 66. Black Mesa Black-on-white pitcher, Twelve Mile site. Height, 4.6 cm.

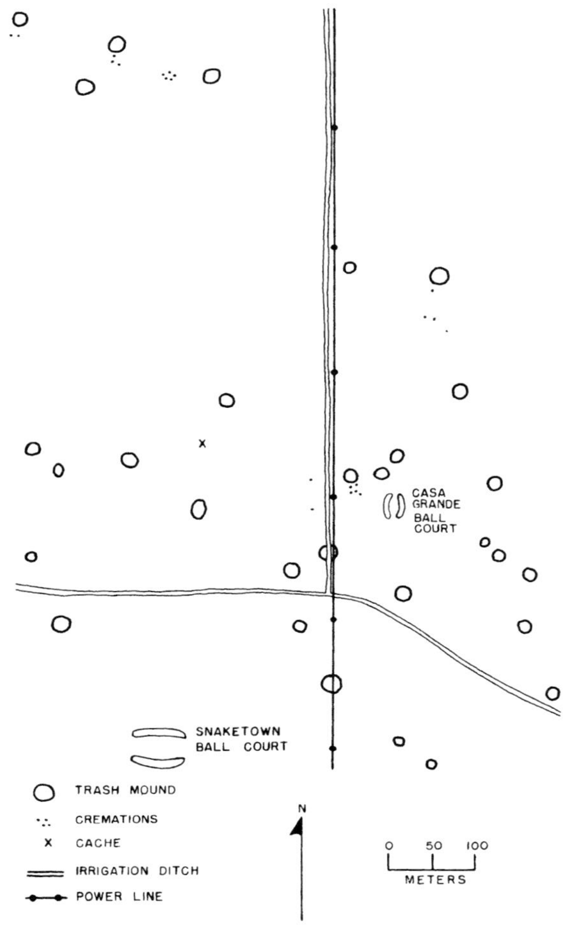

Fig. 67. Norton Allen's sketch map of Citrus site. "X" marks shell cache. Entire area north of irrigation ditch traversing lower portion was leveled for cultivation several years ago.

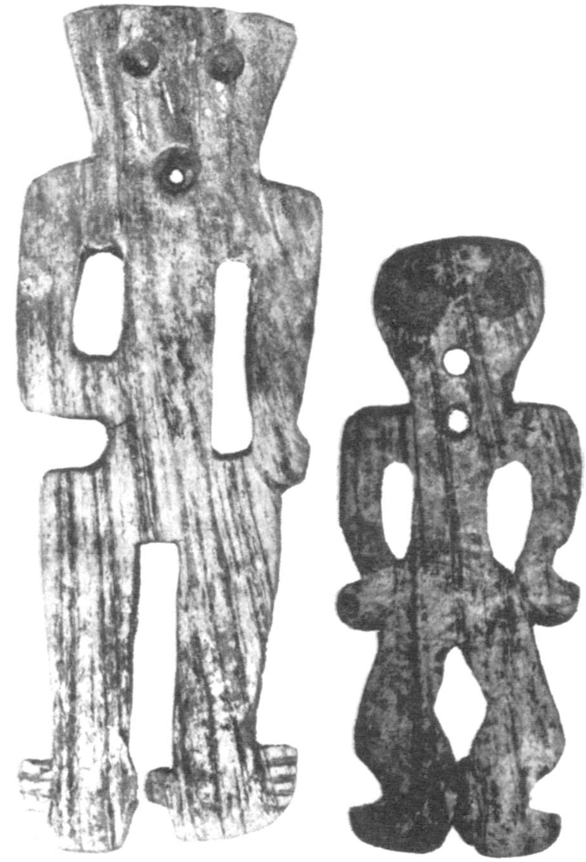

Fig. 68. Carved shell human representations from shell cache, Citrus site. Figure length, left, 7.8 cm.

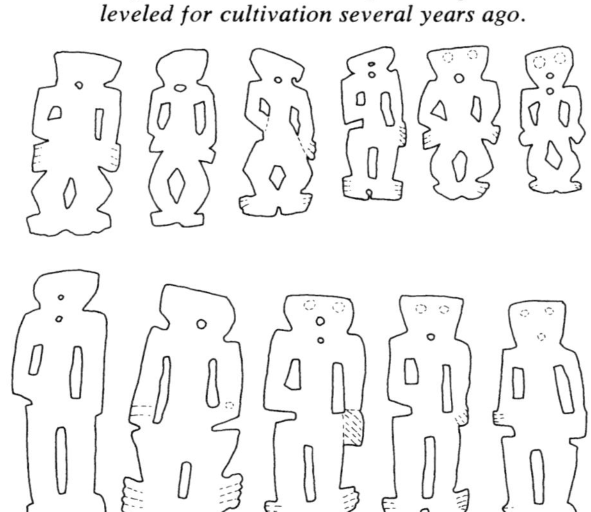

Fig. 69. Outline drawings of the eleven carved shell human representations. Figure length, lower left, 8.8 cm.

Fig. 70. Carved shell birds, shell cache, Citrus site. Bottom figure length, 7 cm. from wing tips.

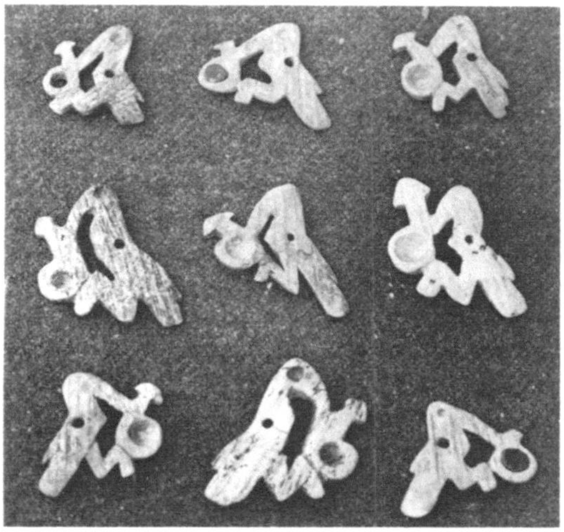

Fig. 71. Carved shell bird-snake representations, shell cache, Citrus site. Head-tail length, lower left, 4.4 cm.

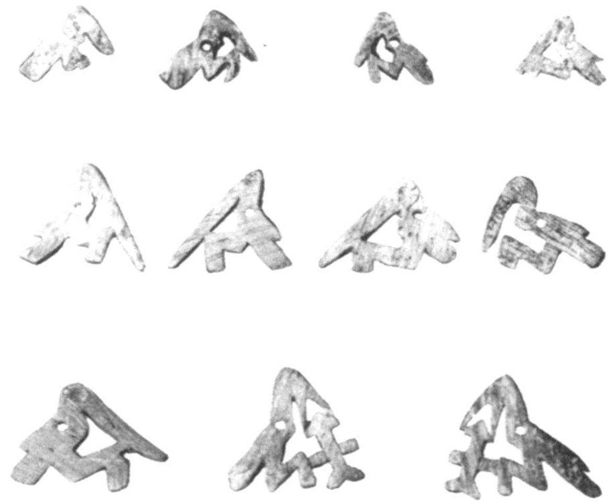

Fig. 72. Carved shell waterfowl representations, shell cache, Citrus site. Head-beak length, lower left, 3.8 cm.

Fig. 73. Close-up of carved shell birds. Head-tail length, upper right, 4.1 cm.

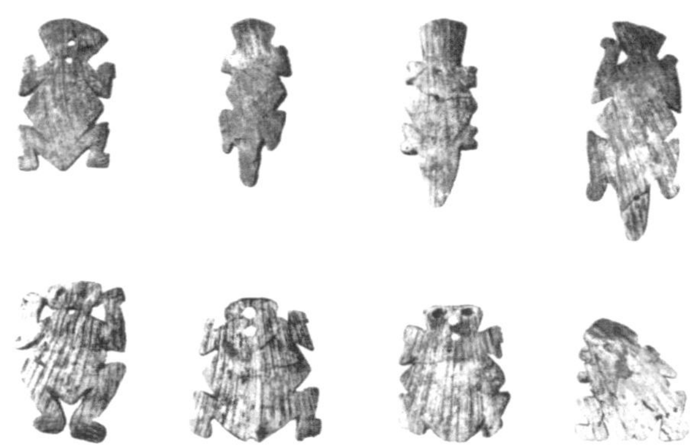

Fig. 74. Carved shell reptiles, shell cache, Citrus site. Length, upper right, 9.3 cm.

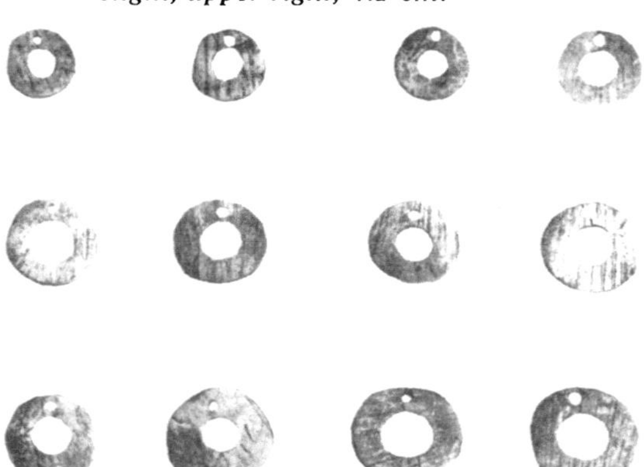

Fig. 75. Disc pendants, shell cache, Citrus site. Diameter, lower left, 3.5 cm.

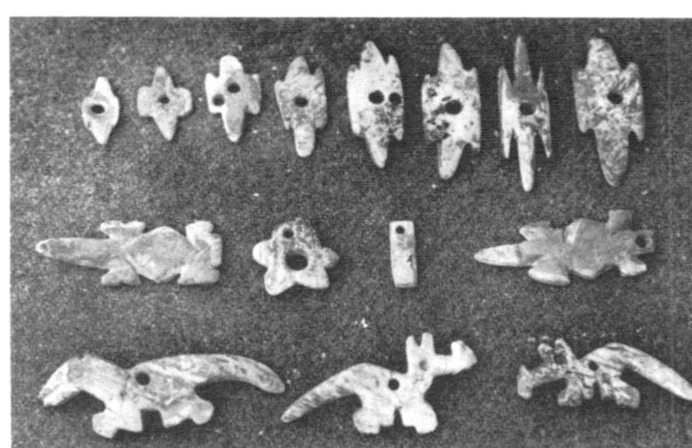

Fig. 76. Miscellaneous ornaments, shell cache, Citrus site. Length, lower left, 5.7 cm.

a garment. This same feature may also be observed for two of the bird ornaments (Fig. 70) and for some of the reptilian representations (Fig. 74).

Two groups of bird representations are of particular interest. One of these groups of ornaments consists of birds holding coiled snakes in their mouths (Fig. 71). Within the coils of two of these (Fig. 71, middle row center and bottom row right) were inlay discs. These also were badly burnt, but the material appears to have been turquoise. Turquoise inlays were described for the two bird-snake ornaments from the Swarts Ruin (Cosgrove and Cosgrove 1932: 67 and Pl. 76). There are depressions for inlays in the coils of the remaining snakes. Shell beads may have been inlaid in the eye depressions (Fig. 73, upper left), as was the case in the examples from the Swarts Ruin.

The second group of bird ornaments seems to represent a pelican-like water fowl (Fig. 72), two of which are shown with fish-like representations in their beaks (Fig. 72, bottom row center and right).

A group of carved shell reptilian representations is shown in Figure 74. There is a question whether the ornament in the lower left corner was intended as a reptile or as a human figure. More stylized ornaments are shown in the bird symbol pendants in the top row of Figure 76, while relatively-plain shell disc pendants are illustrated in Figure 75.

Similarities between the carved shell ornaments from the Citrus site and those from the Swarts Ruin have already been mentioned. The degree of similarity, however, is made more striking by Figure 77 in which objects from the cache at the Citrus site were selected and arranged to simulate the illustration in the Swarts report (Cosgrove and Cosgrove 1932, Pl. 76).

A type of long, white projectile point (Fig. 60) commonly associated with cremations in the Gila Bend area has already been mentioned several times. Another very common type of point, also often associated with cremations, was plentifully represented in the shell cache. Some of these are illustrated in Figure 78.

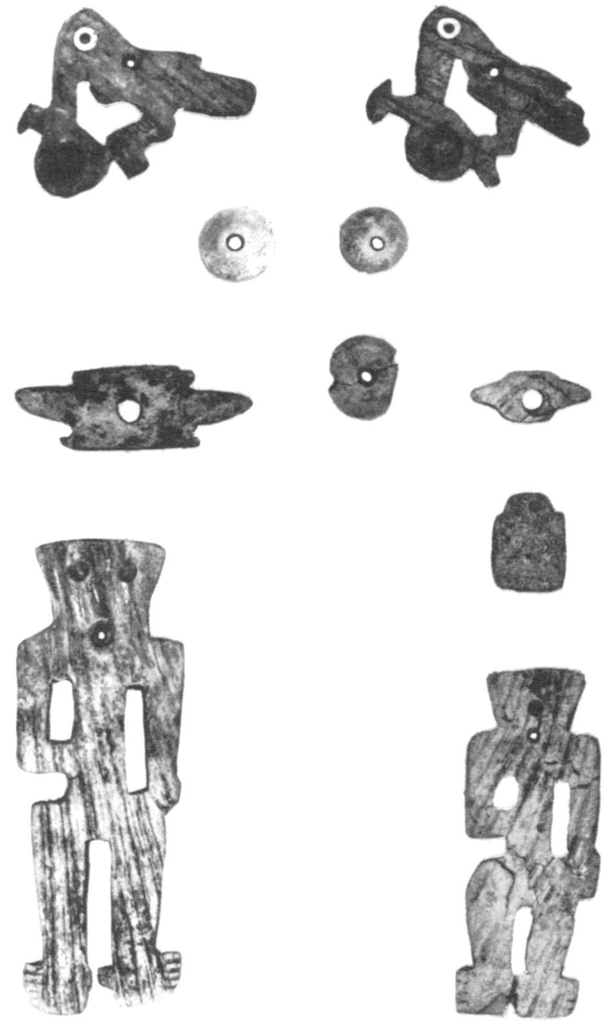

Fig. 77. Shell objects from Citrus site selected and arranged to simulate those illustrated from Swarts Ruin (Cosgrove and Cosgrove 1932, Pl. 76.) Length, lower left, 7.8 cm.

Fig. 78. Some projectile points associated with shell cache, Citrus site. Average length, 4 cm.

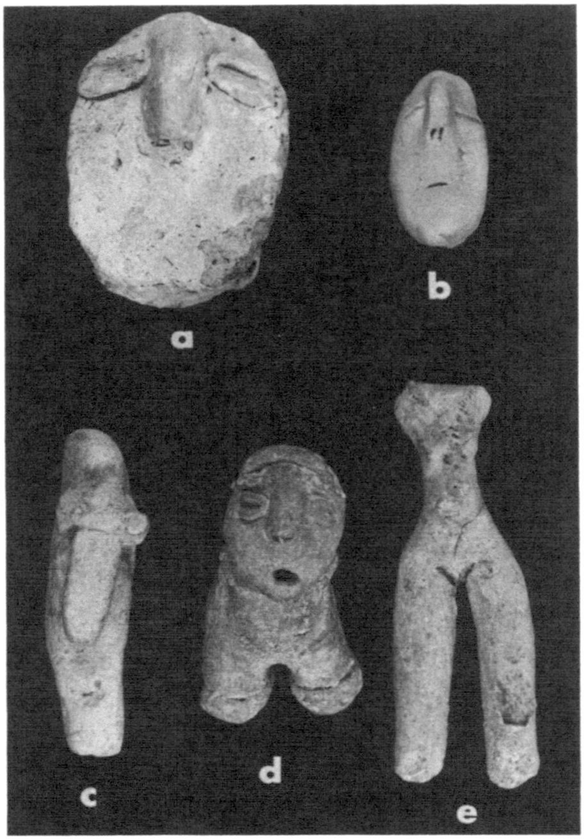

Fig. 79. Clay figurines, Gila Bend area; a, b, *Sacaton phase;* a, *Twelve Mile site;* b, *Citrus site;* c, e, *associated with Gila Butte-phase grooved pottery at Arizona T:14:15;* d, *in mixed Colonial and Sedentary trash at site southwest of old Indian school. Height of c, 8.2 cm.*

Fig. 80. Tanque Verde Red-on-brown bowl from primary cremation, Bartley site. Height, 12.7 cm.

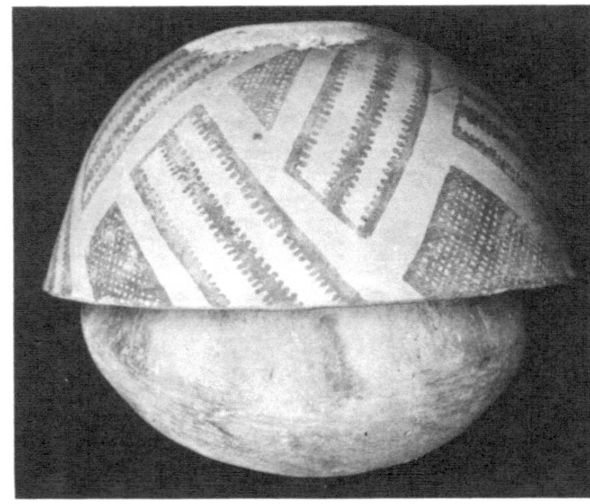

Fig. 81. Jar cremation, Arizona T:14:17, covered with restored Tanque Verde Red-on-brown bowl. Bowl diameter, 29.2 cm.

Fig. 82. Brownware jar and Tanque Verde Red-on-brown bowl from Soho-phase cremation, Arizona T.14:7. Bowl diameter, 25 cm.

Fig. 83. Roosevelt Black-on-white pitcher and brownware bowl from Soho-phase cremation, Arizona T:14:17. Pitcher height, 16.8 cm.

COLONIAL AND SEDENTARY FIGURINES

Fired-clay figurines do not appear to be particularly common in the Gila Bend area. Only two fragmentary specimens were reported from the excavated sites, and these came from the Gila Butte-phase Rock Ball Court site (p. 14). Two additional Gila Butte-phase figurines are illustrated from the Norton Allen collection (Fig. 79*c,e*).

Two other figurines in this collection came from Sacaton-phase associations. Figure 79*a* retains the "coffee bean" eye treatment which is more typical of the Santa Cruz phase, while Figure 79*b* exhibits the more careful modeling characteristic of the Sacaton phase (Gladwin and others 1937: 234–35; Morss 1954: 30–31). A fifth figurine in this collection occurred in mixed Colonial and Sedentary trash, and on the basis of the "coffee bean" eye treatment could be either Santa Cruz or Sacaton in time (Fig. 79*d*).

CLASSIC PERIOD

Most of the Classic-period objects illustrated from the Norton Allen collection have been interpreted by Allen, probably correctly, as coming from Soho-phase associations at the Bartley site (Ariz. T:14:11) and at Ariz. T:14:17.

The Tanque Verde Red-on-brown bowl shown in Figure 80 was found beneath an inverted Soho-phase plainware bowl at the east end of a primary cremation in the Bartley site. The favored burial pattern at the Bartley site appears to have been infant inhumation and adult primary cremation. At Ariz. T:14:17 on the Enterprise Ranch, however, the more typical Hohokam practice of jar cremations appears to have been favored. The Soho-phase plainware jar shown in Figure 81 contained coarse fragments of cremated bone. Two other Soho-phase cremation associations are shown in Figures 82 and 83. The jar in Figure 82 is a hard, smooth, light-brown ware. The bowl in Figure 83 is the same type of pottery, and it has a flat bottom, which is not characteristic of earlier Hohokam pottery.

The shell frog decorated with turquoise mosaic (Fig. 84) was found in a Civano-phase site north of the Twelve Mile site. The square piece in the center is red argillite, sometimes called "Arizona pipestone." This ornament was not found intact, since whatever had been used for "glue" had long ago lost its adhesive properties. However, much of the mosaic patterning marks were still preserved on the shell and were used as the basis for Allen's reconstruction.

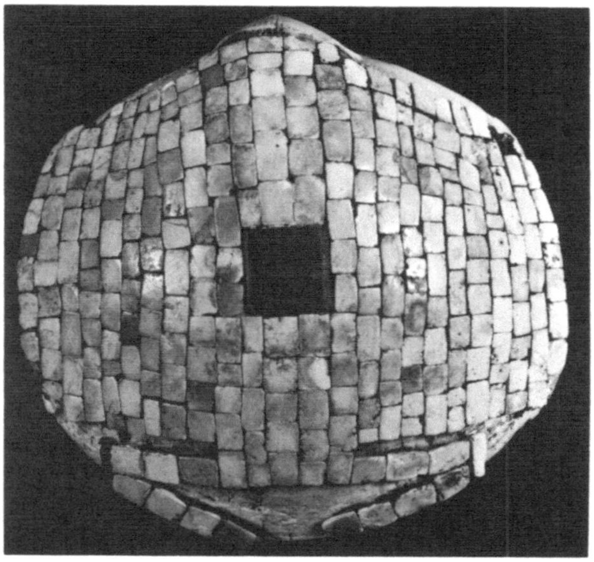

Fig. 84. Carved shell frog decorated with turquoise mosaic. Square center piece is red argillite. Approximate length, 6.5 cm.

APPENDIX B

Prehistoric Plant Remains from the Gila Bend Area

by Hugh C. Cutler

All of the corn from these five sites could be duplicated in a collection of ears gathered among the Pima and Papago Indians about 1912 and now in the collections of the Missouri Botanical Garden. From a number of archaeological sites in and near the Pima-Papago area and from collections made in historic times, it has been possible to work out the general history of corn in this area. The earliest kinds are small-cobbed ears of the race Chapalote. Chapalote was followed by Reventador which is the result of mixtures of Chapalote with other kinds of corn and perhaps with one or more grasses of Mexico. Shortly after this the Pima-Papago race appeared (Cutler 1960). This race probably resulted from the crossing of Reventador or Chapalote with an eight-rowed soft corn, Harinoso de Ocho, in Mexico. Harinoso de Ocho entered the Southwest after its offspring. A complete series of ears can be arranged: Chapalote, Reventador, Onaveno, Pima-Papago, and Harinoso de Ocho. Chapalote is the hardest and smallest-grained, usually a 14-rowed, smoky-colored, flinty pop corn. Reventador has larger and flatter, softer but still hard pop kernels, usually pearly-white or yellow, and may have as many as 20 rows of grains but usually has 12 or 14. Onaveno is still larger and has flatter kernels, is a flint which may become so soft that it approaches Pima-Papago. Pima-Papago, usually 12-rowed, is similar to the soft flour corn of Basket Maker sites in northern Arizona. Until recently it was the most common corn of Papago, Pima, Cocopah, Maricopa, and Yuma Indians, and is still grown to some extent by these Indians and by the Hopi and Zuni. In some places the softer and large-grained eight-rowed Harinoso de Ocho is grown in almost a pure condition although usually it is mixed with Pima-Papago. All races except Chapalote were collected in 1953 in southern Arizona but the dominant kind was Pima-Papago with Harinoso de Ocho and intermediates with Pima-Papago becoming dominant in a few localities. Reventador and Onaveno have almost disappeared from the southwestern United States and Chapalote has not been reported for many years although these races are still grown in many parts of northwestern Mexico.

ARIZONA T:13:9

(Gila Butte phase, A.D. 500–700)

The only corn fragment is 16-rowed, with an extremely small cob. The cupules are very small, 3 mm. wide, and adjacent rows overlap. This fragment belongs to the race Chapalote, the oldest kind of corn known for this region.

A carbonized fragment of a screwbean pod, *Prosopis pubescens* Benthan (= *Strombocarps pubescens* Gray or *Prosopis odorata* Torrey and Fremont), was found. The sweet pods of screwbean are used like those of mesquite.

ARIZONA T:13:2

(Sacaton phase, A.D. 900–1100)

A half-cup-size mass of carbonized, small kernels from the plaza floor probably belongs to the Reventador race of corn. The kernels were too distorted for accurate measurements but they are slightly large for Chapalote and too small to be Onaveno or Pima-Papago. Estimates for the average grain measurements before charring are 5 mm. wide, 3.2 mm. thick, 5.2 mm. long. Practically all were from 14-row ears.

About a cup and a half of carbonized kernels from a trench west from Structure 1 apparently belong to the Pima-Papago race. The kernels are slightly larger, especially in width and length, and were from ears which had 12, 14, and 16 rows of grains. Estimates of the average measurements of the grains before charring are 6.2 mm. wide, 4 mm. thick, and 6.2 mm. long.

A small fragment of a screwbean pod was found in this trench.

ARIZONA Z:2:1 GATLIN SITE

(Sacaton phase, A.D. 900-1100)

The carbonized cobs from the Platform Mound include seven which probably are Reventador (the 14 and 16-rowed ones and the four 12-rowed cobs with the smallest cupules, Fig. 85); six which are typical Pima-Papago corn (12-rowed cobs); three which are Pima-Papago with larger portions of Harinoso de Ocho; and two eight-rowed cobs which are good Harinoso de Ocho. Although this sample is too small to be completely reliable, it is similar to collections of about the same period from southern Arizona, southern New Mexico, and northwestern Mexico (Cutler, unpublished data) in containing a relatively large number of Reventador specimens.

Carbonized corn kernels from the Platform Mound vary from small to medium in size, and came from cobs with 10, 12, and 14 rows of grains. Many were so distorted that they could not be measured or assigned to a race but all races from Reventador to Pima-Papago (but no 8-rowed Harinoso de Ocho) were represented. A small mass of mostly medium-sized carbonized kernels from Structure 1, Fill, is similar except there are proportionately more Pima-Papago race kernels. A small mass of medium-sized carbonized kernels from Structure 1, Level 4 (collapsed roof debris) is similar to the other lot from Structure 1 except that most of the Pima-Papago kernels were uniform in size.

ARIZONA T:14:12

(Classic Period, A.D. 1150–1450)

The 13 charred cobs from the trash mound at this site are relatively uniform (Fig. 86), ten falling within the Pima-Papago race. Some of these may be of the closely-related flinty Onaveno race; the two with the smallest cupules probably being Reventador, and a single eight-rowed cob being Harinoso de Ocho. While this sample is so small that it might consist mainly of cobs from a cache of a single race, this emphasis on the Pima-Papago corn is typical of recent corn in southern Arizona and the proportions may not be far from the true average for this period.

ARIZONA Z:1:11

(Classic Period, A.D. 1150–1450)

Seven carbonized kernels from a 14-rowed ear were small and flat, measuring about 5.3 mm. wide, 3.2 mm. thick, and 6.1 mm. long. They probably came from an ear of the Pima-Papago race (which is a flour corn) but may have come from the closely-related Onaveno, a flint corn one extreme of which approaches Pima-Papago.

About a cupful of small pop corn, distorted, puffed and popped, so that measurements are only approximate, was obtained from Broadside 2. These are from a very small pop corn, a selected form of Reventador or even Chapalote, with average estimated kernel measurements of 4 mm. wide, 3.3 mm. thick, and 4 mm. long.

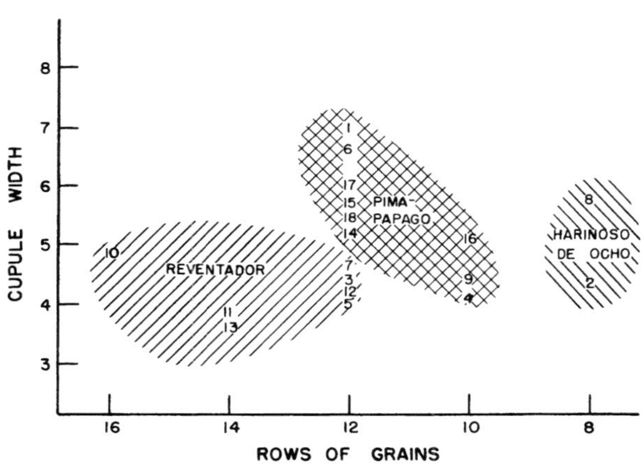

Fig. 85. Diagram showing numbers of rows of grains and cupule width of corn cobs, Gatlin site.

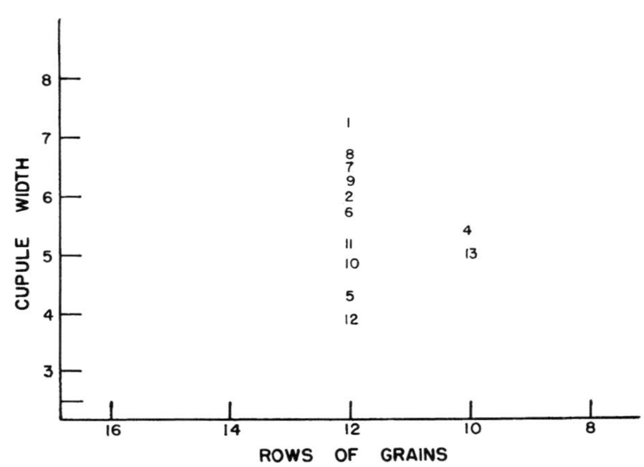

Fig. 86. Diagram showing numbers of rows of grains and cupule width of corn cobs, Ariz. T:14:12.

APPENDIX C

Prehistoric Textiles from the Gila Bend Area

by Mary Elizabeth King

Two small groups of River Hohokam textile material were recovered from sites in the Painted Rocks Reservoir area. Since Hohokam textiles are exceedingly rare, perhaps because dry-cave sites of this culture are generally lacking, a brief summary of the published reports may be worthwhile.

The largest collection of Hohokam textiles recovered to date, from Ventana Cave, is of Desert, rather than River, Hohokam manufacture. More than 70 specimens were found, and the techniques are varied – plain weave, gauze, weft-wrap openwork, tapestry, braiding, and weft twining were reported (Haury 1950).

Only a few examples of River Hohokam weaving have been preserved – almost all in the form of charred fragments or impressions on pottery. In addition to some basketry and sandal fragments and impressions, Snaketown produced one charred textile fragment from a Sacaton-phase (A.D. 900–1100) house (Gladwin and others 1937: 162). This is a fine piece of weft-wrap openwork made of Z-spun cotton. At Casa Grande, Fewkes (1912: 147–48) found textiles of cotton and other plant fiber, as well as animal hair; the first two fibers were apparently sometimes combined in one textile. He reports (1912: 148) feather garments (probably twined feather blankets), a belt with embroidered geometric designs, and a "lace-like" fabric (which could have been gauze, weft-wrap openwork, or a single-element construction such as looping). These textiles probably date from the Soho or Civano phases (A.D. 1100–1450) of Classic Hohokam. Haury (1945a: 163, 172) records plain-weave textile fragments from the Classic period sites of Los Muertos and Las Acequias. The specimen from Los Muertos had cotton warps and wefts of equal size with an average count of 35 elements to the inch. A cotton fragment from Las Acequias had warps which were more tightly spun than the wefts, and there were about 60 warps and 32 wefts to the inch; this textile had a side selvage of multiple-strand twining. Las Acequias also produced an apocynum(?) fragment with two-ply warps re-plied and two-ply wefts; it had a count of 6 warps and 14 wefts to the inch. At Los Guanacos, a Colonial-Sedentary-period site, fragments of two types of cotton plain weave, one with a count of 28x24 elements to the inch and the other with 24x20, and a fragment of cotton twill were found (Haury 1945a: 179). The twill is particularly interesting for its extraordinary state of preservation. It is brown and white broken 2/2 twill with stripes containing small motifs (Kent 1957: 551, Fig. 67 *b,* describes this as a plaid). The brown elements are 2-ply, S-spun, Z-plied, while the white are 3-ply, Z-spun, S-plied.

Jones (1936: 55) reports that Arthur Woodward "discovered cotton seed and what appear to be impressions of cotton textiles in a Colonial Hohokam site." Although Jones does not name the site, it is probably the Grewe site. In 1936 this was the earliest evidence for cotton in the Southwest.

Allen (1953: 16) describes a pottery bell from the Twelve Mile site between Gila Bend and Gillespie Dam, which has textile impressions on the clapper and interior of the bell. Apparently the clapper was wrapped in cloth, the bell fashioned around this and then fired, consuming the textile and leaving the clapper in place inside the bell. No specific data on the textile itself are given. This site dates from the Colonial and Sedentary periods (A. D. 500–1100).

These few examples constitute the sum total of River Hohokam textiles reported in the literature. Spindle whorls – the only other evidence of weaving – are found at Snaketown from the Sweetwater phase (A. D. 500–700) and are common from A. D. 700 on. Both bead and disc-shaped whorls were used.

There is no good evidence for the type of loom used by the Hohokam. Kent (1957: 488) states that the "warp-face belting and specialized bead-type spindle whorls . . . associated with the belt loom in central Mexico, Guatemala, and Peru . . . are found in Hohokam and Hohokam-influenced villages after [A.D.] 1000, and certainly suggest that the belt loom might also have been present. The warp-face blanket from Ventana Cave made of two fifteen-inch wide cloths sewn together, resembles belt loom work." No belt, or backstrap, looms or parts of looms have been recovered archaeologically. On the other hand, the loom in use historically among the Pima, Papago, and Maricopa of the Southwest, and throughout northern Mexico, was the staked-out, horizontal loom. Although many northern Mexican groups today use the backstrap loom (often a slightly aberrant form) for weaving narrow fabrics such as belts, the Tarahumara do make sashes on the staked-out loom, and the Pima apparently also utilized this loom for narrow belts. It seems possible, therefore, that the loom originally used by the Hohokam was a staked-out, horizontal loom rather than the backstrap loom of central and southern Mexico. Kent (1957: 488) also postulates that the "wide, plain weave blankets from Ventana Cave . . . are horizontal loom products." The backstrap loom was probably introduced from Mexico (Kent suggests a date of A.D. 700 or earlier), and may have been used by the Hohokam, though there is no record of its use by the historic Pima or Papago.

The textiles from Painted Rocks Reservoir add no new techniques to the Hohokam inventory; in fact many of those known are missing from this collection (for example, gauze, weft-wrap openwork, and others). However, they add considerably to our limited sample of River Hohokam fabrics.

All of the textiles to be described here are from cremations, preserved by charring. The fragments are small and extremely fragile; the largest fragment was about 14 cm. by 15 cm., and most were much smaller. Although positive fiber identifications could not be made, they appear to be largely of cotton, as were the textiles from Ventana Cave (Haury 1950: 488). The most striking feature of the collection is the extreme fineness of the weaves. Unlike most groups of Anasazi textiles, there are no coarse, heavy fabrics among the Painted Rocks Reservoir fragments. The number of elements to the centimeter ranges from 6 to 20. In most cases, the absence of selvages makes it impossible to distinguish warp from weft. Even when one selvage is present, it is almost impossible to determine whether it is an end or side selvage since in Southwestern fabrics both customarily were twined.

Unfortunately, any color, or dyed pattern such as tie-dye, is now lost. Some of the fragments must once have had some color. Though the Ventana Cave specimens are mostly of natural color, some were red or brown, and the Los Guanacos twill fragment was brown and white. It seems likely that the Hohokam utilized only a limited range of colors in dyeing. Russell (1908: 150) reports that the historic Pima used only "a dark buff ocher bartered from the Papagos" for dyeing cotton.

Two periods are represented in the collection from Painted Rocks Reservoir. The Three Mile site (Ariz. T:14:15) produced textiles of the Sacaton phase, Late Sedentary period (A.D. 900–1100), and the Bartley site (Ariz. T:14:11) produced textiles of the Soho phase, Classic period (A.D. 1100–1400). Since the material from the two sites shows some technical as well as temporal differences, we will consider them separately.

THE THREE MILE SITE

Cordage from this site (Ariz. T:14:15) appears to be largely of yucca or a similar plant fiber. Spins and diameters vary. There is some fine Z-spun, S-plied cordage (which may be of cotton) with a diameter of about .5 mm. There are also some fragments of slightly heavier S-spun yucca (?) yarns, and of S-spun, Z-plied yucca (?) cordage about 1 mm. in diameter. A mass of yucca (?) cordage, which might be the remnants of a "string apron" (reported for the Desert Hohokam by Haury 1950: 429), consists of Z-spun, S-plied yarns, re-plied Z. These are about 3 mm. in diameter.

All of the textile fragments from this site are plain weave, and all appear to be of cotton. Both warps and wefts are Z-spun singles with yarn diameters of less than 1 mm. The following warp and weft counts were observed in balanced, compact, or somewhat open, plain weaves: 12x12, 12x11, 14x12, and 16x9 warps and wefts per centimeter. One of these fragments has a twined

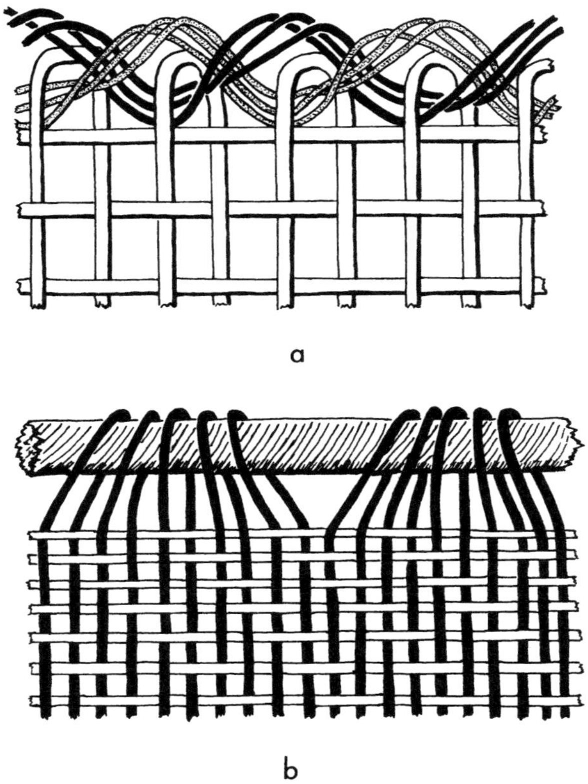

Fig. 87. Techniques of selvage finish; a, *selvage finish of two-strand twining with three yarns used in each strand;* b, *selvage finish on 2/2 twill fragment, with a heavy cord running through the edge loops.*

selvage made up of two or three threads twined together down to the right.

There are also some extremely fine, narrow, folded fragments, possibly from a tape or band. There are no complete widths. These fragments, probably all from one textile, are either weft-faced or warp-faced. The latter is most likely. The warp and weft count per centimeter is 20x10. There is a twined side (?) selvage consisting of three threads twined together down to the left (Fig. 87*a*).

None of these textile fragments shows any trace of patterning. All are very competently woven.

Additional textiles from the Three Mile site were donated to the Arizona State Museum by Norton Allen. These arrived too late for inclusion in this description, and will be discussed in a journal article.

THE BARTLEY SITE

The Bartley site (Ariz. T:14:11) produced two bundles – both wadded masses of completely charred material.

One bundle contained what appeared to be twill matting, but it was insufficiently preserved to determine the order in which the elements interlaced. The elements were of beargrass or split yucca and were about 3 mm. wide.

Under this matting was a layer of twill cloth. The warps and wefts are of Z-spun cotton with a count of 10x6 elements to the centimeter. The twill is over-two, under-two. It appears to be patterned, since there are over-three floats in places, but the direction of the twill does not seem to reverse, and the fragment is too small to determine the nature of the patterning. What at first appeared to be an end selvage, seemed, on closer examination, to be a seam. Each selvage has a heavier (Z-spun, S-plied?) cord run through the weft (?) loops and the two selvages are joined with a whipping stitch.

The bundle also contained fragments of plain-

Fig. 88. Charred twill cloth, Bartley site.

Fig. 89. Twined mending on charred cloth, Bartley site.

weave cotton with Z-spun elements and a count of 12 warps and 12 wefts to the centimeter.

The second bundle again produced bits of 2/2 twill cloth (Fig. 88) which also has floats over or under more than two. In this case the twill diagonal reverses, and the patterning seems to have been a diamond twill. Both warps and wefts are of Z-spun cotton, and there are 12 elements to the centimeter in each direction. The only remaining selvage is not twined, but has a heavy cord consisting of 14 Z-spun threads, plied S, around which the elements pass in groups of 10 or more (Fig. 87*b*). These groups of elements are separated by about 5 mm. This could be either a loom end with spaces left where the cords which lashed the end to the loom bar once were, or a side selvage which was once fastened to another piece by means of a cord dovetailing the two sets of weft loops together.

One piece of plain weave in this bundle has 14 tightly Z-spun cotton warps and 8 cotton wefts (loosely Z-spun) to the centimeter. The wefts do not run at right angles to the warps — possibly they have been pulled out of line by some distortion of the finished fabric. The over-all impression of this textile is of parallel threads with no weft showing. The edge which is preserved consists of 4 threads twined together down to the right.

Other plain weaves are all of Z-spun cotton and have counts of 10x9, 12x11, 14x8, 14x14, 16x12, and 17x10 elements to the centimeter. All intact selvages consist of two groups of 4 threads twined down to the right.

A number of fragments show considerable mending (Fig. 89). In most cases the stitch used is a twined double running stitch (which may slant in either direction) in rows 1 cm. to 2 cm. apart, but one fragment has some areas in which a long plain running stitch was used instead of twining. The rows of stitching may have been decorative as well as useful, and one fragment seems to be gathered by means of the twining rows.

One large fragment has two seams 7.5 cm. apart. Although this dimension could represent the loom width, it seems more likely that the edges were cut. Since the fragment has much twined mending, the seams may simply be another attempt to conserve badly-worn material. At any rate, the edges are rolled together and sewn with a whipping stitch, using paired Z-spun cotton threads.

In addition there are bundles of threads which may represent very worn textiles. One bundle consists of S-spun cotton (?) thread, an unusual occurrence in Southwestern textiles. Others have Z-spun, or Z-spun, S-plied threads.

One small fragment of cloth and wrapped yarns may represent a corner tassel, but the material is too fragmentary to be sure.

There are also a few fragments of twill matting in which the elements seem to cross over and under at least three elements in each direction, but again the state of preservation is such that it is impossible to be definite. The elements are 3 mm. wide and are probably beargrass or split yucca.

Even though the two bundles are from the same cremation, a comparison of thread counts and other features indicates that they represent two distinct groups of textiles.

SANDALS

Four fragments of sandals were also found in

the Painted Rocks Reservoir area from Arizona T:14:10, Primary Cremation 1. These are of the general type described by Haury (1950: 436–39) from Ventana Cave. According to his analysis, the Ventana Cave specimens were worked in chain stitch through a foundation. However, one of the fragments from Painted Rocks Reservoir shows horizontal stitches (?) on the reverse rather than the vertical stitches one would expect from a chain-stitch construction.

All of the specimens found at Painted Rocks Reservoir are, unfortunately, so charred (and, in fact, have an almost petrified quality) that technical analysis was impossible. It therefore seems wiser to wait until a specimen which can be dissected is located before venturing into description of the technique. At the present time, though the appearance of the fragments is the same as those recovered from Ventana Cave, we cannot be sure that the technique used was the same.

There seems to be little doubt that this general type of sandal, which resembles coiled braiding (and has been described as such by Fulton 1941: 25–26), is as typical of Sedentary and post-Sedentary Hohokam sites as "raised pattern" sandals are of Basketmaker III. Examples of these sandals have been found at Snaketown, the Grewe site, Ventana Cave, and Winchester Cave (Haury 1950: 438), as well as Painted Rocks Reservoir.

CONCLUSIONS

Although only plain weave and twill, aside from matting, sandal, and cordage, fragments have been found at Painted Rocks Reservoir, these few specimens are of value in adding to our picture of River Hohokam weaving. The River Hohokam wove plain weave, both balanced and warp-faced, compact and open; 2/2 twills, both balanced and irregular; and weft-wrap openwork. They probably also knew such techniques as gauze and tapestry, but to date these have been reported only for the Desert Hohokam. Unfortunately, we still have no idea of what non-woven constructions were made—with the possible exception of twined(?) blankets from Casa Grande.

All of the Painted Rocks Reservoir fragments are extremely well woven. Threads are evenly spun and fine, and the thread counts of the textiles are relatively high. Cotton seems to have been the preferred fiber for weaving and yucca (?) for cordage; the former is usually spun in the Z direction and the latter in the S direction, but exceptions occur. Yarns used in weaving are not usually plied; those used for cordage almost always are. The extensive use of mending suggests that textiles were too precious to discard until they were completely worn out.

There is no evidence inherent in the weaving for the use of either a backstrap or a staked-out loom, but the presence of patterned twills leaves little doubt that the Hohokam possessed a loom with multiple heddles.

We cannot definitely date any Hohokam textiles before the Colonial-Sedentary periods (A.D. 500–1100). However, these textiles by no means represent an early stage in the development of weaving in the Southwest. Inspiration for such techniques as twill, gauze, weft-wrap openwork and so on, may well have come from Mexico, at least by A.D. 700 and probably earlier. Some textile techniques may have come into the Southwest at the same time as the introduction of pottery.

REFERENCES

ALLEN, NORTON

1953 A Hohokam Pottery Bell. *El Palacio,* Vol. 60, No. 1, pp. 16–19. Santa Fe.

AMSDEN, C.A.

1936 A Prehistoric Rubber Ball. *Masterkey,* Vol. 10, No. 1, pp. 7–8. Southwest Museum, Los Angeles.

ANONYMOUS

1935 Notes and News: Southwestern Area. *American Antiquity,* Vol. 1, No. 2, pp. 154–55. Menasha.

BARTLETT, J.R.

1854 *Personal Narrative of Explorations and Incidents in Texas, New Mexico, California, Sonora and Chihuahua.* Vol. 2. D. Appleton and Company, New York.

BRAIDWOOD, R. J.

1957 Prehistoric Men. *Chicago Natural History Museum, Popular Series: Anthropology,* No. 37 (3rd Edition). Chicago.

BRAINERD, G. W.

1951 The Place of Chronological Ordering in Archaeological Analysis. *American Antiquity,* Vol. 16, No. 4, pp. 301–313. Salt Lake City.

BRANDES, RAYMOND S.

1957 An Early Ball Court near Globe, Arizona. *Kiva,* Vol. 23, No. 1, pp. 10–11. Tucson.

BRETERNITZ, D. A.

1959 Excavations at Nantack Village, Point of Pines, Arizona. *Anthropological Papers of the University of Arizona,* No. 1. Tucson.

BROWNE, J. R.

1950 *A Tour Through Arizona, 1864, or Adventures in the Apache Country.* Arizona Silhouettes, Tucson.

BULLARD, W. R., JR.

1960 Maya Settlement Pattern in Northeastern Peten, Guatemala. *American Antiquity,* Vol. 25, No. 3, pp. 355–72. Salt Lake City.

COLTON, H. S.

1938 Names of the Four Culture Roots in the Southwest. *Science,* Vol. 87, pp. 551–52. Lancaster.

1939 Prehistoric Culture Units and Their Relationships in Northern Arizona. *Museum of Northern Arizona, Bulletin* 17. Flagstaff.

1941 Winona and Ridge Ruin. Part 2. *Museum of Northern Arizona, Bulletin* 19. Flagstaff.

1945 The Patayan Problem in the Colorado River Valley. *Southwestern Journal of Anthropology,* Vol. 1, pp. 114–21. Albuquerque.

1946 The Sinagua. *Museum of Northern Arizona, Bulletin* 22. Flagstaff.

COLTON, H. S. AND L. L. HARGRAVE

1937 Handbook of Northern Arizona Pottery Wares. *Museum of Northern Arizona, Bulletin* 11. Flagstaff.

COSGROVE, C. B.

1947 Caves in the Upper Gila and El Paso Area. *Papers of the Peabody Museum of American Archaeology and Ethnology, Harvard University,* Vol. 24, No. 2. Cambridge.

COSGROVE, H. S. AND C. B. COSGROVE

1932 The Swarts Ruin. *Papers of the Peabody Museum of American Archaeology and Ethnology, Harvard University,* Vol. 15, No. 1. Cambridge.

COUES, ELLIOT

1900 *On the Trail of a Spanish Pioneer: The Diary and Itinerary of Francisco Garces.* Francis P. Harper, New York.

CUTLER, H. C.

1960 Cultivated Plant Remains from Waterfall Cave, Chihuahua. *American Antiquity,* Vol. 26, No. 2, pp. 277–79. Salt Lake City.

DICE, L. R.

1943 *The Biotic Provinces of North America.* University of Michigan Press, Ann Arbor.

DIPESO, C. C.

1951 A Ball Court Located on the San Pedro River in Southeastern Arizona. *American Antiquity,* Vol. 16, No. 3, pp. 257–60. Salt Lake City.

1956 The Upper Pima of San Cayetano del Tumacacori. *Amerind Foundation,* No. 7. Dragoon.

DIXON, K. A.

1956 Archaeological Objectives and Artifact Sorting Techniques: A Re-examination of the Snaketown Sequence. *Western Anthropology,* Vol. 1, No. 3, n.p.

DUNNE, P. M. (TRANSLATOR)

1955 *Jacobo Sedelmayr, Missionary, Frontiersman, Explorer, in Arizona and Sonora: Four Original Manuscript Narratives 1744–1751.* Arizona Pioneers' Historical Society. Tucson.

ECCLESTON, ROBERT

1950 *Overland to California on the Southwestern Trail, 1849,* edited by G. P. Hammond and E. H. Howes. University of California Press, Berkeley and Los Angeles.

EDDY, F. W.

1958 *A Sequence of Cultural and Alluvial Deposits in the Cienega Creek Basin, Southeastern Arizona.* MS, master's thesis, University of Arizona, Tucson.

EMORY, W. H.

1848 *Notes of a Military Reconnoissance from Fort Leavenworth, in Missouri, to San Diego, in California, including part of the Arkansas, Del Norte, and Gila Rivers.* Thirtieth Congress, First Session, Ex. Doc. No. 41. Wendell and Benthuysen, Washington.

EZELL, P. H.

1937 Shell Work of the Prehistoric Southwest. *The Kiva,* Vol. 3, No. 3, pp. 9–12. Tucson.

1961 The Hispanic Acculturation of the Gila River Pimas. *Memoirs of the American Anthropological Association,* No. 90. Menasha.

1963a The Maricopas: An Identification from Documentary Sources. *Anthropological Papers of the University of Arizona,* No. 6. Tucson.

1963b Is There a Hohokam-Pima Culture Continuum? *American Antiquity,* Vol. 29, No. 1, pp. 61–66. Salt Lake City.

FERDON, E. N.

1955 A Trial Survey of Mexican-Southwestern Architectural Parallels. *Monographs of the School of American Research,* No. 21. Santa Fe.

FEWKES, J. W.

1912 Casa Grande, Arizona. *Twenty-eighth Annual Report of the American Bureau of Ethnology,* pp. 25–179. Washington.

FORDE, C. D.

1931 Ethnology of the Yuma Indians. *University of California Publications in American Archaeology and Ethnology,* Vol. 28, No. 4, pp. 83–278. Berkeley.

FULTON, W. S.

1941 A Ceremonial Cave in the Winchester Mountains, Arizona. *Amerind Foundation,* No. 2. Dragoon.

GIFFORD, E.W.

1936 Northeastern and Western Yavapai. *University of California Publications in American Archaeology and Ethnology,* Vol. 34, No. 4, pp. 247–354. Berkeley.

GILMORE, R. M.

1950 Fauna and Ethnozoology of South America. In "Handbook of South American Indians," edited by J. H. Steward. *Bureau of American Ethnology, Bulletin* 143, Vol. 6, pp. 345–464. Washington.

GLADWIN, H. S.

1942 Excavations at Snaketown III: Revisions. *Medallion Papers,* No. 30. Gila Pueblo, Globe.

1945 The Chaco Branch, Excavations at White Mound and in the Red Mesa Valley. *Medallion Papers,* No. 33. Gila Pueblo, Globe.

1948 Excavations at Snaketown IV: Reviews and Conclusions. *Medallion Papers,* No. 38. Gila Pueblo, Globe.

GLADWIN, H. S., E. W. HAURY, E. B. SAYLES, AND NORA GLADWIN

1937 Excavations at Snaketown: Material Culture. *Medallion Papers,* No. 25. Gila Pueblo, Globe.

GLADWIN, WINIFRED AND H. S. GLADWIN

1930 The Western Range of the Red-on-buff Culture. *Medallion Papers,* No. 5. Gila Pueblo, Globe.

1931 Some Southwestern Pottery Types, Series II. *Medallion Papers,* No. 10. Gila Pueblo, Globe.

1933 Some Southwestern Pottery Types, Series III. *Medallion Papers,* No. 13. Gila Pueblo, Globe.

1934 A Method for the Designation of Cultures and Their Variations. *Medallion Papers,* No. 15. Gila Pueblo, Globe.

GRIFFIN, J. B.

1952a Culture Periods in Eastern United States Archaeology. In *Archaeology of the Eastern United States,* edited by J. B. Griffin, pp. 352–64. University of Chicago Press.

1952b Radiocarbon Dates for the Eastern United States. In *Archaeology of the Eastern United States,* edited by J. B. Griffin, pp. 365–70. University of Chicago Press.

HARGRAVE, L. L.

1938 Results of a Study of the Cohonina Branch of the Patayan Culture in 1938. *Museum Notes,* Vol. 11, No. 6, pp. 43–50. Flagstaff.

HARNER, M. J.

1958 Lowland Patayan Phases in the Lower Colorado River Valley and Colorado Desert. *Reports of the University of California Archaeological Survey,* No. 42, pp. 93–97. Berkeley.

HAURY, E. W.

1932 Roosevelt:9:6, a Hohokam Site of the Colonial Period. *Medallion Papers,* No. 11. Gila Pueblo, Globe.

1936 Some Southwestern Pottery Types, Series IV. *Medallion Papers,* No. 19. Gila Pueblo, Globe.

1937 A Pre-Spanish Rubber Ball from Arizona. *American Antiquity,* Vol. 2, No. 4, pp. 282–88. Menasha.

1943 A Possible Cochise-Mogollon-Hohokam Sequence. *Proceedings of the American Philosophical Society,* Vol. 86, No. 2, pp. 260–63. Philadelphia.

1945a The Excavation of Los Muertos and Neighboring Ruins in the Salt River Valley, Southern Arizona. *Papers of the Peabody Museum of American Archaeology and Ethnology, Harvard University,* Vol. 24, No. 1. Cambridge.

1945b The Problem of Contacts between the Southwestern United States and Mexico. *Southwestern Journal of Anthropology,* Vol. 1, No. 1, pp. 55–74. Albuquerque.

1950 *The Stratigraphy and Archaeology of Ventana Cave.* University of New Mexico Press and University of Arizona Press, Albuquerque and Tucson.

1956 Speculations on Prehistoric Settlement Patterns in the Southwest. In "Prehistoric Settlement Patterns in the New World," edited by G. R. Willey. *Viking Fund Publications in Anthropology,* No. 23, pp. 3–10. Wenner-Gren Foundation for Anthropological Research, Inc., New York.

1957 An Alluvial Site on the San Carlos Indian Reservation, Arizona. *American Antiquity,* Vol. 23, No. 1, pp. 2–27. Salt Lake City.

1958 Evidence at Point of Pines for a Prehistoric Migration from Northern Arizona. In "Migrations in New World Culture History," edited by R. H. Thompson. *University of Arizona Bulletin,* Vol. 29, No. 2 (Social Science Bulletin, No. 27), pp. 1–6. Tucson.

HAWLEY, H. G.

1953 The Manufacture of Copper Bells Found in Southwestern Sites. *Southwestern Journal of Anthropology,* Vol. 9, No. 1, pp. 99–111. Albuquerque.

HAYDEN, J. D.

1957 Excavations, 1940, at University Indian Ruin. *Southwestern Monuments Association, Technical Series,* Vol. 5. Globe.

HINTON, R.J.

1954 *The Handbook to Arizona.* Arizona Silhouettes, Tucson.

HOWARD, E. B.

1935 Evidence of Early Man in North America. *University of Pennsylvania Museum, The Museum Journal,* Vol. 24, Nos. 2–3, pp. 53–171. Philadelphia.

JENNINGS, J. D.

1952 Prehistory in the Lower Mississippi Valley. In *Archaeology of the Eastern United States,* edited by J. B. Griffin, pp. 265–71. University of Chicago Press.

1956 The American Southwest: A Problem in Cultural Isolation. In "Seminars in Archaeology: 1955," edited by Robert Wauchope, pp. 59–127. *Memoirs of the Society for American Archaeology,* No. 11. Salt Lake City.

1957 Danger Cave. *Memoirs of the Society for American Archaeology,* No. 14. Salt Lake City.

JOHNSON, A. E.

1961 A Ball Court at Point of Pines, Arizona. *American Antiquity,* Vol. 26, No. 4, pp. 563–67. Salt Lake City.

1963 The Trincheras Culture of Northern Sonora. *American Antiquity,* Vol. 29, No. 2, pp. 174–86. Salt Lake City.

JOHNSON, A. E. AND W. W. WASLEY

1961 Pottery and Artifact Provenience Data from Sites in the Painted Rocks Reservoir, Western Arizona. *Archives of Archaeology,* No. 18. Society for American Archaeology and University of Wisconsin Press. Madison.

JOHNSON, A.E. AND R. H. THOMPSON

1963 The Ringo Site, Southeastern Arizona. *American Antiquity,* Vol. 28, No. 4, pp. 465–81. Salt Lake City.

JOHNSTON, A. R.

1848 *Journal of Captain A. R. Johnston, First Dragoons.* Thirtieth Congress, First Session, Ex. Doc. 41, pp. 565–614. Wendell and Benthuysen, Washington.

JONES, V. H.

1936 A Summary of Data on Aboriginal Cotton of the Southwest. In "Symposium on Prehistoric Agriculture," edited by D. D. Brand. *University of New Mexico Bulletin, Anthropological Series,* Vol. 1, No. 5, pp. 51–64. Albuquerque.

KENT, K. P.

1957 The Cultivation and Weaving of Cotton in the Prehistoric Southwestern United States. *Transactions of the American Philosophical Society,* Vol. 47, Pt. 3, pp. 457–732. Philadelphia.

LATCHAM, R. E.

1922 Los animales domesticos de la America precolombiana. *Publicaciones del Museo Etnológico y Antropológico de Chile,* Vol. 3, No. 1, pp. 1–199. Santiago.

LEHMER, D. J.

1950 Review of "Excavations at Snaketown IV: Reviews and Conclusions" by H. S. Gladwin. *American Anthropologist,* Vol. 52, No. 3, pp. 415–18. Menasha.

LLOYD, F. E.

1911 Guayule: A Rubber-Plant of the Chihuahuan Desert. *Carnegie Institution of Washington, Publication* 139. Washington.

LUMHOLTZ, CARL

1912 *New Trails in Mexico.* Charles Scribner's Sons, New York.

MANJE, J. M.

1954 *Luz de Tierra Incognita.* (Translated by H. J. Karns.) Arizona Silhouettes, Tucson.

MARTIN, P. S. AND J. B. RINALDO

1950 Sites of the Reserve Phase, Pine Lawn Valley, Western New Mexico. *Chicago Natural History Museum, Fieldiana: Anthropology,* Vol. 38, No. 3. Chicago.

MARTIN, P. S., J. B. RINALDO, E. A. BLUHM, H. C. CUTLER, AND ROGER GRANGE, JR.

1952 Mogollon Cultural Continuity and Change: The Stratigraphic Analysis of Tularosa and Cordova Caves. *Chicago Natural History Museum, Fieldiana: Anthropology,* Vol. 40. Chicago.

MCGREGOR, J. C.

1936 Ball Courts in Northern Arizona. *Museum of Northern Arizona, Museum Notes,* Vol. 8, No. 11, pp. 55–58. Flagstaff.

1941 Winona and Ridge Ruin, Part I: Architecture and Material Culture. *Museum of Northern Arizona, Bulletin* 18. Flagstaff.

MEIGHAN, C. W.

1959 New Findings in West Mexican Archaeology. *Kiva,* Vol. 25, No. 1, pp. 1–7. Tucson.

1960 Prehistoric Copper Objects from Western Mexico. *Science,* Vol. 131, No. 3412, p. 1534. Lancaster.

MORRIS, E. H.

1939 Archaeological Studies in the La Plata District, Southwestern Colorado and Northwestern New Mexico. *Carnegie Institution of Washington, Publication* 519. Washington.

MORSS, NOEL

1954 Clay Figurines of the American Southwest. *Papers of the Peabody Museum of American Archaeology and Ethnology, Harvard University,* Vol. 49, No. 1. Cambridge.

NORDENSKIÖLD, ERLAND

1922 Deductions Suggested by the Geographical Distribution of Some Post-Columbian Words Used by the Indians of South America. *Comparative Ethnographical Studies,* No. 5. Göteborg.

OLSON, A. P. AND W. W. WASLEY

1956 An Archaeological Traverse Survey of West Central New Mexico. In *Pipeline Archaeology,* edited by Fred Wendorf, Nancy Fox, and O. L. Lewis, pp. 256–390. Laboratory of Anthropology and Museum of Northern Arizona. Santa Fe and Flagstaff.

PENDERGAST, D. M.

1962 Metal Artifacts from Amapa, Nayarit, Mexico. *American Antiquity,* Vol. 27, No. 3, pp. 370–79. Salt Lake City.

PINKLEY, F. H.

1935a Seventeen Years Ago. *Southwestern Monuments Monthly Report, November,* pp. 383–89. Casa Grande National Monument.

1935b Seventeen Years Ago. *Southwestern Monuments Monthly Report, December,* pp. 455–62. Casa Grande National Monument.

POMEROY, J. A.

1959 Hohokam Etched Shell. *Kiva,* Vol. 24, No. 4, pp. 12–21. Tucson.

1962 *A Study of Black-on-white Painted Pottery in the Tonto Basin, Arizona.* MS, master's thesis, University of Arizona, Tucson.

PROSKOURIAKOFF, TATIANA (ASSEMBLER)

1956 Notes and News: Middle America. *American Antiquity,* Vol. 21, No. 4, pp. 441-42. Salt Lake City.

RINALDO, J. B.

1959 Foote Canyon Pueblo, Eastern Arizona. *Chicago Natural History Museum, Fieldiana: Anthropology,* Vol. 49, No. 2. Chicago.

RINALDO, J. B. AND E. A. BLUHM

1956 Late Mogollon Pottery Types of the Reserve Area. *Chicago Natural History Museum, Fieldiana: Anthropology,* Vol. 36, No. 7. Chicago.

ROBINSON, W. S.

1951 A Method for Chronologically Ordering Archaeological Deposits. *American Antiquity,* Vol. 16, No. 4, pp. 293–301. Salt Lake City.

ROGERS, M. J.

1945 An Outline of Yuman Prehistory. *Southwestern Journal of Anthropology,* Vol. 1, No. 2, pp. 167–98. Albuquerque.

ROUSE, IRVING

1958 The Inference of Migration from Anthropological Evidence. In "Migrations in New World Culture History," edited by R. H. Thompson. *University of Arizona Bulletin,* Vol. 29, No. 2 (Social Science Bulletin, No. 27), pp. 63–68. Tucson.

RUSSELL, FRANK

1908 The Pima Indians. *Twenty-sixth Annual Report of the Bureau of American Ethnology,* pp. 3–390. Washington.

SAUER, C. O.

1952 Agricultural Origins and Dispersals. *The American Geographical Society,* Series 2. New York.

SAYLES, E. B.

1945 The San Simon Branch: Excavations at Cave Creek and in the San Simon Valley I: Material Culture. *Medallion Papers,* No. 34. Gila Pueblo, Globe.

SAYLES, E. B. AND ERNST ANTEVS

1941 The Cochise Culture. *Medallion Papers,* No. 29. Gila Pueblo, Globe.

SCANTLING, F. H.

1940 *Excavations at the Jackrabbit Ruin, Papago Indian Reservation, Arizona.* MS, master's thesis, University of Arizona. Tucson.

SCHROEDER, A. H.

1940 *A Stratigraphic Survey of Pre-Spanish Trash Mounds of the Salt River Valley, Arizona.* MS, master's thesis, University of Arizona. Tucson.

1949a Cultural Implications of the Ball Courts in Arizona. *Southwestern Journal of Anthropology,* Vol. 5, No. 1, pp. 28–36. Albuquerque.

1949b A Preliminary Examination of the Sacred Mountain Ball Court. *Plateau,* Vol. 21, No. 4, pp. 55–57. Flagstaff.

1951a Snaketown IV vs. the Facts. *American Antiquity,* Vol. 16, No. 3, pp. 263–65. Salt Lake City.

1951b A New Ball Court Site in the Verde Valley. *Plateau,* Vol. 23, No. 4, pp. 61–63. Flagstaff.

1952a A Brief Survey of the Lower Colorado River from Davis Dam to the International Border. *National Park Service, Region Three Office.* Santa Fe.

1952b The Bearing of Ceramics on Developments in the Hohokam Classic Period. *Southwestern Journal of Anthropology,* Vol. 8, No. 3, pp. 320–35. Albuquerque.

1957 The Hakataya Cultural Tradition. *American Antiquity,* Vol. 23, No. 2, pp. 176–78. Salt Lake City.

1960 The Hohokam, Sinagua and the Hakataya. *Archives of Archaeology,* No. 5. Society for American Archaeology and University of Wisconsin Press. Madison.

1961 An Archaeological Survey of the Painted Rocks Reservoir, Western Arizona. *Kiva,* Vol. 27, No. 1, pp. 1–28. Tucson.

SELLERS, WILLIAM

1960 *Arizona Climate.* University of Arizona Press, Tucson.

SMILEY, T.L.

1952 Four Late Prehistoric Kivas at Point of Pines, Arizona. *University of Arizona Bulletin,* Vol. 23, No. 2 (Social Science Bulletin, No. 21). Tucson.

SMITH, A. L.

1955 Archaeological Reconnaissance in Central Guatemala. *Carnegie Institution of Washington, Publication* 608. Washington.

THWAITES, R. G. (EDITOR)

1905 Pattie's Personal Narrative. In *Early Western Travels, 1748–1846,* Vol. 18. Arthur H. Clark Company, Cleveland.

TUOHY, D. R.

1960 *Archaeological Survey and Excavation in the Gila River Channel between Earven Dam Site and Buttes Reservoir Site, Arizona.* MS, report prepared for the National Park Service. Arizona State Museum, Tucson.

TURNEY, O. A.

1929 Prehistoric Irrigation, Part II. *Arizona Historical Review,* Vol. 2, No. 2, pp. 11–52. Phoenix.

TUTHILL, CARR

1947 The Tres Alamos Site on the San Pedro River, Southeastern Arizona. *Amerind Foundation,* No. 4. Dragoon.

1950 Notes on the Dragoon Complex. In *For the Dean,* edited by E. K. Reed and D. S. King. Hohokam Museums Association and Southwestern Monuments Association. Tucson and Santa Fe.

VOGT, E. Z.

1956 An Appraisal of "Prehistoric Settlement Patterns in the New World." In "Prehistoric Settlement Patterns in the New World," edited by G. R. Willey. *Viking Fund Publications in Anthropology,* No. 23, pp. 173–82. Wenner-Gren Foundation for Anthropological Research, Inc., New York.

WASLEY, W. W. (ASSEMBLER)

1959 Notes and News: Southwest. *American Antiquity,* Vol. 25, No. 1, pp. 147–49. Salt Lake City.

1960a Notes and News: Southwest. *American Antiquity,* Vol. 25, No. 3, pp. 443–46. Salt Lake City.

WASLEY, W. W.

1960b A Hohokam Platform Mound at the Gatlin Site, Gila Bend, Arizona. *American Antiquity,* Vol. 26, No. 2, pp. 242–62. Salt Lake City.

WHEAT, J. B.

1954 Crooked Ridge Village. *University of Arizona Bulletin,* Vol. 25, No. 3 (Social Science Bulletin, No. 24). Tucson.

1955 Mogollon Culture Prior to A.D. 1000. *Memoirs of the Society for American Archaeology,* No. 10. Salt Lake City.

WHEAT, J. B., J. C. GIFFORD, AND W. W. WASLEY

1958 Ceramic Variety, Type Cluster, and Ceramic System in Southwestern Pottery Analysis. *American Antiquity,* Vol. 24, No. 1, pp. 34–47. Salt Lake City.

WILLEY, G. R.

1953 Prehistoric Settlement Patterns in the Viru Valley, Peru. *Bureau of American Ethnology, Bulletin* 155. Washington.

WITHERS, A. M.

1941 *Excavations at Valshni Village, Papago Indian Reservation.* MS, master's thesis, University of Arizona. Tucson.

WOODWARD, ARTHUR

1931 The Grewe Site. *Los Angeles Museum of History, Science and Art, Occasional Papers,* No. 1. Los Angeles.

ZEUNER, F. E.

1963 *A History of Domesticated Animals.* Hutchinson and Company, Ltd. London.